COMORE

ANJOUAN

Jimilimé
Bimbini
ouni
Foumbani
Quani
Sima
Mutsamudu
Tsembehou
Bambao
Lac de Dziaiandze
Pomoni
Domoni
Moya
eli
Chiroroni
ni
Itsamia Beach
Iconi
_I

Accoua
Soulou
Mamoudzou
Dzaoudzi
Kombani
Pamandzi
MAYOTTE
Sada
D
Dembeni
Bweni
Bandrele
Kani-Keli
Saziley
s map

REFERENCE	
▬▬▬	Main road
───	Secondary road
∿∿∿	Road or track
═══	City street
⌇⌇⌇	Coral reefs
✚	Hospital
❶	Information bureau
⊠	Post office
✈	Airfield
▲	Places of interest
🚌	Bus terminal
Ⓟ	Police station
▲	Spot height
Ⓗ	Hotel
Ⓡ	Restaurant
⛴	Port

VISITORS' GUIDE TO
THE COMOROS AND SEYCHELLES

VISITORS' GUIDE TO
THE COMOROS
AND
SEYCHELLES

HOW TO GET THERE · WHAT TO SEE · WHERE TO STAY

Marco Turco

SOUTHERN
BOOK PUBLISHERS

This book is dedicated to the dream wanderer in all of us

ISBN 1 86812 584 X

First edition, first impression 1995

Published by
Southern Book Publishers (Pty) Ltd
PO Box 3103, Halfway House 1685

While the author and publisher have endeavoured to verify all facts, they will not be held responsible for any inconvenience that may result from possible inaccuracies in this book.

Cover photograph by Jody Turco
Cover design by Insight Graphics
Maps by Colin Stevenson
Set on 10/11.5 pt Palatino
by Kohler Carton & Print, Pinetown
Printed and bound by Kohler Carton & Print, Pinetown

ACKNOWLEDGEMENTS

Writing a book of this kind requires the assistance of numerous people and organisations. To everyone who helped me with information, accommodation, transport or in any other way, I extend my deepest gratitude.

South Africa

Yolande Weaich and Air Seychelles; Dave Barry and Backpacker for supplying travel-packs, day-packs and other accessories; Urbans Footwear for supplying boots; Bruce Hutchison, Barbara Beauchamp and World Leisure Holidays for a wonderful stay at La Galawa Beach Hotel and Casino.

Jody Turco, for the companionship, excellent photographs, support, trust, time and freedom to go wandering about the world.

Louise Grantham and Southern Book Publishers; John Michell; Colin Stevenson for the maps; and family and friends for the encouragement and love.

Comoros

Roukiat Ahmed, PRO at La Galawa Beach Hotel, and the management and staff of the hotel; Arnold Wernersson; Hakim Allaoui; Nadia Ahmed; Zalhata Sidi; Fatouma Bacar Chehou; John Mazamba; Mouhmar-Kadaffi Mohamed; Kamal Eddine and the Hotel Al-Amal; Salim Abodou, Curator of the Musée des Comores; Hassan Moussa.

Seychelles

Conrad Benoiton and Air Seychelles; John Benoiton; Joel Hoarau of Auberge de Bougainville; Serge Robert and Mason's Travel; Helen Etienne of La Retraite Guesthouse; Rosemarie Adrienne and La Louise Lodge; Anthony Hunt and Mountain Rise Hotel; Nicole La Buschagne-Smith and staff of the Hotel Coco de Mer; Marie-Jose d'Oger de Speville of the Indian Ocean Lodge; Oliver Dupont and the Paradise Sun Hotel; Cecile Hodoul of L'Archipel Hotel; Choppy's Bungalows; Nicholas Mederick of the Manresa Guesthouse; AE Geers and the staff of the

Sunset Beach Hotel; Edward Holloway and Beau Vallon Bay Hotel; Therese Blanc of Auberge Club des Seychelles; Paddy Brearley and Equator Sun Hotel; the management and staff of Mahé Beach hotel; Maryse Eichler de Saint Jorre and Northolme Hotel; Marie-Anne Hodoul of La Résidence; John Cruise-Wilkins; Stella Dowey, Curator of the National Museum of the Seychelles; Jean-Claude Pascal Mahoune, Senior Archivist at the Bastille; the management of Bird Island Lodge.

CONTENTS

HOW TO USE THIS GUIDE

To get the most enjoyment out of a visit to the Comoros or Seychelles, some form of prior planning is recommended. Although many tourists leave their itinerary to a travel agent or tour operator, independent travellers must have some idea of where they are going to stay, what they want to see and how they plan to get around.

Once you have decided which islands you would like to visit, turn to the relevant chapter in this guide book, and embark on the exciting task of working out a route, using the maps and suggestions provided. The description of each island is divided into sections, which take the prospective visitor gently into the magic of the locale.

Facts about the country include introductory information on its history and government, geography and climate, festivals and holidays. Facts for the visitor detail the nitty-gritty of travel. Information is provided on a range of topics from visas through to money, accommodation and places to eat. The sections on getting there feature international transport to the island, and those on getting around cater for those wanting to find the cheapest, easiest and most enjoyable way of seeing their chosen destination.

Each chapter also has a comprehensive section on the island's capital city. Here you will find where banks, post offices, tourist information and embassies are situated. The text offers a guided walk through the city and a street map for quick orientation.

The next section details various regions of each island. Visitors are advised on accommodation, places to eat, shopping and sights, and there are personalised notes on things travellers should try.

The text contains ample general information on health, planning, photography, money and suggested length of stay.

I have attempted to furnish visitors with as much detailed information as possible. However, countries do change; often very abruptly. If you encounter problems that could affect future travellers, or have suggestions that may benefit visitors to the area, please write to me care of my publishers. All letters will be acknowledged; the material will be incorporated in updated editions of this guide book.

Note: Comoros is the correct English name of the country, but the islands are commonly referred to as the Comores, which is the French spelling.

1 GENERAL INFORMATION

While the majority of visitors to the Comoros and Seychelles islands go on organised package tours, there is a growing number of travellers who are more interested in discovering the region without the assistance of guides and tour operators. This section is directed particularly at these people.

PLANNING

Contrary to what many prospective visitors may presume, the two island groups detailed in this book are rich with unique things to see and do. No two of the islands are entirely alike. Although it may be true that all have stretches of white beaches, palm trees and turquoise lagoons, there is a great deal more to attract and interest travellers. If you decide to visit one of the islands, ask yourself several questions before settling on a destination: What is it that you hope to do on the island? Is there a particular standard of accommodation you want? What type of flora and fauna would you like to see? Are you looking for a beach holiday, an adventure holiday or a little of both? How much money do you have in your budget? How do you plan to travel to and around the island? Do you want to meet the locals and learn about their culture? Would you like to see the island with other tourists or explore the remote areas on your own?

From the answers to these questions you will be able to formulate your ideal island vacation. The following synopsis may provide a useful, quick reference.

Comoros: Expensive. Largest active volcanic crater in the world. Islamic culture. Rainforests. Scuba diving. Livingstone's giant fruit bat. Poor tourism infrastructure. Limited tourist-class hotels. Good public transport network. Remote villages. Spice plantations. Opportunity of staying with the locals.

Seychelles: Expensive. Typical tropical island paradise. Beaches. Well-developed tourism industry. Good hotel accommodation. Forests. Water sports. Scuba diving. Uninhabited atolls. Excellent inter-island transport. Friendly locals. Creole culture. Large marine nature reserves. Black parrot. Black paradise flycatcher. Coconut groves. Remote coves and bays.

Once you have decided which island to visit, it is important to know its size, especially if you plan to hike or hire a vehicle. This guide gives the size of all the popular islands. Many visitors are surprised, upon arrival, to discover just how small the islands actually are. About six weeks prior to departure, it is advisable to have all the necessary vaccinations and dentist check-ups, and apply for International Driving Permits, visas and traveller's cheques.

LENGTH OF STAY

The length of time you spend on an island often depends on things beyond your control, e.g. budget, employment, university terms. The average tourist spends 10-14 days on an island group. In that time it is quite possible to get a good overall view of either the Comoros or Seychelles. Provided you do not spend every day lying in the sun outside your hotel, you will be able to see most of the important sites, plus experience many of the delights that each of the island groups has to offer its visitors.

Travellers who have lots of time, but little money, should consider a stay of at least three weeks. This will allow you sufficient time to use public transport, to track down cheap accommodation and local restaurants, to hike to the sites and to mix with the islanders.

Any visit under seven days is hardly worth the expense of getting there. Arrival and departure formalities will leave you with only five days in which to discover the islands you have chosen. With four islands in the Comoros and 117 in the Seychelles, visitors staying less than seven days will not be able to reach many of the fascinating outer islands. Inter-island transport takes time, although an aircraft speeds things up by a few hours. Taking the ferry or a trading vessel may require at least half a day to reach the inner islands and several days to reach distant ones.

BEHAVIOUR

This is one of the most vital aspects of island travel. Attention to your conduct will make the difference between the best or worst trip of your life. Sunbathing topless or in a G-string is permissible on the beaches of tourist hotels, but forbidden on all public beaches. Drinking in public is frowned upon on many of the islands, and will result in your arrest if you try it in the Comoros. Smoking cannabis or hashish on the street is illegal, but acceptable if done in the privacy of your room or private house. Exchanging money on the black market is expressly forbidden on all the islands, although it may not seem so in the Comoros. If caught, you run the risk of having the money confiscated and spending a few hours in some deplorable island prison.

Be polite, smile a great deal, and above all else, remain calm, no matter what the situation. The military and police on some of the islands feel that they have to exert their authority occasionally. Be courteous but firm. There have seldom been reports of any violence being perpetrated by paramilitary forces against tourists.

You will have to deal with petty government officials if travelling independently. Allow them their power and grandiose gestures. Within a few minutes they lose interest and complete the necessary paperwork. If a situation becomes too unpleasant, ask to see their superior; this usually evokes surprise and then swift assistance.

It is necessary to understand that you are a foreigner, with different principles, traditions and values. You are bound to make cultural blunders at some stage of your travels. Quickly apologise for breaking any taboo, and immediately ask that someone explain the correct procedure or behaviour. Through years of Third World travel I have learned that a sincere, humble attitude goes a long way towards assuring one's acceptance by traditional people. Do not get angry; this will only cause more annoyance and could possibly prevent you from getting to know the people of the island.

PHOTOGRAPHY

Take along plenty of film and spare batteries. The number of opportunities for photographers is staggering. For taking photos of those exotic night shows, so popular at tourist hotels, you will need a pivotal flash, and preferably a tripod. The best film to use for travel photography is 64 ASA colour reversal film for slides. Print photographs have a tendency to lose depth of colour and often appear overexposed. In addition to this, colour reversal film is cheaper to process and offers photographers the required medium should they wish to sell any of their photos to libraries or tour companies.

Your camera's biggest enemy on the islands, apart from the sun, is the fine coral or volcanic sand. Keep all rolls of film tightly closed in their cases, and whenever possible keep your camera in its bag or case. It is advisable to purchase yourself a camera cleaning kit before departure.

Use this daily on your equipment. Keeping your camera equipment dry is another problem. Given the high heat, intense humidity and frequent rain, it may make more sense to take along an underwater camera. If your camera does get wet, immediately strip it down and thoroughly dry all the parts, preferably with pressurised air, or else a soft cloth.

Visitors from northern climes may be rather disappointed by their photographs of the islands. The main reason for this is the degree and intensity of light in the tropics. Tropical sunlight is a great deal more concentrated than the light in temperate latitudes. The best time to take photographs is early morning and late afternoon or early evening. Photos taken around midday are inevitably "washed out" or overexposed. The only reasonable solution to taking photos at this time is to use shade filters. But even these are often not enough to dull the strong sunlight of the Indian Ocean islands.

Always ask permission before taking photographs of people. On the Seychelles and Comoros many people are averse to having their pictures taken, because they believe that having their photo taken is akin to having their souls stolen. The women on the Comoros are very particular in this regard. You will usually be asked for money before being allowed to take a photo. Whether you agree to pay for the privilege, or rather not take the photo, is entirely up to you. Remember, though, the image you must present to poverty-stricken islanders, as you walk around with thousands of dollars' worth of camera equipment around your neck, but refuse to pay a few francs for taking their photograph. What several unscrupulous photographers have done in the past – to the detriment of all future travellers – is to steal photographs by using a zoom lens. Not only is this insensitive and selfish, it also creates difficulties for other visitors. Be polite, ask, and if they say no, respect their wishes.

Airport X-ray equipment may damage film, irrespective of whether it is exposed or not. Lead-lined bags are one solution. A better idea, however, is to get a letter written in French stating that you are a photographer and want your equipment hand-checked. Most airport authorities will comply. If they refuse, ask to see the Chief Inspector.

HEALTH

It is highly unlikely that you will fall ill while visiting the Comoros or Seychelles. However, some knowledge of what may go wrong is necessary, especially for independent travellers. Get yourself as fit and healthy as possible before leaving home. Have your injections at least six weeks prior to departure. All the islands have good medical facilities, so do not be afraid to visit a hospital, clinic, dentist or doctor should you feel ill. Many of the tourist-class hotels have both a nurse and doctor on call.

All visitors should carry a first-aid kit. It need not be large, but should include basic remedies and equipment for emergency first-aid. The kit I have carried around with me during several years of travel to Third World destinations includes:

- Antihistamine – for allergies, poisonous stings and bites.
- Antibiotics – a broad-spectrum antibiotic is useful for a whole range of medical problems. Consult your doctor on the best course to take with you. Do not forget to keep the prescription with the tablets.
- Antiseptic (solution or cream) – for cuts and scratches.
- Bandages and plasters – at least one long bandage, one triangular bandage and an assortment of plaster strips.
- Calamine – for sunburn, insect bites and stings.
- Diarrhoea remedy – the change of food could cause a slight stomach upset for a few days.
- Glucose – most people perspire profusely during their first few days in the tropics. Make sure to keep your electrolytes up.
- Syringes and needles – if you need an injection while on the islands, ask the medical staff to use your sterilised equipment.
- Insect repellent – you will be astounded by the number of creepy-crawlies on the islands. The suggested repellents to take along are smouldering coils, a rub-on stick and aerosol spray.
- Prescriptions for glasses, scheduled drugs you may need and a letter detailing any potentially dangerous allergies you may have, e.g. bee stings, penicillin or sulpha drugs. Also carry a contact number and address for your next of kin and private physician.
- Scissors, pocket-knife, tweezers, mirror, eyewash and a course of multivitamins (this must include high doses of calcium and vitamin A to help you cope with the heat).

All visitors must have an International Certificate of Vaccination. These are available from your home country's Department of Health. Visitors will be issued with the certificate when they have had their vaccinations. The suggested inoculations are: yellow fever, cholera, infectious hepatitis, typhoid and tetanus. You should already have been vaccinated against polio and smallpox as a child. If not, you can have these vaccinations done with the others.

Sun

The biggest threat to your health while visiting the islands is the sun. It is fierce, with a high UV factor every day. All visitors must wear a hat and adequate sun-protection cream. Anything under factor 8 strength suntan lotion is useless. Take special care during your first few days outside. The light reflected off the ocean is enough to burn you, let alone lying for hours on end in direct sunlight. Children, especially, should be kept in the shade as much as possible. Areas most prone to severe sunburn are your feet, backs of legs and head. Try to wear a hat even in the water. Avoid doing anything too strenuous in the tropical heat. Keep body fluids up by drinking lots of water and fruit juice. Drinking alcohol in the sun is a sure way of not only getting horribly drunk, but also heat stroke.

Diarrhoea

Relatively few visitors develop diarrhoea. Those who do usually feel well again within a few days, especially if they stop eating the spicy island food until they are better. Eat dry, bland food such as bread. Avoid fruit and dairy products, but remember to keep taking lots of fluids – something like black tea or flat cola. Do not immediately resort to the contents of your first-aid kit. If the situation persists after two days on a bland diet, try Lomotil. If you are still ill by the fourth day, consult a doctor.

Malaria

This is the biggest disease threat to a visitors' health in the tropics. The disease is caused by a bite from an infected female anopheles mosquito. These mosquitos are mainly active during the hours of darkness. The best policy is to ensure that you do not get bitten: use insect repellant on exposed areas of your body at night and burn an anti-mosquito coil.

Symptoms of this potentially lethal disease are severe headaches, alternate bouts of sweating and shivering and a general decline in your health. Professional help must be sought immediately.

Just as fast as chemists devise new drugs for combating malaria, so the mosquito becomes resistant to the chemicals. Consult your doctor on the latest recommendations. At the time of writing, the prescribed anti-malarial programme is chloroquine tablets once a week, on the same day each week. Combine this with proguanil taken daily. Start the regimen about two weeks before leaving for the islands, and then continue for three weeks after your return. The most powerful anti-malarial prophylactic is mefloquine – this should only be taken under a doctor's guidance.

MONEY

On all the islands of the south-western Indian Ocean the French franc is accepted. On the Comoros it is legal tender, even though the Comorians have their own currency. On the Seychelles it is the easiest money to exchange at banks and hotels. The strongest currency to take to the islands is pounds sterling, which banks are willing to convert into local currency. US dollars are always easy to use and exchange. On islands that have a well-developed tourist industry, foreigners are often required to pay for hotels and airline flights in a foreign currency.

Cash remains the best way to take money to the islands, but is also the most unsafe. Your next alternative is traveller's cheques: American Express and Thomas Cook are still the best. Keep a careful record of each transaction and write down all your cheque numbers. Put this information in a safe place. The suggested currency for traveller's cheques is French francs, US dollars, German marks and pounds sterling. Other currency is not only grossly undervalued, but in some places will not be accepted.

Credit cards are useful if you plan to stay at expensive hotels. French credit cards, such as Carte Bleu, are most readily accepted by local banks. Diners Club, Mastercard and Visa can be used to pay bills, but may be difficult to draw cash from. No hotel will allow purely a cash withdrawal from a credit card. One solution is to ask the cashier to charge your bill at a higher price and then give you change.

Personal cheques from foreign visitors are not accepted anywhere in the Indian Ocean islands.

WHAT TO TAKE

Take as little as possible. The islands are warm, some might say downright hot. Humidity is high, the sun is strong and even breezes can become too balmy. Obviously, if staying at upmarket hotels you will need to take along a lot more clothing than if you spend your trip using local transport and sleeping in huts. Such travellers are advised to pack all their gear into a backpack, and include a large plastic bag with which to cover the pack for aircraft flights and against rain. Tourists staying in hotels will be comfortable with a suitcase and a small day-pack.

A suggested list of clothing:
one pair of denims, two pairs of cotton shorts, one swimming costume, one sarong, one dress-up set of clothes, one windcheater, one raincoat or poncho, one lightweight jersey, two T-shirts, one pair of sneakers, one pair of sandals, one hat and sunglasses.

Finally, do not forget those small items that never seem important until you are far from home:
a penknife (Swiss Army type), sewing kit, two small and two medium-sized locks, a length of cloth you can wear and on which you can lie, toiletries, one towel, clothes washing kit, including an elastic line and a few pegs.

PART 1

COMOROS

2 FACTS ABOUT THE COUNTRY

The Comoros are the "dream islands" of the adventurer in all of us. From their shores, pirates, buccaneers and corsairs sailed out to prey on cargo-laden East Indiamen. Persian and Omani sultans once ruled the islands, amassing huge fortunes from their dealings in the infamous slave trade. Today the Comoros are still filled with an intrigue, mystery and allure that make them irresistible to many travellers.

More than anything else, a Comoros vacation is about people and natural splendour. Meeting the Comorians requires effort. Sadly, this is something many tourists neglect. Visitors who try to understand and respect the ways of Sunni Muslims will discover the kind hearts of the hospitable and gracious Comorian natives. Their faith is of paramount importance to them.

The Comoros have only recently become an important tourist attraction. Since then they have lost some of their original unspoilt atmosphere; the wilderness and the Comorian culture are dying fast, and may not survive even 20 more years of coups d'état, industrialisation and mass tourism. Visitors who wish to experience the traditional Comorian way of life should visit these winsome islands in the Indian Ocean now.

HISTORY

The history of the Comoros has been inextricably linked to three other countries: Persia and Africa during the pre-colonial era, and France in modern times. Despite continuing disagreements, it is generally accepted that the first inhabitants of the Comoros arrived from Polynesia. Following the south equatorial current and driven by seasonal southeast monsoons, the first seaborne arrivals landed on the tiny cluster of islands almost 2 000 years ago. Many scholars, however, believe that the islands' discoverers were emissaries from the Middle East. Legend has it that King Solomon and the Queen of Sheba married and spent their honeymoon on Grande Comore.

It is definite that Arab sailors made landfall on the Comoros around AD 620. This was the origin of Islam in the country. Yet, visitors will soon notice that the biggest racial influence on the Comoros is not

COMOROS ARCHIPELAGO

0   10 km

N

Le Galawa Beach
hotel & casino
Bangoi-Kouni
Mitsamiouli
Lac Sale
Île Aux
Tortues
Haoveni
Bouni Beach

HAHAYA
INTERNATIONAL
AIRPORT

GRANDE COMORE

Itsandra Sun hotel
& casino
Itsandra
Moroni
Karthala
Volcano
Iconi
Pidjani

ANJOUAN

Jimilimé

Singani
Foumbouni
Bimbini
Foumbani
Quani
Tsembehou
Chindini
Sima
Mutsamudu
Bambao

Lac de Dziaiandze

Domoni
M'Batse
Hotel
Pomoni
Domoni
Fomboni
Airport Mohéli
Moya
Wallah
Niumashuwa
Wawani
Itsamia Beach
Chiroroni
Sambia
Iconi

Ilots de
Niumashuwa
MOHÉLI

Accoua
Soulou
Mamoudzou
Dzaoudzi
Kombani
Pamandzi
MAYOTTE
Sada
Dembeni
Bweni
Bandrele
Kani-Keli
Saziley

Arabic, but African. Less than 500 km away to the west, Africa offered a lucrative supply of human resources for the slave-trading Arabs. Striking deals with African tribal chiefs, the slave traders often interned slaves on the Comoros while European and Arab buyers were sought. Then, as the islands started to develop, many of the slaves were kept to work the plantations. Intermarriage was inevitable, and the result is the pleasing mixture of people who inhabit the Comoros today.

Sultans were the early rulers of these islands. Getting rich on the spice and slave trade, they lived lives of indolent luxury. The Shirazi Arabs from Persia dominated the Comoros during this period. They continued trading in slaves until 1904 when international pressure succeeded in putting a stop to the trade in humans.

On Grande Comore alone there were nine sultans, who each governed and owned a portion of the volcanic island. Anjouan had two sultans, and Mohéli and Mayotte one each. Internecine strife between the sultans was common and hastened the eventual collapse of Arabic rule on the Comoros.

Until the arrival of the colonising French, the only enemies that had to be faced by forces of the sultans were the marauding Sakalava pirates from north-west Madagascar. Their Viking-like strikes on coastal settlements were a constant threat to the Arab settlers. Abducting women, looting and killing, the Sakalava buccaneers were hated and feared by the Comorian sultans who were virtually powerless against them. The Sakalava continued to foray and rampage through the islands until well into the 19th century, when superior French naval power halted their attacks.

The first recorded Europeans to land on the Comoros were the Portuguese navigators Diaz and Suarez. But they seemed to have little interest in the islands: water, food and fuel were available in abundance, but the tiny islands were too far off the main ocean routes to be of any benefit to Portuguese traders. The Dutch, too, landed on the islands. But they had found richer pickings on the African mainland and on the islands east of Madagascar. Even the Germans waded ashore to plant a flag at Foumbouni, on the south-east of Grande Comore.

None of the Europeans stayed or settled these isolated islands between the bulk of Africa and the wilderness of Madagascar, until the French happened along and struck a deal with the Sultan of Mayotte in 1843. The old sultan, Sahalave Andriantsoli, ceded the island in return for an annual rent and the promise of an education, in France, for his sons. The French wasted no time in stationing troops on the island and battleships off the coast, and establishing a colonial administration.

The sultans on the other islands were aghast. All manner of plans were laid by each one to evict the French, but none ever came to fruition. In a colonial display of arrogance, the French simply annexed Mohéli in 1886. The sultan on the island was powerless in the face of the French military. Turning their attention to Grande Comore and Anjouan, the invading French found themselves up against greater opposition. But as the French navy bombarded the islands and staged a blockade, the sultans realised that their rule was over. Landing triumphantly in 1912, French troops proclaimed Grande Comore and Anjouan part of the French empire.

However, the islands needed better administration and development if they were to provide France with income. So, the French government placed the Comoros under the jurisdiction of its administration in Madagascar. At first apathetic and defeated, the Comorians soon began to fight back. There were several demonstrations, all savagely put down by French soldiers. To further enforce their authority, the French banned all newspapers and political parties were disbanded. No native was allowed either to arrive at or leave the Comoros without written permission, which was granted only under exceptional circumstances.

In 1946 the Comorians were granted their first step on the road to liberation. They were permitted to be independent of Madagascar and have their own French administration on the islands. In 1961 the Comoros became self-governing within the framework of French colonialism: a so-called *Territoire d'Outre-Mer*. In 1961 Saïd Mohammed Cheik became the first lackey President of the Comoros.

For the youths, things were changing too slowly; they demanded total autonomy and took to the streets en masse in 1968. France was enraged and sent in crack units of the army to quash the rebellion. This they did so violently that world governments voiced their displeasure. In an effort to appease the critics, France allowed political parties to form and campaign publicly.

Pressure was now mounting against colonial powers. Both international and local demands were forcing Great Britain, Germany and France to reconsider their positions. But another problem loomed on the Comoros in 1970. President Saïd Mohammed died and was replaced by a prince, Saïd Ibrahim. Being under the rule of an aristocrat did not sit well with many Comorians, and they continued fighting for independence and a general election. The French government, loath to surrender any territories, decided to hold a referendum on the Comoros in 1974.

Ninety-two per cent of the population voted for independence; the remainder were nearly all on the island of Mayotte. To please the international community, France gave Grande Comore, Anjouan and Mohéli a greater degree of autonomy and political representation within the French administration. This was not enough for many. On 6 July 1975 Ahmed Abdallah Abderemane declared unilateral independence on behalf of all the islands; only Mayotte excluded itself. The French government initially did nothing, but then started withdrawing financial investment, personnel and trading houses.

Within a month, Abdallah was deposed in a coup led by French mercenary Bob Dénard (of Benin and Biafra notoriety), and went into exile in Paris. Replacing him, for the interim, was Saïd Mohammed Djaffar. Grudgingly, in December 1975, France acknowledged the new Comorian government.

More trouble started almost immediately. On 2 January 1976 Ali Solih grabbed power from the transitional government and attempted to install a unique form of rule that involved a mixture of Koranic teachings and Chinese Communism. He expropriated all the remaining French holdings in the Comoros and dismissed all civil servants. Giving supreme power to his Jeunesse Révolutionnaire (Revolutionary Youth), he allowed them to run the country. This they did – into the ground! They burned all government documents, abolished purdah for women and forbade the practice of traditional rituals and ceremonies. To further entrench himself, Ali Solih declared himself a Muslim prophet and then, God.

France suspended all aid. Solih's popularity plummeted. The youth brigades turned into bullying tyrants who kept the populace terrified and subservient. Adding to the already volatile situation, violent persecution of Comorians on the west coast of Madagascar saw 20 000 of them return to the already overpopulated Comoros in December 1976. Then the mighty Karthala volcano erupted in 1977.

Things got steadily worse and the people became more rebellious. There were four coup d'état attempts against the dictatorial and obviously mentally unstable Ali Solih; none was successful. In a desperate attempt to remove him, Ahmed Abdallah, several exiled businessmen and the French Secret Service decided to use Bob Dénard and his mercenaries again.

Sneaking into the country, Dénard and 29 mercenaries stormed the presidential palace in the early hours of 13 May 1978. Ali Solih was arrested after only 33 months in power, his Revolutionary Youth disbanded and Ahmed Abdallah reinstated as ruler, although he had to share power with Mohammed Ahmed. Three days later, while supposedly trying to escape, Ali Solih was shot and killed.

Despite having his new Comorian delegation kicked out of the OAU, Abdallah was not about to rule without help, and he kept the mercenaries on as his Presidential Guard. He claimed complete control in December 1978. Declaring the Comoros an Islamic Republic, he set about the awesome task of rebuilding the economy.

Coups d'état, however, seem to be a feature of Comorian politics. In early 1985 a plot devised by a career diplomat, Saïd Ali Kemal, was thwarted in Australia where he tried to recruit mercenaries to fight in the Comoros. Still in 1985 another plan to overthrow Ahmed Abdallah was uncovered among Comorian members of his personal guard. Towards the end of 1985, 70 members of the banned Front Démocratique (FD) were jailed for planning a coup against Abdallah.

To show the world that he was still acceptable to the islanders, Ahmed Abdallah held an election in March 1987 and was re-elected. There were murmurs from the opposition parties concerning fraud and ballot lists, but nothing was ever publicly proven. Confident in his popularity, Abdallah accepted an invitation to attend talks in France. While he was away, several high-ranking officers and soldiers staged another coup attempt. But Abdallah's highly trained, not to mention highly paid, mercenaries suppressed the attack, emerging victorious heroes.

Not unexpectedly, another bloody coup was staged on 26 November 1989. This time Abdallah was assassinated. Although the exact details have never been made public, rumours of murder, chicanery and France's involvement are still heard among the Comorians. What is known from court proceedings is that Bob Dénard, the soldier of fortune, was with the president when he was killed. According to a statement made by Dénard, radical elements within the armed forces had attacked the Presidential Palace. In a state of panic, one of Abdallah's bodyguards rushed into the room and shot the president five times around the heart. In turn, one of the most infamous of the mercenary leaders, Captain Marques, shot the guard and then, for some unexplained reason, gutted him with a knife. No-one was ever brought to trial for the assassination of the president. Readers who are interested in the cover-ups, lies and manipulation surrounding the coup and death of Abdallah are advised to read *Last of the pirates* by Samantha Weinberg (Jonathan Cape Books, London, 1994).

The mercenaries had thankfully gone, and Saïd Mohammed Djohar – elder brother of the murdered anti-French president, Ali Solih – became the unpopular head of state. Bob Dénard, who had married a Comorian woman, was deported from the islands, but his house and holdings remain his own.

The Comoros are now again part of the OAU. Although the UN supports Comorian claims to ownership of Mayotte, the Mahorais of Mayotte are adamant that they want to remain part of France – just as another Indian Ocean island, Réunion, still is.

As the Comoros struggle out of decades of civil strife, a collapsed economy and harsh religious laws, they are gaining respect and acceptance worldwide. A major advance was made when they were admitted to the exclusive Indian Ocean Commission in 1985.

GOVERNMENT

According to the Comorian constitution, elections must be held every six years, with no one person holding the office of president for longer than 12 years. There is a council of 11 ministers and a federal assembly of 42 delegates. Each of the three islands has a governor, chosen by the incumbent president.

Mayotte continues under French administration. She is controlled by the Ministère d'Outre-Mer in France as a Collectivité Territoriale. There is a prefect and council of ministers to govern the island. A detachment made up of divisions from the Third Infantry Regiment of the French Foreign Legion is stationed on the island to prevent any rebelliousness or ideas that the Comorian government may have about claiming Mayotte.

GEOGRAPHY

Twenty-two million years ago, 5 km beneath the Indian Ocean, a volcanic cousin of the south-western Indian ridge started erupting. For another 10 million years liquid rock continued spilling from the mantle until the summit emerged above the surface of the sea about 12 million years ago. The first of these mountain peaks to appear was the island of Mayotte, nearly 500 km east of Africa. The last to emerge from the

depths was Grande Comore, about 300 km east of the African mainland, its volcano still active today.

The four main islands which make up the Comoros are Mayotte,
Anjouan, Mohéli and Grande Comore. Over millions of years the mass
of the islands will force the sea floor down and surface erosion will
flatten the now mountainous islands into plains. Slowly the islands will
disappear beneath the waves to form what is known, in oceanographic
terms, as a guyot: a flat-topped submarine mountain.

On Grande Comore, which is 70 km long, Karthala volcano (2 400 m)
still occasionally erupts. The Comoros islands are the summits of a
volcanic ridge.

Lying at the northern entry to the Mozambique Channel, the islands
are washed by the warm waters of the south-flowing Mozambique
Current coming from the equator. The volcanic soils of the Comoros,
much younger than those of either Africa or Madagascar, are porous
but rich in nutrients.

There are no streams on Grande Comore as most of the surface run-
off is quickly percolated into the volcanic earth. The water needed by
the population is collected in giant water tanks set up around the island
in catchment areas and led to public cisterns in each settlement. Waterfalls, rivers and forests are features of Anjouan, Mohéli and Mayotte.

Geologically young, the islands are still growing in size. Only Mayotte
has eroded sufficiently to form an encircling reef from the coral living
in these nutrient-rich waters. Visitors may see the crater of the active
volcano on Grande Comore, plus some of the islands' interesting black
beaches.

CLIMATE

Warmed by equatorial air masses in January and cooled by tropical air
masses in July, the Comoros have two distinct seasons: summer and
winter. Spring and autumn hardly exist.

Summer, also known as the hot, wet season, lasts from November
to April. At this time, high humidity is the most striking characteristic
of the climate. Temperatures range from a pleasant 24 °C to a sweltering
33 °C. The highest temperatures – and highest humidity – occur in
March-April and November-December. January has the highest rainfall
and heavy rainstorms are common. This is also the southern cyclone
season. Raising both sea and land temperatures, the warm "kashkazi"

winds blow in from the north-west, creating high-altitude atmospheric turbulence in the confines of the Mozambique Channel.

Winter, known as the cool, dry season, extends from May to late October. This is the best time to visit the Comoros. There is little of the oppressive humidity, temperatures hover between 19 °C and 25 °C, and nights are still warm enough to go about in shirtsleeves. The lowest temperatures are experienced from July to September, but they never fall below 17 °C. October is the month of lowest rainfall, a mere 85 mm. Even the "kusi" breezes that blow from the south during winter are pleasant.

POPULATION

With almost 600 000 people and only 2 250 square km of land the Comoros face serious overpopulation. Despite clinics and family-planning programmes the Muslim populace maintains its belief that birth control and abortion are wrong. The Grand Mufti (the main Islamic religious leader) has remained surprisingly silent on this serious matter. Visitors will be amazed by the large number of children everywhere. With an estimated 68% of all Comorians under the age of 30, it is only a matter of time before the country's already weak infrastructure is overburdened, perhaps even to the point of collapse.

An attractive people, Comorians are a mixture of Arab, south-west Asian, African and a little French. This polyglot of races and cultures has created a nation of passionate, wily and astute people. Many visitors may be surprised at the high level of literacy among the islanders, in spite of regular strikes by school teachers, boycotting of classes and the other vagaries of the unstable educational system. Politics is a favourite topic, and anti-French sentiment is strong. If you venture beyond the glitzy confines of the tourist hotels, you may well end up chatting to a local about Dénard, the French and the present government. It is useful to have some background knowledge of what has happened and what is going on politically and economically on the islands.

CULTURE

Over 99% of Comorians are Muslim, mostly Sunni. About 20% of Comorian men practise polygamy, but strictly according to the injunctions of Mohammed. Recently, however, there have been influential arrivals preaching the need for fanatic fundamentalism. Many Comorians are somewhat averse to these extremist teachings, especially the older people. Among the unemployed youth the call for drastic religious changes and whispers of "jihad" against the French are gaining popularity. In the male-dominated world of Islam, it is mostly young males who are in favour of these changes. The young women remain as peaceful, attractive and beguiling as ever.

During the week men wear Western-style clothing, occasionally adding a yamatso, a beautifully embroidered cap. Over weekends there is a noticeable change in men's attire. The long white kandou becomes prevalent. These dress-like outfits are worn by Muslims throughout the Arab world, especially in Saudi Arabia. Long trousers are worn underneath. For all religious and public functions the wearing of a kandou and yamatso is *de rigueur.*

Women wear a colourful length of cotton cloth called a chiromani, which they wrap about themselves. Older women tend to cover their heads with it as well, but the young usually leave their braids exposed, preferring to throw the chiromani over their shoulder as a traditional accessory, rather than the main item of dress. The dominant colours appear to be red and white, though some of the older women wear more demure green, gold and black.

Should you be one of the rare *mzungus* (Europeans) fortunate enough to be invited to a *grand mariage* (as I was), you will be given the appropriate clothing to wear, whether you are male or female. Women should remember that if they attend a public gathering where the Koran is read, the head must be covered, and preferably the face as well, with just a slit for the eyes to peer through.

The bright yellow face-packs that you see women wearing on the Comoros serve a multitude of purposes. Made of powdered sandalwood, tumeric and water, the pack is used as a beauty treatment. It protects the wearer from the harsh Comorian sun, acts as an astringent and keeps the skin clear of blemishes. Unlike self-conscious European women, the Comorian ladies wear the face-packs at any time. You will see the protective masks worn in the markets, at festivals, at home, in nightclubs and at work.

Dance

No visitor to the Comoros will leave without at least one night of dancing. Dancing is a way of life for the islanders. Whether you insist on spending every evening at your hotel, or go out to the discos and palm-frond nightclubs, rest assured that you will dance. Guests at weddings or parties are in for hours of abandoned revelry that always involves dancing.

The traditional dances are all carefully choreographed according to ancient routines. Although at the outset of festivities the dances are decidedly Arabic in their movements, towards the end they become predominantly African in movements and rhythms. The *mougodro* dance, seen most frequently at dances on Mohéli, is typically African in its sequences. In the villages, women use the excuse of pounding cassava and maize to dance what is known as the *danse de pilon*. The women move around a wooden pestle exchanging the long, heavy mortars without breaking rhythm. This is a beautiful dance to watch.

Crafts

Curios are strangely lacking in the Comoros.

However, the islanders seem to believe that their front door must always be a work of art. In keeping with Arab tradition, the doors of homes are embossed and carved by craftsmen using traditional tools. The best place to see these experts at work is in the village of Domoni on Anjouan.

Boatmaking is another of the traditional crafts still practised in the Comoros. On the beach at Mitsamiouli village you can see workmen carving *galawas* out of tree trunks. At Ouani, planks are hewn and pegged together for the making of fishing smacks.

On Anjouan, the villagers at Sima, Bangweni and Dzindri specialise in raffia dolls dressed up in traditional clothing. The islanders themselves put these dolls in their houses; the animist influence is much stronger on Anjouan and Mohéli than on Grande Comore or Mayotte.

Grand mariage

Arguably the most wonderful cultural event to see or attend in the Comoros is a traditional *grand mariage* or wedding feast, supposedly based on the original *grand mariage* of King Solomon to the Queen of Sheba. Despite the concerted efforts of President Ali Solih – during his short reign – to eradicate the expensive ritual, it is still occasionally indulged in today.

Getting married in the Comoros is a thoroughly joyous and festive occasion. A strict set of laws and traditions must be followed before the couple are allowed to be together. The old way of an arranged marriage is being shoved aside by the idea that love is the main pre-requisite for a happy union.

The wedding is divided into two parts. First the man approaches his father and tells him of his intention to marry. Then the father, together with his son, pays a visit to the family of the woman. The son's request is put forward by his father to the parents of the woman. If the proposal is acceptable to the mother and father, the daughter is summoned and the proposition put to her by her own father. If she agrees, a date is set. On the agreed date the local Mufti or religious leader, in the presence of the parents and a few relatives, reads a few scriptural injunctions from the Koran, and then commands the pair to be faithful and supportive, no matter what, until death separates them. He then places their hands together and the marriage is sealed.

That, however, is only the first part. The public manifestation or second part of the wedding only takes place once the man has enough money to hold a lavish reception and buy his wife her dowry. This can take anything from four to 12 years, depending on his income. The idea is that the bigger and more elaborate the reception, the higher will be his standing in the community. He may even achieve the rank of "Notable", getting invited to voice his opinions in village affairs and becoming one of the elite. You can usually see these "Notables" sitting around in village squares, dressed in kandou and yamatso, with an emerald green or sapphire blue length of cloth around their necks.

The second part of the wedding is obviously the major event. First the bridegroom, dressed in a long, black, gold-edged robe and sombre turban, is paraded through the village streets, accompanied by young boys singing, dancing and playing musical instruments. At the public square he is joined by a representative (a sort of best man) dressed in identical clothing. Both carry 24-carat Saudi Arabian gold scimitars. In the square are seated all the men who have been invited; the women stand to the side, their faces covered by chiromanis. Once again the Mufti reads passages from the Koran. Then everyone rises and does a slow jig, on the spot, before sitting down to hear the music of the band and youths. Roasted peanuts, biscuits and cold drinks are then handed out to all the men before the procession sets off through the streets again, this time to the bride's house.

Mention should be made here as to why the bridegroom goes to the bride's house. All over the Comoros visitors will notice numerous half-built houses. When a daughter is born the father immediately begins to construct a house for her. There is no rush to finish, but he does what he can, when he can afford the money and time. Upon her marriage, the family's gift to her is the house; the husband moves into the wife's new, and hopefully completed, house. The main implication of such a wise tradition is obvious – even after divorce, which is quite common on the Comoros, the wife retains her own house.

The bridegroom is met by the bride on the steps of her house. With a chivalrous bow he requests her permission to enter and reside in the house. She agrees and goes down the steps to take his hand. Followed by bridesmaids, whose hair is covered in honeysuckle, jasmine and ylang-ylang, the pair enter the house to a tumultuous welcome. All those invited must then walk past the gifts given to the bride by her husband. The gifts always include gold, precious stones and money. A *grand mariage* remains one of the best places for seeing the legendary skill of Comorian goldsmiths.

With the women clicking their tongues and the band playing, the men commence dancing in a circle, or several circles depending on the number present. Still secretive behind their chiromanis, the ylang-ylang-scented women then select dance partners. They do this by placing a scarf over the shoulder of the desired man. This can result in several scarfs ending up on one man's shoulders, while another man gets none. This is one of the very few instances in their religion-ruled lives that women are allowed a free choice. There is no animosity if a wife selects another man; chances are that her husband will end up with someone else anyway.

Then the dancing men stop for the ceremony of "slaughtering the bulls", which is merely symbolic nowadays: two groups of men play the bulls and the hunters. In ancient times men fought real bulls to the death.

Once this rite is over, the real feast can begin. And what a feast it is! First there is a period of eating and drinking. (Remember, no alcohol . . . well, at least until the Mufti leaves.) Invariably one of the women who has graced you with her chiromani or scarf will serve you food and cold drink. After a suitable time, the band strikes up and dancing begins. Each of your partners will expect at least four to six dances with you during the evening. As the night wears on and the musical beat accelerates from the restrained sounds of the Middle East to the enthralling rhythms of Africa, so too does the dancing tempo change. Whereas careful steps, coy glances and distance mark the early-evening dances, exuberance, sensuality and open smiles are a feature later at night.

When the sun peeps over the horizon and the mullah's call to prayer heralds a new day, the official celebration ends. You can, however, be certain that the unofficial festivities will continue for quite some time.

Getting invited to a *grand mariage* is not only a privilege granted to few foreigners, but also offers a nonpareil insight into a unique tradition. No-one must ever refuse such an invitation, the insult is unforgivable. There is no need to take a gift along, this is the bridegroom's time to give presents to his bride.

Theatre

Details about theatre productions, exhibitions and educational films may be obtained from the Musée des Comores (Centre National de Documentation et de Recherche Scientifique). This impressive white building is located next to the Nouveautés, opposite the Caisse Française de Développement, in Moroni.

ECONOMY

The Comoros' economy is desperate. Inflation is high, unemployment even higher (even among highly educated and qualified people), the Comorian franc devalued and exports almost non-existent. Over 60% of all food and 82% of consumer goods are imported. While the government tries to combat the problems, the people blame their economic woes on France. For years dependent on French assistance, the Comoros' production of food and necessities has waned. Even rice, the staple diet, is imported or provided by aid organisations. In remote villages you will see bags of rice from the USA, stamped: "Aid food, not to be sold", being sold at exorbitant prices in shops.

Ylang-ylang, vanilla and cloves are the main agricultural crops intended for foreign sale. Sadly, the demand and therefore price of these products has plummeted recently, leaving many estate owners bankrupt. Cassava, bananas and citrus are grown for family use, while fish is provided by the bounteous seas around the islands. Coconuts are simply plucked from the numerous palms all over the islands. Most people have chickens, a few cattle or goats, which are slaughtered for meat.

Because of the unstable political situation, tourism has not flourished as it has on other Indian Ocean islands. On Grande Comore there are only two top-class tourist hotels, La Galawa Beach and Itsandra Sun, while on the other islands you will be hard-pressed to find any tourism infrastructure at all. Plans are afoot to improve the situation. Already several international organisations have started working on creating a viable tourism industry.

Most visitors to the Comoros come from France and South Africa. The government has made several concessions concerning visas and taxes for the tourist trade, hoping to draw more holiday-makers. But until the country is more stable, prices are dropped and a tourist marketing plan is presented, the Comoros will continue to be an unlikely destination for most big-spending vacationers.

Electricity is another major problem. It is not uncommon for the capital, Moroni, to lose all electrical power at peak times. (Always take a torch with you to the Comoros.) On Grande Comore electricity is generated by huge diesel engines; this has made electricity on Grande Comore the most expensive in the world. On the other islands hydro-electric power has replaced diesel generators.

Water is another headache on Grande Comore. The soil is porous and there are no rivers or dams on the island. The entire water supply comes from rainwater caught in giant reservoirs and fed to metal cisterns in villages and towns. During the dry season there are frequently severe water restrictions. There are rumours that the Saudis may assist with the construction of a seawater desalination plant on Grande Comore, but nothing seems definite and I could get no confirmation from government officials.

Roads, on the other hand, are in good condition. Public transport is cheap and frequent, although it can be dangerous. You can reach virtually all villages by taking a bush-taxi (taxi-brousse).

Smuggling and racketeering reach huge proportions. With government corruption rampant, you are bound to encounter these activities several times while exploring the islands. Gold and precious stones from Madagascar and Saudi Arabia, inflated exchange rates for dollars and sterling, hashish from Zanzibar, local cannabis and firearms of East European origin can all be illegally purchased in the narrow alleys of Moroni, Mutsamudu, Fomboni and Mamoudzou.

RELIGION, HOLIDAYS AND FESTIVALS

Ninety-nine per cent of all Comorians are Muslim. There is only one Christian church on Grande Comore, and two on Anjouan. A visit to these places of worship on a Sunday morning will reveal how small the community of Christians is. On the other hand, Friday is the Muslim Comorians' day of prayer. Most people attend services and prayers at one of the numerous Friday (Jami Masjid) mosques. Shops are usually closed from about 11h00-14h00.

Islam is one of the newer religions to appear on the world's stage. Based on the visions recorded from AD 610 by the prophet Mohammed and contained in the Koran, Islam flourished since his death in AD 632. Taken to the Comoros by Arab sea-traders, the religion found instant favour with the islanders. To gain firsthand knowledge and receive direction, the Comorians sent one of their own to track down Mohammed in Saudi Arabia. Unfortunately their envoy arrived too late; the prophet was already dead. Nevertheless the envoy gained as much information and directives as he could and returned to the Comoros. The message of the Great Prophet was spread all across the islands by Islamic missionaries.

Not having suffered the violent split that affected Muslims in the Middle East in AD 662, the faith practised in the Comoros remains essentially a pure form of Islam. Though not as fanatic as Muslims in, say, Iran, Comorians do expect visitors to respect their traditions, laws and beliefs. Women are still held in low esteem by most Muslim men, but there is a noticeable change in this attitude now. Purdah, the custom of keeping women in seclusion and requiring that they be covered from head to toe when they go out, is virtually extinct nowadays. Nevertheless, most women still carry a length of cloth, the chiromani, with them, with which they cover their heads. During religious festivals and weddings women still cover their faces completely, with only their kohled eyes peeping through.

Despite the predominance of Islam, the ancient animist and shamanic traditions, brought from Africa, have not altogether disappeared. In the remote mountain villages of Anjouan and forest settlements of Grande Comore, you may still encounter rituals and practices that have barely changed since the arrival of the first slaves. The best time to see these secretive ceremonies is in autumn or spring, when offerings, incantations and trances are a feature of the festivals honouring the dead, thanking the spirits of the earth and invoking the 20 aspects of the medicine wheel. The villagers are wary of strangers attending these ceremonies and visitors are seldom allowed to just arrive unannounced. Speak to the curator at the museum in Moroni for details. Alternatively, head into the forests and hills a few days before the full moon in April or October and ingratiate yourself with a local village elder, who may invite you to attend their clandestine tribal ceremonies.

Steeped in the religion of Islam, and for many years under French rule, the Comorians' festive and public-holiday calendar is an amalgam of Muslim and Christian celebrations. Only Muslim celebrations are observed on Grande Comore, Anjouan and Mohéli, while both Muslim and Christian holidays are observed on Mayotte.

The Comoros observe the following Islamic festivals, based on the lunar year:
Ramadan (*Lailatul-Qadr*) – falls in the first quarter of the year. (A month of daily fasting, during which disciples are allowed to eat and drink only before sunrise and after sunset. This is a bad time to visit the Comoros: everyone is short-tempered, hungry and stressed.)
Id-ul-Fitr (public holiday) – the end of Ramadan, when the new moon appears. This is the biggest celebration in the Islamic calendar.
Id-el-Kabir (public holiday) – in honour of Abraham, for his unswerving devotion to God, even to the point of being prepared to offer his son as a sacrifice.
Maoulid or *Rabi-ul-Awwal* (public holiday) – celebration observing the birth of the Great Prophet, Mohammed.
Leilat ul-Miradj (public holiday) – marks the ascension of Mohammed to heaven.
Muharram (public holiday) – the Islamic new year.
Ashoura (public holiday) – mournful day in honour of the martyr Imam Hussein.
Republic day (public holiday) – 6 July.

Other Islamic holidays and religious days are the following (with the secular months in which they fall):
January – *Meerajun-Nabie*
January – *Lailatul-Baraat*
May – *Zil Hajj* (Day of Haj)
May – *Eid-ul-Adha*
August – *Rabi-ul-Akir*
August – *Gyarwin Shareef*
December – *Miraajun-Nabi*

Additional holidays on French-governed Mayotte:
1 January – New Year's Day
April – Good Friday
May – Ascension Day
25 December – Christmas Day

WILDLIFE

Fauna

The Comoros have few terrestrial faunal species. While the sea holds
a profusion of fish, including several submarine oddities, land animals
are restricted to birds, bats and domestic creatures. A few lemurs, imported from Madagascar as pets in the last century, escaped and established small populations now inhabiting the vanishing forests on
Grande Comore and Mohéli. It is highly unlikely that you will see any
lemurs in the wild. Pigs broke out of their sties and became feral in
the forest. You may hear them snuffling around if you camp in the
rainforest on the slopes of Karthala volcano. Chameleons, also from
Madagascar, and huge snails inhabit the cool depths of the forests on
Anjouan and Mohéli.

One creature that every visitor to the Comoros should endeavour to
see is the giant Livingstone fruit bat, on Anjouan island. The species
was first described by David Livingstone, but the bats' existence had
already been recorded in the travel works of Ibn Battuta in 1377. Guides
to these enormous bats, which often have a wingspan in excess of 2 m,
can be arranged from the Hotel Al-Amal in Mutsamudu. Trek up into
the forested hills south-west of Bambao. Here, on the slopes of Trin-
drini, these enormous furry bats can be seen leaving their tree-perches
during early morning and evening to scour the island for food.

Flying foxes (another species of fruit bat) can be seen in the trees on
the steep sides of Lac Salé, on northern Grande Comore. Colonies of
other bats inhabit the forests around Lac de Boundouni on Mohéli and
the ruins at Kombani on Mayotte.

There are no dangerous or poisonous creatures on the Comoros. But
be warned: mosquitoes, gnats, spiders and insects are plentiful. Anti-
malarial preparations are a must for all visitors, as is some form of
insect repellent.

Ask virtually anyone what they know of the Comoros and chances
are they will mention the coelacanth. Considered extinct for at least 70
million years, a recently dead specimen of this fish, washed up on a

South African beach, was identified in 1938 by JLB Smith, a South African marine biologist. A concerted search was launched for more specimens and a living coelacanth was caught in a fishing net off the Comoros in 1952. Rushing to Grande Comore JLB Smith apparently broke down in tears when he first saw the creature. A fascinating account of the whole episode is contained in his informative, often humorous and sad book, *Old four legs: the story of the coelacanth* (Pan Books, London, 1958). Since then, several have been caught off the islands. A well-preserved specimen can be seen in the museum in Moroni.

Other fish that populate the warm waters around the Comoros include marlin, sailfish, barracuda, shark and tuna. By far the most exciting encounters in the sea are with dolphins and whales. Even turtles occasionally make their way to the isolated beaches of eastern Mohéli and south-western Anjouan.

There is a marine reserve off the south coast of Mohéli. The best places to see the multitude of colourful sea creatures are:

• west of Fassi (north-western Grande Comore)
• in the sea between Ifoundihe and Chindini (south-west Grande Comore)
• between N'Droude and Île aux Tortues (north-east Grande Comore)
• along the coast from Niumashuwa and Iconi (south Mohéli)
• between Île de la Selle and Bimbini (north-west Anjouan)
• off Chiroroni (south-west Anjouan)
• west of Accoua (north-west Mayotte)
• north of Kungu (north-east Mayotte)
• off Dembeni (east Mayotte)
• in the bay between Bweni and Kani-Kéli (south-west Mayotte).

Remember that the removal of seashells is expressly forbidden. If you are caught trying to take shells out of the country, you are in for a hefty fine and possibly spending a few days in one of the Comoros' notorious prisons.

Scuba divers on night dives should look out for the luminous fish which inhabit the depths of the ocean by day but rise to within a few metres of the surface at night. These weird fish use "spotlights" (large light organs) below each eye and rows of light organs along their jaws to attract prey and to see. Rising at night from depths as great as 300 m, these fish are frequent visitors to the waters off western Grande Comore and western Mohéli.

Flora

Comorian flora is a sheer delight to the senses. Sadly, deforestation is causing the variety and numbers of flowers and plants to shrink rapidly. Particularly on Grande Comore, you will see fires destroying virgin forest where villagers use the slash and burn technique in cultivating their subsistence crops. Unless something is done to curb this destructive practice, it will only be a matter of years before all the rainforests on the Comoros have disappeared.

No visitor to the islands should miss a walk in the forests or through the plantations. Those people in search of beautiful and delicate orchids are recommended to explore the forests on the sides of Mt Karthala on Grande Comore and Mt Mtsapéré on Mayotte. In these forests you will see towering takamaka, wild fig and camphor trees. Many of them are festooned with moss and lichens, the so-called old man's beard. The higher you go, the greater the number of wild orchids that can be seen.

Of the plantations, coconut, cloves, ylang-ylang and cinnamon are the most common. Aptly known as the Perfumed Isles, the Comoros also have estates growing such fragrant crops as jasmine, honeysuckle, lemon grass and gardenia.

Ylang-ylang is the principal export crop of the Comoros. The best place to see the distilling of this heady-scented flower is on Anjouan, in the village of Bambao. Eastern Mohéli also has vast estates of ylang-ylang. Visitors will be able to identify these estates as much by the wonderful fragrance as the gnarled appearance of the trees, the result of continuous pruning to picking height.

Clove tree plantations can be seen on southern Grande Comore and western Anjouan. The red-calyxed clove flowers are laid out to dry on sacking, often in the road. Slowly, over several days of exposure to sun, the fleshy part of the flower shrivels up, leaving only the clove behind, to turn black in the tropical sun.

Vanilla is prolific on all the islands, and in November to December its fragile orchid flowers can be seen bursting forth on the vines.

LANGUAGE

Comorian is a derivative of Kiswahili from East Africa and Arabic, and includes many words of French and Malay-Indonesian origin. French is used for all business transactions, taught in schools and spoken by everyone. However, with the strong anti-French feeling on Grande Comore, Anjouan and Mohéli, visitors may find that they are received more readily and assisted much quicker if they can speak a few words of Swahili or Comorian. Even if you speak English, you may find more doors opening for you than if you use only French. Obviously, on Mayotte the opposite is true: speak English to expats and nothing is achieved, except the odd sneer. The Mahorais (natives of Mayotte) all speak impeccable French and, naturally, Comorian.

There are no English-Comorian dictionaries, but you can buy a French-Comorian dictionary from Nouveautés, next to the museum in Moroni. No matter how atrocious your pronunciation, Comorians will respond positively if you try to address them in their own language. Women, in particular, are shy about speaking in any language other than Comorian. Travellers who use a combination of sign language, body language and a smattering of Comorian will be able to communicate with the locals far more easily than those who insist on speaking only their own language.

Useful words

Greetings	Salaam aleikum (this is the universally accepted Muslim greeting)
Hello	Jeje (on Grande Comore pronounced as gege)
How are you?	Habari gani?
I am well	Djema
Goodbye	Kwa heri ya kuonana
Yes	Aiwa
No	Siyo
Day	Mtsana
Night	Uku
Yesterday	Jana
Today	Leo
Tomorrow	Meso
Where is . . .?	Wapi/ndahu . . .?
Post office	Poste

Mosque	Maukiri/masjid
Boat	Markabu
Where is the taxi rank?	Wapi kituo cha motokaa ya kukodi?
Where is the beach?	Wapi mtsangani?
How long will it take?	Muda gani?
How much is this?	Hii ngapi?/ryali nga?
What is your name?	Jina lako nani?
Thank you	Marahaba
Excuse me	Uniwie radhi
Eat	Houla

3 FACTS FOR THE VISITOR

VISAS

There are sufficient quirks and oddities in the Comorian visa legislation to make writing guidelines almost impossible.

If you are in transit through the Comoros and will be staying for less than five days, there is no need for a visa at all.

At the time of writing, all foreign visitors to the islands require a visa. These are unobtainable outside the Comoros! What is more important to officials, however, is that you have a valid onward ticket. Chances are that on arrival no-one will even tell you that you need a visa. You therefore have two options: either you arrive and then get a visa from the Ministère de L'Intérieur, Sureté Nationale, in Moroni, or you wait until departing, at which time you buy a visa from the immigration authorities at the airport. The price is the same either way. Whereas getting a visa from the ministry usually takes a day, at the airport it is issued while you wait.

An advantage of getting a visa from the ministry is that you are able to specify the length of your stay and can avoid all the questions asked at roadblocks. Do not expect a visa for a stay beyond the departure date on your ticket, though. Make certain that there are three État Comorien, Timbre Fiscal, stamps on your visa if you get it from the ministry offices, otherwise you will have to pay for the extra revenue stamps when leaving.

Independent travellers may encounter problems when applying for a visa on departure, and may have to produce receipts of all currency exchanges, hotel bills and curio purchases. Tourists who are members of a package tour or stayed their whole visit at La Galawa Beach Hotel or Itsandra Sun Hotel simply breeze through.

Any passport holder may enter the Comoros (Bob Dénard and his cronies excluded). An airport departure tax must be paid by all passengers. Even this is rather eccentric. Some people have the tax included in their air ticket price, others are asked to pay when checking in their luggage, and still others (myself included) are waved through to the departure lounge without paying at all. It would be prudent to keep the required amount on hand, just in case. There has recently been talk of adopting a similar policy to that of Madagascar's international airport: non-residents must pay departure tax in foreign currency, preferably French francs.

Most hotels on Grande Comore are able to obtain a visa for guests. La Galawa Beach Hotel and Itsandra Sun Hotel are still a little vague on this. It seems that it is unusual for guests there to request a visa before departure. The best hotel for assistance to solo travellers in getting a visa is the Karthala Hotel, opposite Iconi Airport in Moroni. The hotel will send a staff member to the relevant offices for you. Visitors can make enquiries about the price from the immigration officials at the airport, or from Tourism Services Comoros, which has a desk in La Galawa Beach Hotel.

Those visitors wishing to go on to Mayotte will need a French visa unless they hold an EU or French passport. These can be obtained from the French Embassy on Grande Comore or in your home country. Allow about 14 days for the return of your passport. It's pointless writing to the embassy in Mayotte for a visa: they send your application either to the embassy in your country of residence or to the Ministry of Immigration in France.

EMBASSIES AND CONSULATES

Very few countries have diplomatic representation in the Comoros. Most rely on communiqués via the French Foreign Ministry to the islands. Those that do have offices in the archipelago are all based in Moroni. France, however, also has a sub-branch at Mutsamudu, Anjouan. Countries with consuls in the Comoros are:

Consul of Belgium
Situated less than 100 m north of Volo-volo market on the main west coast road going towards Mitsamiouli. Also represents the Benelux countries.

Chinese Embassy
Turn east at Restaurant Rahat El-Lahil. This narrow road is the one crossing the centre of Grande Comore to the east coast. About 50 m down this road, on the left, is the embassy building.

Embassy of France
Located across the road from Iconi Airport, this is the largest foreign embassy on the islands. The easiest way to find the entrance is to walk south from the Hotel Karthala. The embassy is next door, behind the graffiti-adorned white wall.

The consular office in Mutsamudu is in the suburb of Hombo. Go south from the Hombo Hospital and past the football ground. Near the French school is the consulate.

Consul of Madagascar
This is also the Air Madagascar representative. The consulate is on Magoudjou Street next to the EEDC building, opposite Volo-volo market. If needing an air ticket to Madagascar or a visa for that country, you will need to visit the consulate. You may also try to confirm Air Madagascar flights here. The success of this depends on how busy the consul is. He may direct you to Iconi Airport where all airline tickets are reconfirmed by Air Comores staff. (Locals call Air Comores Air Comic – you'll soon see why!)

CUSTOMS

Tourists with luggage are unlikely to be searched upon arrival at Hahaya Airport. Backpackers, on the other hand, are virtually assured of having their packs inspected. Leaving the Comoros via the airport is relatively painless; seldom are your belongings examined.

Each visitor is allowed to bring in 1 ℓ of spirits or wine, 25 ml of perfume, 200 cigarettes and 20 cigars. Scuba diving gear is allowed but is limited to face-mask, fins, snorkel, wetsuit, weight-belt, delivery-valve, gauges, buoyancy compensator and one cylinder. Spear-guns are forbidden, as are dive knives. Dive computers, digital compasses and specialist equipment must be declared on entry. You may not be requested to do this on arrival, but will definitely have to explain on departure. Ask the customs officials for the Tourist Baggage Declaration Form.

Plant material, animals and marine life may not be brought into the country. It is also expressly forbidden to take any of these things out of the Comoros. Shells, plant cuttings, reptiles and coral are all protected by Comorian law. If caught removing these or trying to take them out of the country, you will receive a hefty fine and will probably have to spend an interesting few hours explaining your actions to the local police chief. Known as Comorian gold, the local cannabis is obviously also on the list of non-exportable goods. Arrive back in Europe or the Americas after visiting the Comoros and you are almost guaranteed of being searched for drugs.

With their legacy of coups d'état, the Comorians are understandably paranoid about firearms. No visitor is permitted to bring a firearm into the country. Not even knives over 10 cm long are allowed. Any item that may be considered useable in a military sense is taboo. This can get rather ridiculous at times: walking sticks, umbrellas and pen-knives will all be carefully scrutinised by officials.

If wanting to remove items of historical or cultural significance, you will first need to obtain written permission from the relevant authority. This will be issued by the Musée des Comores in Moroni. Speak to the curator at least three days before your intended departure.

MONEY

Local currency is the Comorian franc (CFr). It was linked to the French franc for quite some time, but now stands on its own. As a result, it is grossly undervalued and useless outside the Comoros. French francs (Ff) are, however, accepted as legal tender throughout the islands. On Mayotte it is the only currency.

Visitors arriving at Hahaya may be asked to pay for their taxi ride in French francs. Make certain that you are able to calculate the difference in value between the franc and local currency. There have been several reports of tourists getting ripped off. As a rule of thumb, the CFr is about half the value of the Ff. Another problem concerning the CFr and foreign currency is that many places try to insist on payment in francs, dollars, pounds or marks. There is no law in the Comoros that mandates this.

Visiting a bank to change foreign currency, cash traveller's cheques or draw from credit cards is a test of patience. There are always long queues at the foreign-exchange counter, and usually only one clerk who takes frequent tea breaks. The most efficient banks are on Mohéli and Anjouan. Those on Grande Comore, particularly in Moroni, would stretch the patience of Ghandi.

The banks in the Comoros are Banque Centrale (BC), Caisse Centrale de Coopération Economique, Banque Internationale des Comores (BIC) and Banque de Développement. On Mayotte there is also a branch of Banque Française Commerciale (BFC).

The recommended bank for doing any foreign currency transactions is BIC, situated on Grande Comore across the road from the central post office in Moroni, and also near Djema Bonbons in Mitsamiouli. On Anjouan, the BIC has branches next to Agence Bon Voyage Comoria in Mutsamudu and near the post office in Domoni. The BIC branch on

Mohéli is in Fomboni, across the road from the post office. On Mayotte there are branches near the harbour in Mamoudzou on Grande Terre and south of the gendarme post in Dzaoudzi.

The suggested foreign currency to take to the Comoros is French francs. All banks, hotels, restaurants and vendors accept this in the form of cash. The easiest currency to change at banks and hotels is US dollars. Sterling and marks yield a high rate on the thriving black market in Moroni and Mutsamudu. Although illegal, the black market trade in foreign currency is conducted quite openly. You are likely to be approached by dealers even as you queue at the foreign-exchange counter in a bank. You may bring into the country as much hard currency as you like.

Note that it is impossible to change Comorian money back into an international currency after departure. This means that you must calculate all financial transactions very carefully; once you are through the international departure lounge the Comorian franc becomes worthless. Getting CFr outside the islands can be a problem. Unless you know someone who has recently returned from the Comoros, it is highly unlikely that you will find any CFr available. To avoid the feeling of vulnerability caused by arriving in a foreign country without useable cash, have a few hundred French francs in cash on hand.

Traveller's cheques are used by most independent visitors to the Comoros. American Express is the most popular, followed by Thomas Cook and then numerous lesser known brands. Stick to American Express and Thomas Cook if possible. The currency to use for traveller's cheques is dollars, pounds sterling or marks. Lire are accepted, as are yen, but the exchange rate is very unfavourable. South African rand (ZAR) traveller's cheques can be changed only at La Galawa Beach Hotel. Several jewellers are prepared to accept traveller's cheques as payment. The major drawback of traveller's cheques in the Comoros is that there are no representatives of American Express or Thomas Cook on the islands – a problem if the cheques get lost or stolen. To prevent losing all your negotiables, split your money into hard cash, traveller's cheques and credit cards (although the latter are rather useless on the Comoros).

The only credit card accepted at banks is the French Carte Bleu. Visa, Master, Diners Club and Amex are accepted only at La Galawa Beach Hotel. Many of the other hotels are at present awaiting approval of their application to accept credit cards. French visitors may use their Carte Bleu to draw cash from the BIC. No other card is accepted for cash withdrawals. An obvious solution is to buy something from a boutique at a hotel, have the cashier charge you more than the purchase price and give you change. Speak to the hotel or boutique manager about this; they are usually very helpful.

Transferring money from abroad to the Comoros is fraught with problems. The only banks that will even consider accepting an international money order are BIC and BFC. Even then, they are prepared to deal only with international banking institutions. Expect to wait about three days for your money to be processed. If you have completely run out of money, the BFC will give you a letter detailing the pending transaction. This can be used to placate hotel managers who demand payment.

COSTS

The Comoros are costly. An accurate forecast of costs is difficult and obviously depends on what you plan to do on the Comoros. If you are staying at a top-class hotel, scuba diving, eating three meals a day in a hotel dining room, shopping at boutiques and hiring a car, you are looking at a very expensive holiday indeed. On the other hand, if you can accept staying at medium-tariff hotels, eating twice a day in restaurants and using taxis, then a vacation in the Comoros will be no more expensive than in Switzerland or Germany.

Budget travellers are in for a tough time. Visiting the Comoros on a tight budget is not for the inexperienced, although it can be done. Live in *pensions* or with locals, eat one large meal a day in a Comorian café, have a few snacks for lunch and breakfast and use public transport. This will keep your overall costs down, but the visit will still be rather expensive. Also, even when travelling on a small budget, it is necessary to splash out occasionally on a good meal and somewhere pleasant to stay.

Apart from accommodation, the biggest expense is inter-island transport. Flying is really expensive. Medium-budget tourists may elect to use the ferry service from Grande Comore to the other islands, while budget travellers are advised to rely on the island trading vessels and fishermen for their transport.

A hired car is the most expensive way of getting about each island. Taxis are costly, but their prices are negotiable. Bush-taxis (taxi-brousses) are the cheapest method of transport.

An evening out needs careful consideration. A trip to the casino and bar of La Galawa Beach Hotel will see your finances plummet quickly. Going to a tourist disco or bar is not much better: the entrance price and a few drinks will set you back a few thousand CFrs. However, if you attend instead a Comorian dance hall and sip palm wine, your budget will hardly be affected at all. This is also the best way of meeting Comorians.

TIPPING

Thanks to European influence, guests at tourist-class hotels are expected to tip the staff for services. The usual 10% of the bill is customary for waiters in hotel dining rooms. But in cafés and local restaurants a few francs will suffice. Hotel porters, tour guides and touts all expect a tip for their assistance. The amount you give is really up to you.

A host of surprises await those who practise judicious tipping on the Comoros. Give a taxi driver a few extra francs and you have a car on call. At the post office, tip the woman who works in the poste restante section and your letters will be filed away in a special cabinet just for you. Tip the boatman on the ferry and you are certain of getting a berth in a cabin for the crossing. The problem is deciding who to tip, why and how much. Avoid doing what affluent tourists do: shelling out money as though it were sweets. The receiver must appreciate the value of your tip and be able to render some service in return.

TOURIST INFORMATION

Getting useful tourist information about the Comoros is difficult. The literature available is inevitably outdated and the tourist authorities on the islands are far from helpful. The best information is available from tour operators, travel agents and consular representatives abroad. You are far more likely to be helped by a Comorian embassy than the Ministry of Tourism on Grande Comore. Still, you may want to try contacting the Ministère des Transports et du Tourisme, B.P. 97, Moroni, Grande Comore, Comoros, tel. 73.27.29.

The Southern African Regional Tourism Council (SARTOC) puts out a few colourful brochures but is unable to provide detailed information for prospective visitors. Their pamphlet is recommended at the planning stage of your trip. You may receive a free copy by contacting SARTOC, PO Box 564, Blantyre, Malawi, tel. (09265) 63-4888, or SARTOC,

PO Box 600, Parklands 2121, South Africa, tel. (011) 788-0742, fax (011) 788-1200.

Prospective tourists are advised to contact one of the Comorian attaches in the following countries for tourist information: Belgium (Brussels), France (Paris), Luxembourg; Egypt (Cairo), Kenya (Nairobi), Senegal (Dakar), Tanzania (Dar es Salaam), Zanzibar; Saudi Arabia (Jeddah); Japan (Osaka), Singapore.

The most detailed information you can get prior to arriving on the Comoros is from World Leisure Holidays, whose several years' experience on the islands makes it the most reliable source of tourist information about the Comoros. Contact it for all your tour requirements or to have specific questions answered:
World Leisure Holidays, PO Box 1474, Randburg 2125, South Africa, tel. (011) 886-9710, fax (011) 886-9709.

You could also try contacting one of the tour operators before departure. They are, however, loath to send brochures or pamphlets unless you are actually booked on one of their tours. They do provide basic tour outlines and a little relevant tourist information upon request.

The best of them is Tourism Services Comoros, B.P. 1226, Moroni, Grande Comore, Comoros, tel. 73.17.40, fax 73.17.50.

Other operators who may offer some assistance are:
Royal Transit Express, B.P. 19, Moroni, Grande Comore, Comoros, tel. 73.00.10, fax 73.08.06
Tourisme Comoros International, B.P. 544, Moroni, Grande Comore, Comoros, tel. 73.07.28

On the islands, Tourisme Services Comoros is the most helpful to tourists and gives maps, brochures and pamphlets to all who contact its desk in La Galawa Beach Hotel. The PRO staff at this hotel are also able to provide useful information about touring the islands, especially Grande Comore.

The Ministère des Transports et du Tourisme, in Moroni, is far from the ideal place to get tourist information. The staff are rude, there is precious little literature in English, and even that in French is hopelessly outdated. They do have some good maps though. You may visit the office near the Ministère de Finances et du Budget building.

The Musée des Comores (CNDRS) has a great deal of information that will prove useful to tourists. Speak either to the curator or to the person who runs the archives. Both have an encyclopedic knowledge of the islands, what to see, where to stay and what to do.

On Anjouan, contact the general manager of the Hotel Al-Amal for assistance. He will even mail you details if there is enough time:
The General Manager, Hotel Al-Amal, B.P. 59, Mutsamudu, Anjouan, Comoros, tel. 71.15.80.

For tourist information about Mohéli, it will be necessary to write at least 90 days before arrival. Although there is a tourism civil servant on the little island, the information he has available is pitiful. Rather contact the following people, who will be glad to send you written information about Mohéli:
Mouhmar-Kadaffi Mohamed, Fomboni, Mohéli, Comoros. He may also be contacted at 107 Rue de la Mairie, 97610 Pamandze, Mayotte, tel. 60.08.08.
Fatouma Bacar Chehou, Moni-Moimoudji, Fomboni, Mohéli, Comoros, tel. 72.03.10.

Mayotte has tourism offices in Mamoudzou and Dzaoudzi. Although they offer a great deal more information than other places, allow them at least three months to reply to a request.
Office du Tourisme, B.P. 169, 97600 Mamoudzou, Mayotte
Office du Tourisme, B.P. 42, 97610 Pamandze (Dzaoudzi), Mayotte

POSTAL SERVICES

Comorian postal services are fast and reliable. The poste restante service is dependable and letters are nearly always received. Note that you will be required to pay a fee for each letter collected from poste restante. Letters are generally kept for 42 days before being returned to the sender. Letters are not filed, but just thrown into a huge box that you will need to rummage through. An alternative is to tip the person who controls the poste restante box. This usually ensures that your letters are kept separately for you to collect.

The main post office on the Comoros is in Moroni, opposite the BIC bank. To find poste restante, go in through the main doors, turn right and ask at the first door you encounter. Mailing letters is traumatic. Go in through the entrance and around the corner to the left. There you will find one counter, one clerk and a crowd of people. Forget about an orderly queue. Just push and shove, like everyone else does, until you get to the glass window. Slide your letters through and immediately block the opening with your arms – people will try to slip their letters in over yours.

There is also a post office in Mitsamiouli, opposite the mosque.

La Galawa Beach Hotel handles postcards and letters for residents and sells stamps.

On Anjouan, the most efficient post offices are in Mutsamudu and Domoni. The post office in Mutsamudu is located downtown across the road from the little park and fountain, opposite the bush-taxi rank. There is another smaller post office east of the CBD, actually an annex post office, but providing all the services of the main post office. Look for the pink and white communications aerials; the post office is directly below them. In Domoni the post office is opposite the magnificent mausoleum of Abdallah.

On the island of Mohéli the most reliable post office is in Fomboni. It is at the end of a gravel road near a tall telecommunication antenna, on the opposite corner from the BIC bank.

On Mayotte there is a post office in Mamoudzou near the gendarme (police) station south of the port, and in Dzaoudzi (Pamandzi) the post office is on the rock of Dzaoudzi near the Ylang-ylang Restaurant, at the western end of Boulevard des Crabes.

PHONE

The international dialling code for the Comoros is 269, which must be preceded by your own country's access code.

The Comorian telephone system is efficient, if expensive. Calls made from Grande Comore, Anjouan and Mayotte are direct, while those from Mohéli may occasionally have to be pre-booked. Telephone calls can be made from any of the hotels and all post offices. Making telephone calls from hotels is the most expensive. Moreover, the operators have a tendency to listen in on conversations.

The best way to make international telephone calls is through ACTEL: calls are satellite-linked and instantaneous. The ACTEL offices are next to the main post office in Moroni, opposite Banque Central.

Phonecards can be used at many public telephone booths. They can be bought from the post office and at several shops around Grande Comore. They allow you a specified number of units. The advantage of phonecards, apart from convenience, is that they are cheaper than using coins.

Telex and fax are used throughout the islands of the Comoros. Most hotels now have their own fax machines, while all post offices and the larger tourist hotels have telex machines as well. Telex machines are cheap to use, although many international destinations now rely almost exclusively on faxes. Fax machines are horribly expensive to use on the Comoros. Expect to pay at least three times the price of a telephone call when sending a fax.

To call ships, yachts or ferries at sea you must use INMARSAT. This is a costly undertaking and only recommended in dire circumstances. To use this, call via ACTEL 0900.

TIME

The Comoros are three hours ahead of Greenwich Mean Time. That makes them one hour ahead of South Africa, two hours ahead of Europe and five hours behind Australia.

ELECTRICITY

Power cuts are a feature of the Comoros, especially during high demand at peak periods. Although some of the larger hotels have their own backup generators, expect to spend at least a few minutes of your holiday in darkness while electricians try to restore the power. Always take a torch and spare batteries with you to the Comoros. However, no-one seems to mind the power cuts. And during those glorious Comorian moonlit nights, artificial lights are the last thing you'll want anyway.

Electricity on Grande Comore is provided by giant diesel generators. This makes electricity on Grande Comore the most expensive in the world. On the other islands, hydro-electric power is the main supply. It is more reliable, quiet and aesthetically pleasing.

The current is 220 volts on all the islands. There is a mixture of French two-pin plugs and South African three-pin plugs in the hotels. To avoid any problems, visitors should take along their own adaptors. Those visitors from countries using other voltage currents should bring a small transformer for electrical appliances. Some hotels have transformers and adaptors for use by their guests, but it is safer to bring your own.

BUSINESS HOURS

Post offices are open Monday to Thursday 7h30-12h00 and 15h00-17h00; Friday 7h00-11h30; Saturday 7h30-12h00.

During the Islamic fasting month of Ramadan, post offices are open Monday to Thursday 7h00-13h30; Friday and Saturday 7h00-11h30.

On the French-governed island of Mayotte, post offices are open Monday to Friday 8h00-17h00; Saturday 7h30-12h00.

Government offices and business offices are open Monday to Thursday 8h00-12h00 and 14h00-16h00; Friday 9h00-12h00. Most administrative offices are closed on Saturday.

Banks are open Monday to Thursday 8h00-12h30; Friday 7h30-11h30. If stuck for cash after closing time you will need to try one of the hotels.

Shops are generally open Monday to Thursday 7h30-17h00; Friday 7h00-11h30; Saturday 8h00-13h30. Street vendors and markets do business Monday to Thursday roughly 6h30-17h30; Friday 6h30-11h00; Saturday and Sunday 7h30-12h00.

Tourist restaurants are open for lunch 11h00-14h30; dinner 19h30-22h30. Cafés and bistros start early at 7h00 and do not close until 22h00. Local eating houses are open Monday to Thursday 8h30-22h30; Friday 8h30-12h00 and 16h00-0h00.

Discos, nightclubs and dance halls start from 21h30 and, while those at hotels close around 2h30, the Comorian ones stay open until sunrise.

MEDIA

There are two local newspapers in the Comoros, *L'Archipel* and *Al-Watwany*. *L'Archipel*, an independent weekly newspaper, is considerably more liberal and probing than the state-controlled *Al-Watwany*. The latter, a bi-monthly, has recently begun to exercise a certain degree of editorial autonomy, which has increased its circulation. Both newspapers are in French and Comorian, with occasional snippets in English. Neither carries much international news. If you are merely interested in what is happening locally, read *Al-Watwany*. For those interested in in-depth articles, exposés and alternative editorial views, *L'Archipel* is recommended. Both newspapers can be purchased from Nouveautés, near the museum in Moroni, or at La Maison du Livre, opposite Agence des Musulmans d'Afrique, also in Moroni. They are also sold at shops and cafés in all the other islands.

In addition to these newspapers, French Sunday papers arrive in the week of their publication. You will need to get to a newsagent fairly early on Tuesday morning if you hope to get a copy; they sell out very quickly. These papers carry all the latest international news, with detailed commentary. Visitors spending a few weeks on Grande Comore can place an order for a French newspaper at Nouveautés.

On Mayotte, the weekly *Le Journal de Mayotte* covers affairs relating to the island and has a few columns of international news. This paper can be bought at supermarkets and general trading stores on Mayotte. Several French newspapers, both dailies and weeklies, are sold on Mayotte. Visitors may read the latest French newspapers at the Centre Culturel (CMAC), near the Tribunal building in Mamoudzou.

Forget trying to buy an English-language newspaper. Occasionally La Galawa Beach Hotel is able to obtain a *Sunday Times* or *Sunday Tribune* from South Africa. However, if you befriend members of the Canadian aid organisation CARE, you may be allowed to read their weekly newspapers.

Magazines, as can be expected, are almost all French: *Vogue, Le Monde, Paris Match,* etc. They are expensive. Among the few English-language magazines are *Time* and *Newsweek.* A number of British and American magazine publishing houses have recently begun showing an interest in sending their editions to the Comoros. This is still being negotiated. Final notices are due in mid-1995.

An amazing thing about the Comoros is the lack of secrecy of government communiqués and documents. Every fax or important document that arrives on the islands is photostatted and distributed to the populace. In some instances the entire document is reprinted in one of the local newspapers. This is obviously unofficial but very effective in keeping Comorians abreast of developments.

The Comoros do not have their own television station. However, several people have purchased satellite dishes with which they can receive programmes broadcast by RFO, the Réunion-based French television network. RFO sends signals across the Indian Ocean to Mayotte, from where the other islands are able to pick up the broadcast every afternoon and evening.

Videos are extremely popular on the Comoros and video-rental shops have flourished in recent years. The locals have a penchant for martial arts movies. Despite the poverty and high unemployment, television aerials adorn most roofs around the islands. As not everyone can afford a satellite dish, a few enterprising individuals have found a way of cashing in on theirs. On Anjouan, for example, there is only one satellite dish in Ouani. All other television owners pay a small subscription to the chap who owns the dish and link their sets to his. Obviously, only what he decides to watch can be viewed by everyone else.

Radio is popular with all Comorians. Radio Comoros broadcasts throughout the day and offers several news bulletins at different times in Comorian, Swahili, Arabic, Malagasy and French. English listeners can tune in to the BBC or Voice of America every evening, on short-wave bands.

One interesting thing about Radio Comoros is its choice of music whenever there has been a coup d'état. Usually blaring out Comorian or reggae music, it switches to sombre classical tunes when the government has been overthrown. Talking to locals, visitors will soon learn that everyone expectantly switches on their radios each morning and listens with bated breath what music is being played.

ACCOMMODATION

Accommodation on the Comoros is expensive, no matter where you decide to stay. The cheapest way of staying on the islands is to get yourself invited to board with a local family. Initially this is not easy, because of the natural reserve of the Comorians. But with perseverance travellers will be able to befriend locals who are only too willing to have you stay with them.

At the top end of the scale are the extravagant La Galawa Beach Hotel and Casino and Itsandra Sun Hotel and Casino on Grande Comore. This is luxury at its best on the Comoros and the usual accommodation of package tourists. Breakfast and dinner are included in the rate. Rooms are lavish and all amenities are provided for guests. Staff are highly trained and many of them speak English, German and Italian.

Other hotels that fall into this classification, though not anywhere near the standard of La Galawa Beach Hotel, are the Hotel Coelacanthe, La Grillade, Moifaka Studios and Novotel Ylang-ylang.

Next is the so-called medium-tariff accommodation in privately owned hotels. On Grande Comore the best of these is the Hotel Karthala. Breakfast is included in the rate, but all other meals must be paid for separately. On Anjouan the hotel in this category is the Hotel Al-Amal. Mohéli has the Relais de Cingani. Mayotte has Le Rocher, the Hotel Ngouja, Le Tortue Bigotu and Trévani Village. These hotels are all comfortable, clean and situated in locales suitable for tourists. Managers at these places are usually able to speak English and arrange island tours.

Hardened travellers may find cheaper accommodation in any number of *pensions* and small hotels scattered across each of the islands. Although not as clean as higher priced rooms, the lodgings in *pensions* are adequate. Meals are not included in the tariff, but staff are normally willing to cook food if you supply the ingredients.

On Grande Comore, these places are all located in or around Moroni. The following suggested *pensions* have good reputations and friendly staff, and provide the opportunity to mix with the locals: Pension Kohinoor, Pension Zilmadjou, Pension Karibu, Pension Zam-Zam and Pension Maharajah.

Staying with Comorians is an exciting way of visiting the islands. On Mayotte this is very difficult. The French influence has caused most people to shun association with foreigners. However, on the other islands it is not too difficult with some effort on your part. In the larger towns it may take two or three days before someone is friendly enough to invite you home. But in the rural areas no-one will go without a bed for the night. If you arrive in a village at sunset, without pre-planned accommodation, ask to speak to one of the settlement's "Notables". Within minutes something will have been arranged for you. Although payment is usually not demanded, it is considered proper to contribute something towards the meals. You may either give the hostess money to buy food or do some shopping yourself. Should you be carrying any dehydrated food, supply this.

The friendliest settlements to try for accommodation with locals on the various islands are:
Grande Comore – Haoueni, Koimbani and Tsinimoipanga
Anjouan – Sima, Lingoni, Dzindri and Mremani
Mohéli – Fomboni, Iconi and Miringoni
Mayotte – Kombani and Mtsangamuji

FOOD

Comorian food is delicious. With the abundance of spices and herbs grown locally, no dish is bland or tasteless. Most families have their own plots of land on which they cultivate vegetables, keep a few livestock and plant fruit trees. From the ocean comes a daily harvest of seafood delicacies.

Hotels have à la carte menus of mostly Continental food. Top-class hotels have buffets on certain nights – the largest and most lavish at La Galawa Beach Hotel. You do not need to be a guest to eat here, but must make table reservations at least 24 hours before. The Hotel Karthala specialises in Moroccan dishes. There are restaurants catering to the tourist trade on Grande Comore and Mayotte. On the other islands, visitors must take their meals in the hotel or find a restaurant frequented by Comorians.

Rice, of the long-grained variety, is the staple of most meals and is added to all meat dishes. The Comoros used to be self-sufficient in rice but have now become reliant on foreign and second-grade rice donated by aid agencies.

Rice is followed closely by bananas as a staple. The long, fat bananas are fried in a batter and offered with a bowl of chili sauce. They are not at all sweet. The sweet bananas are the small yellow ones you will see on sale in the fresh produce markets. Bananas grow wild on the islands, and visitors will frequently see men carrying bunches from the forests.

Beef is in plentiful supply. Most of it is imported, either from Africa or Madagascar, although a fair amount is from locally grown animals. It is cooked in a variety of ways, the most common being grilled or roasted. On the seafront in Anjouan, beef is made into brochettes (kebabs) and flame-grilled by sidewalk street vendors. If you are a meat eater, avoid visiting any of the butcheries – you will definitely not eat the stuff again. The Comoros being a Muslim country, naturally no pork is eaten. Sheep are a rarity; you have little chance of eating lamb or mutton. Goats are common and no-one should miss tasting a fiery hot, spiced Anjouani goat stew. Chicken is a favourite, mostly grilled or fried over an open fire. A sauce is always added.

Sauces are one of the greatest delights of Comorian food. It seems as though each housewife or cook has her own secret ingredients for her sauces. Every traditional meal you eat will be served with some sort of sauce. Coconut appears to be a common base to these thick, colourful concoctions. Some are downright hot, others mild, while a few are even sweet. There are several regional specialities. On Anjouan the traditional sauce comprises chili, cloves and cinnamon. The people on Mohéli enjoy their sauces with the addition of peppercorns and a quill or two of vanilla. Cooks on Grande Comore nearly always add nutmeg to their sauces, while on Mayotte the islanders combine all these ingredients with garlic and ginger. You will not find these sauces at tourist-class hotels and, therefore, must venture into the local tin-shack restaurants and cafés.

Seafood, together with rice, is the main component of daily meals. It is always fresh, usually caught that day. The islanders enjoy frying fish or roasting it in coals. Squid is often eaten, as is shark and marlin.

Everything is eaten, the bones and skin being fed to cats and dogs or left for the birds.

There is an abundance of fruit on the islands, from coconuts to bananas, citrus to pineapples. Many of these fruits can simply be picked from roadside trees as you walk around. Some of the more exotic varieties can be bought from fresh produce markets.

Vegetables for sale are a rarity. Most people only grow enough to feed their families. This excludes tomatoes, which are sold at all markets and are delicious. Depending on the season, visitors may find leafy green vegetables for sale. These include spinach, spring onions, lettuce and the odd cabbage. Onions, garlic, ginger, herbs and spices are available at the larger markets in Moroni, Mutsamudu, Mamoudzou and Fomboni.

Bread and pastries do not rate highly on the list of Comorian foods. Bread is typically French in appearance and texture. Long loaves are baked daily in Moroni, Mutsamudu and Mamoudzou. However, on Mohéli there is only one bakery for the entire island. Bread is baked four or five times per week, depending on the arrival of flour from Grande Comore. Pastries are limited to urban centres and are a far cry from anything European. They are always filled with fruit and spices, and make for wonderful breakfast food. The Salon de Thé Salimamoud, across the lane from Volo-volo market, makes some of the biggest, cheapest and tastiest pastries available on the Comoros.

DRINK

Islam forbids the drinking of alcohol, but hotels, cafés, stores, discos and dance halls all serve beer, wine and spirits. While you may drink as much alcohol as you like at these places, don't even think about stepping outside with a glass in your hand. Drinking on the street is illegal. Most alcohol is imported. Beer comes from South Africa; wine and spirits are from Europe, South Africa and the Americas. Drinking in licensed places is expensive.

In the rural settlements, where Islam is not practised as ardently and ancient animist traditions are still in evidence, visitors are likely to be offered palm wine. This alcoholic drink, usually served in 1 ℓ bottles, is really pleasant, but pour it into your glass through a tea strainer. The effect is slow but dramatic. Cancel all activities or sightseeing after a bout in a local palm wine bar.

These local bars are not advertised, you must ask around. The children are very helpful in this regard. The patrons will initially be extremely surprised to see a foreigner entering their bar, but within minutes you will be offered a drink and the people's reserve will disappear.

Imported fruit juice and soda are sold at all food shops. To taste the local fruit juice, pay a visit to the remote villages in the forests or along the coasts. When strolling through coconut groves, get one of the workers to open a green coconut for you. The coconut water is delicious, nutritious and very filling. The flavour of the water depends on the stage of growth of the coconut. The thick, sweet coconut milk is equally pleasant. In the village of Fomboni, on Mohéli, several of the shops have coconut milk for sale. It is kept in a bucket in the fridge.

Should you be invited to eat with a Comorian family it is highly recommended that you accept the offer. Not only will it be a unique experience, but the opportunity to taste authentic cuisine should not be missed. You all sit on the floor on a grass mat. The meal usually starts off with a glass of fresh fruit juice, followed by fried bananas and piment sauce. Fresh salad is served, then a stew, either goat or beef, with slices of French bread. After the stew, plates of spiced rice and seafood or chicken are offered. Cold drinks are handed out and then fresh coconut. After the coconut, visitors may be surreptitiously offered a glass of palm wine. You then all sit back and show good Comorian manners by burping.

BOOKS

There is a dearth of books on the Comoros. The only places that regularly sell any are La Maison du Livre and Nouveautés in Moroni. You are unlikely to find any English books. Those that are on sale are meant for school or tertiary education.

The library is located in the Musée des Comores and includes a reference section and archives. It has a good selection of books on the Comoros, if you can read French. The librarians are helpful and go out of their way to assist with translations and finding English reference books for you.

One of the best books available on modern history and the recent upheavals in Comorian politics is *Last of the pirates: the search for Bob Dénard*, by Samantha Weinberg (Jonathan Cape, London, 1994). Once you start reading this enthralling book it is almost impossible to put down. As a pre-trip primer this is the ideal book. Travellers hoping to mix with the Comorians must have some idea of current history. You are bound to get involved in at least one political discussion while on the islands, usually concerning the French, Bob Dénard, his mercenaries and South Africa.

A more serious historical work, in French, is the collection of two volumes entitled *Comoros: quatre îles entre pirates et planteurs*, by Jean Martin (L'Harmattan, Paris, 1984). This covers Comorian history in great detail. It can get a little dull in places, but is still worth the read. The chapters on buccaneers are sure to excite the imagination of those visitors planning to explore the forests and hills of Mohéli and Anjouan.

Africans by David Lamb (Random House, New York, 1982) has a section devoted to the Comoros, especially the history of Ali Solih and Ahmed Abdallah.

Another book worth reading before departing for the Comoros is *The Comoros islands: struggle against dependency in the Indian Ocean*, by Malyn Newitt (Gower Publications, London, 1984). This is very much a text book, but offers astute observations into the Comorian way of life and the reasons behind many of the occurrences in the politics of the islands.

There are two books about Mayotte that visitors might consider buying. Both are available on the island. *Mayotte: île aux parfums*, by Christian Bossu-Picat (Éditions Delroisse, Paris, 1989) is a coffee-table book of fascinating photographs and accurate text. *Regards sur Mayotte* is more of a pocket-guide to the island. It is useful once there, but should not be relied on totally as a guide book. It omits several points of interest and some important information for visitors.

MAPS

Possibly the best map of the Comoros available for tourists is produced by Éditions Baobab. Entitled Archipel des Comores, this fold-out map is ideal for travelling with and may be obtained free from the Consulate of Madagascar, across the road from Volo-volo market, or by writing to Éditions Baobab, B.P. 575, Moroni, Grande Comore, Comore. This map is not only large enough to show major points of interest, but also includes hotels, roads, beaches and hiking routes. On the reverse side it has detailed street maps of Moroni, Mutsamudu, Mamoudzou and Fomboni.

Apart from this, getting accurate maps of the Comoros before arriving there is difficult. Most maps put out by the likes of Bartholomew or

Michelin portrait the Comoros in a ridiculously small scale of about 1:5 000 000. This is useless for planning a route around the islands. SARTOC is able to supply prospective visitors with an A4 sized map of the four islands, but it has no scale from which to work. An alternative is to write for the maps of the Comoros produced by the Institut Géographique Nationale in France: 136 bis, Rue de Grenelle, 75700 Paris Cedex, France. These maps, in six parts, are somewhat outdated but are useful for travellers.

The Comoros are small enough to allow for changes in your planned itinerary. So the best option may be to get hold of the SARTOC maps, or use the ones in this book, and then buy the relevant maps when you arrive in Moroni.

The Institut Géographique Nationale maps are obtainable from Nouveautés, next to the Musée des Comores in Moroni. There are two sheets for Grande Comore, two for Anjouan, one for Mohéli and one for Mayotte. It is awkward trying to travel about using these large maps. Instead, choose the area you want to visit and have the relevant map photostatted to a reduced size at the museum.

THINGS TO BUY

Finding suitable curios on the Comoros requires a concerted effort. There are none of the usual curio shops found on other Indian Ocean islands. Although Volo-volo market in Moroni has several stalls that sell handmade curios for tourists, the quality of workmanship is low, especially compared to items made in rural villages. Inspect items at markets very carefully before making your purchase. And remember to bargain hard for everything you buy.

Comorian craftsmen are renowned for two things in particular: their fine woodwork and intricate jewellery. For woodwork, look in the town of Domoni, on Anjouan. Visitors will notice how beautiful the entrance doors to Comorian homes are. While the inside of houses may be spartan and practical, the doorways are works of art. Here Comorian creativity is given full expression. It may be impractical to order an entire door for yourself, but a tooled piece of rosewood or takamaka makes a unique memento. You can watch the artists at work in any number of small workshops on Anjouan. One of the best is down the alley from the BIC bank in Domoni. Across the lane from the workshop are shops selling the products. The carved furniture, including fold-up stools and tables made from a single piece of wood, is exquisite. Tourists may also be tempted by boxes or folding Koran holders unique to Islam. On the Comoros their design and construction reach amazing heights of skill and ingenuity. Whatever you buy, rest assured that there is not another identical object anywhere in the world.

Yellow-wood is used for many of the works, and special items such as game boards and screens are chiselled from ebony and palm trunks. One of the oddest pieces of furniture visitors will come across is the coconut peeler. This is in fact a chair for the person doing the peeling and shredding. The seat is always intricately carved, with a chiselled backrest. At the raised front there is a round metal disc with a serrated edge. The person sits on the carved seat, faces the metal disc and grates the coconut across the serrated edge.

Clothing plays an important part in Comorian culture and religion. At religious ceremonies most men wear white or cream-coloured cotton kandous. These are long, dress-like outfits worn by Muslims throughout the Arab world. Long trousers are worn underneath. Visitors interested in buying a kandou can find them for sale in any of the clothes shops in the alleys below the old market in Moroni. They are fairly cheap and ideal for wearing in the heat and humidity of the Comoros. In addition to the kandou, each man wears a yamatso cap. No two are alike. These caps are usually intricately embroidered by the man's wife, mother or girlfriend. If you are fortunate enough to find one for sale, be prepared to pay a high price. Alternatively, Tourism Services Comoros may be able to arrange for a local woman to make you one if you buy the material and cotton. Give her about seven days to finish the entirely handmade cap. It will be expensive, but certainly worth the price.

Women all own at least two chiromanis. These brightly coloured lengths of cloth serve a similar purpose to the chador of Shi'ite Muslim countries. Travellers will find them useful for a multitude of purposes. Heaps of them are offered for sale at most markets. The biggest selection is available from the old market in Moroni. Once you have returned home they can be used as wall hangings, tablecloths or even bedspreads.

Comorian jewellery is magnificent. Working with 24-carat gold and white silver from Saudi Arabia and Madagascar, the jewellers craft intricate pieces of art that sell for prices far below that asked in First World jewellery stores. From filigreed dolphins and flowers to bangles and necklaces, everything is on sale in the little bijouteries in urban centres. Many "Notables" carry ebony walking sticks topped with tooled silver handles as a sign of social standing in the community. The jeweller at Bijouterie Omar in Moroni is sometimes prepared to fashion such a unique silver handle for visitors if they supply the walking stick.

If you are looking for pieces in gold, then a visit to Bijouterie Jogia, behind the Friday Mosque in Moroni, is a must. The jeweller, one of only a handful of Hindus living on the Comoros, will gladly make you a special item in gold. Discuss the design with him and allow about three days for the item to be completed. You will be asked to pay a deposit.

Silver jewellery is sold in large quantities across the square from Jogia, at Bijouterie Khodidas in Moroni. A serious problem about shopping here is that the jeweller uses turtle shell, shells and even ivory in his work. Potential customers should consider the disastrous environmental impact that the trade in such products has before buying anything from such a place.

Bangles, earrings and necklaces are sold in stores on all the islands. But for the largest selection of bangles and necklaces, many ornate with black, yellow and pink coral, visit Bijouterie Khodidas in Mamoudzou or Bijouterie Essak in Moroni.

No visitor to the Comoros should return home without at least one bottle of ylang-ylang perfume. Ask at La Galawa Beach Hotel and some will be obtained for you at a small commission. Travellers using local transport and touring the islands on their own should ask in the districts where ylang-ylang is grown. The manager of the factory at Bambao is willing to sell independent travellers a small bottle of pure ylang-ylang oil poured straight from the still. It is very cheap considering that this is the most sought-after base for international perfumes.

Places to buy ylang-ylang perfume are Salimani, on Grande Comore, Iconi, at the eastern end of Mohéli, Bambao, in the eastern hills of Anjouan, and Kombani, west of Mt Mtsapéré on Mayotte.

Two curios seldom bought by tourists are the easiest and most interesting to purchase. The first is the raffia dolls made on Anjouan. There is a display of them in the boutique of the Hotel Al-Amal. These dolls are not only for tourists. In many homes on Anjouan, raffia dolls are used as ornaments. Each doll is dressed in a distinct way that signifies something. If you do buy one from the Anjouani islanders, ask them to explain the symbolism of that particular doll.

The second curio missed by many visitors is the vast selection of spices on sale. Vanilla, especially, is very cheap on the Comoros. The quills are normally wrapped in bundles of about 20, or else sealed in little plastic bags. You can find them for sale at most urban markets. Cloves, too, are abundant, as are peppercorns and nutmeg. Spices make cheap but exotic gifts.

Among religious artefacts for curio-hunters, Koran holders have already been mentioned. Grass prayer mats and candle and incense holders are also sold. One of the most beautiful, although costly, things one can buy is a hand-finished Koran. They are all written in the delightful Arabic script and embossed with gold and silver lettering. Many are enhanced by colourful hand-drawn pictures on silk pages.

THINGS TO DO

Hiking

This is one activity on the Comoros that is still wide open to adventure travellers. All the islands have trails and paths that lead through some of the most spectacular landscapes on the Indian Ocean islands. From plunging waterfalls to rainforests, from deserted beaches to remote villages, hiking in the Comoros will always be a truly memorable experience.

A backpack is necessary and a tent is recommended, especially if you plan to sleep in the depths of the forest. Good hiking boots, wet weather gear and food should also be included in your equipment. If you want to explore the interior of Anjouan or Mayotte it is suggested that you hire a guide. On Anjouan this can be done via the Hotel Al-Amal. On Mayotte, contact the management of La Tortue Bigotu for assistance. Walking across Mohéli is easy on your own. The paths are well marked and you are free to camp anywhere in the forests or hills. Grande Comore is crisscrossed by trails. Several of these may be hiked without a guide, but once into the forests around the volcano it is easy to get lost in the darkness of the tall trees.

A number of the hikes described below require that you overnight in rural settlements or sleep in your own shelter. But there are also those that can quite comfortably be walked in a few hours. Even if going out on a day hike, remember to take along a small pack with some water, food and wet weather gear. A hat and suntan cream are very useful when traipsing across open country.

Grande Comore

- Get an early start from Mitsamiouli and walk to the hill village of Pidjani, a few kilometres south-east of La Galawa Beach Hotel. Turn south here and proceed to Mandza. From Mandza walk across the fringe of ancient craters to Haoueni. Turn left (north) in this hamlet and onto the sides of a tall crater. There are impressive views from the summit. Continue east across wooded hills to Dimadjou. It is a stroll down to Moidja and the main east coast road. There you can flag down a bush-taxi. The entire walk should not take more than about 10 hours. If you would like to sleep out on the trail, the villagers in Haoueni are a friendly bunch.

- From Mitsamiouli go south-east to Pidjani. At this village turn north-east and cross the grassy hills to the settlement of Ouela, where there are historical Arab ruins to the left of the road. Swing south from Ouela to reach Idjoinkode. Then it is a fairly strenuous climb over shallow craters to one of the most isolated places on Grande Comore: Koua. Spend the night with the wonderful villagers here. The next morning you return to Idjoinkode and turn east for Ouzio. From this lowland village the road continues north to near Lac Salé, on the north coast. Bush-taxis are frequent along this tarred road and you will not have to wait long for a lift.

- A long hike in the north of Grande Comore can take about three days. Follow the directions in the first route described above as far as Haoueni and spend the first night there. Leave Haoueni at about 6h00, walking south across the line of gentle craters and through montane forest to the main cross-island tarred road. You may need to sleep one night on this section. There is no habitation and you will only have the scented breezes and wide vistas as your companions.

- A walk to the summit of Karthala volcano is a must for all visitors. It can be done in one day, but most people do it over two, sleeping in the outer crater for one night. You will need an expert guide for this walk, which is the most visually pleasing of all Grande Comore's hikes. Not only do you walk through dense rainforest and across hillsides of dead trees, you also cross open grasslands. Then there is the volcano itself. All the effort and struggle to reach the summit is rewarded by the sight of the inner crater.

- In the south of the island are forest trails that will test the skills of any hiker. From Singani, go north-east to the village of Mdjoyezi. There you will need to recruit a guide for the arduous trek through the jungle to Tsinimoipanga. Fit hikers will probably have to spend at least one night in the forest. Others should count on about two nights on the trail.

- One of the shortest hikes that visitors can do on Grande Comore is from Simboussa, which you can reach by bush-taxi, to the beach near

Mâle. From Simboussa it takes less than two hours to walk down to the palm-lined beach opposite the village of Mâle. This is not a difficult walk and is suitable for those who do not enjoy long hikes across difficult terrain.

Anjouan

- Take the bush-taxi from Mutsamudu to Patsy. From there walk southeast into the hills and forests. Near where the road forks, there are paths either side. Each leads to a delightful waterfall in the mountains. Both are impressive and worth the detour. Having seen the waterfalls proceed to Tsembehou. Here you may either take the bush-taxi back to Mutsamudu or continue into the thicker rainforest to the south. It is advisable to hire the services of a guide if you do this part of the hike. Follow the road into the primeval jungle. One of the best places to camp the night is on the edge of Lac de Dzialandzé. You will be alone at this lake. There are no villages nearby, and birdsong and sky are all around. The next day walk down to the waterfall close to Lingoni. Once past Lingoni, the hike is easy all the way to the main west coast road at Pomoni.

- A shorter route can be taken from opposite Lac de Dzialandzé. Turn east and go down the forested slopes to where they give way to savanna, south of Koni-Djodjo. Immediately south of Koni-Djodjo is a small waterfall worth seeing. The village children will be delighted to show you the way. Beyond this settlement the road meets the east coast tarred road between Bambao and Domoni. It is suggested that you sleep one night at Lac de Dzialandzé.

- The most demanding hike on Anjouan is from Lac de Dzialandzé through the least explored part of the island back to Mutsamudu. It will be impossible to walk this route without a guide. The most experienced guides can be contacted through the manager of the Hotel Al-Amal. Take along all your own camping equipment, food and water for the trek. During the dry season the walk will take you about a day. When it rains, however, give yourself at least two days to cover the distance. This route is not recommended for people without hiking or outdoor experience. It is tough but memorable.

Mohéli

Most of Mohéli is attractive to hikers. There are few roads, but numerous scattered hill villages, waterfalls and forests to be seen and visited. Trail guides are not really needed anywhere on Mohéli.

- Take a bush-taxi to Miringoni. Where the main road ends, continue south-east. This trail skirts the base of old calderas and leads into a dense forest, which contains a splendid little waterfall. Exit the forest again and follow the coast. There is a deserted little beach south of the waterfall. You will not find anyone else here. Continue along the route to the remote village of Wallah. In the rainforest to the south-east of Wallah is another waterfall, with a pool at the bottom deep enough to swim in. The path swings towards the coast again and then veers east to end at Niumashuwa, where you will find boats to take you out to the marine reserve and the offshore islands.

- A less demanding but no less beautiful walk can be taken on the eastern side of Mohéli. You can catch a bush-taxi from Fomboni to Wanani. At Wanani there is path that winds through the ylang-ylang estates to Lac de Boundouni. It is a fragrant hike across gentle hills and occasionally through the last vestiges of rainforest on this part of the island. From the lake you have the choice of either going down to Iconi village or north-east to Itsamia and the beach. There is also a strip of beach off Iconi. But the main reason for visiting Iconi is to meet some of the friendliest people on the Comoros. If you arrive with a backpack, they quickly invite you to spend the night, arranging a bed in one of the palm-frond huts.

Mayotte

- One of the best hikes to take on Mayotte starts at the settlement of Mtsapéré. Follow the trail going west into the hills. This takes you on a steep climb to the summit of Mt Mtsapéré. The views of Mayotte from this peak are unparalleled. From the top of the mountain, the route descends through rainforest to the ylang-ylang distilling village of Komboni. Komboni is a good place to find accommodation for the night. From here, continue south along forest paths to the main cross-island road. A regular bush-taxi service operates between the two coasts from about 7h30-17h30.

- From Mamoudzou catch a bush-taxi to Accoua, on the north coast. Where the taxi drops you off, turn south and cross the slopes and grasslands to Mtsangamuji. Close to this village is the most beautiful beach on Mayotte: Baie de Soulou. There is a waterfall near the bay.

There are many other paths across the Comoros islands. Those travellers with experience, not afraid to live with locals and eager to encounter the dwindling Comorian wilderness, can easily venture off the beaten track and find their own trails to follow.

Water sports

For many visitors, the main attraction to visiting the Comoros is scuba diving. La Galawa Beach Hotel is able to provide tourists with scuba diving contacts. The one most frequently recommended is Island Ventures Limited, which offers unqualified people a Resort Diving Course. This starts in the morning and by the afternoon you will be underwater, exploring the shallow reefs offshore. Be advised that this only qualifies you to dive at that particular resort. It is a much better idea to arrive already scuba qualified.

The Boat House on the beach of La Galawa Beach Hotel also offers diving courses and specialised diving, and reputedly has the best divemaster and instructors, who have spent several years charting the area and now offer divers unique locations.

The waters off north-western Grande Comore, although rather disappointing compared to other Indian Ocean islands, are ideal for beginners. There is enough submarine life to encourage most newcomers to pursue scuba diving.

Scuba diving off Itsandra or Moroni is poor. The effluent from the densely populated coast has virtually destroyed all the colourful sea life.

With its reputation as one of the best diving sites in the world, Bonne Aventure Reef, about 40 km south-west of Grande Comore, is a must for all serious scuba divers. It is very expensive to hire a boat to take you there, but the diving is excellent. Still largely unexplored, this reef teems with the most incredible sea life. Its distance from land has kept it protected. From brightly coloured reef fish to sleek deep-water predators, from swaying plants to vibrant coral, divers are in for a treat.

Although there are not really any good places to scuba dive around Anjouan, this author had a once-in-a-lifetime experience while scuba diving in Anjouan Bay. A humpback whale surfaced within a few hundred metres of me, and made no move while I swam around it. Locals say that whales ("baleen" in Comorian) often come into Anjouan Bay.

Scuba diving can be organised through the Hotel Al-Amal in Mutsamudu, Anjouan.

Off southern Mohéli lies the only Comorian marine reserve, around the islands off Niumashuwa. Here, too, there has been little interference from humans, and the sea life has flourished. The water is not deep and Openwater I divers will find conditions suitable. Contact the Relais de Cingani for assistance with scuba gear and an underwater guide. You can arrange a boat with the fishermen of Niumashuwa village.

Two places scuba divers should try on Mayotte are off Dembeni and in the bay between Bweni and Kani-Kéli. Contact the Hotel Ngouja at Kani-Kéli and Le Baobab Hotel in Mamoudzou.

Snorkelling in the Comoros is not for the inexperienced. The strong currents that wash around many of the shallow bays and reefs can prove treacherous, even for experienced swimmers. Mayotte is the best place for snorkellers. The large reef which surrounds the island has created shallow lagoons. Beware of sea urchins, though, they can inflict a nasty wound. Should your skin be punctured by a sea urchin get yourself to medical help quickly. Do not try to remove the spine yourself. It is very brittle and could easily break off in the wound. Locals use paw-paw to draw the spine and poison out.

Guests can hire snorkelling equipment from most tourist-class hotels. A substantial deposit is required if you are not a resident of the hotel. The top-class tourist hotels all offer water sport equipment to their guests. This usually includes pedalos, windsurfers, dinghies and Hobie-cats. If you are staying at the hotel you may use all non-motorised water sport equipment free. Otherwise a small fee is charged. If you are staying at a hotel that does not offer these amenities, speak to the management. The hotel can normally arrange for a day's outing to another hotel that does have these facilities.

Big-game fishing is another of the water sports popular with tourists and can be arranged through all tourist-class hotels. Royal Transit Express tour service is also able to arrange boat charters. Tackle is included in the fee, but you might have to pay for each catch. Lunch is part of the package, while alcoholic drinks are extra and paid for separately. It is much cheaper to make arrangements directly with the charter-boat skippers.

Fishing with the local fishermen is an interesting alternative to trophy hunting. Very few tourists ever do this and the fishermen will be surprised by your wanting to join them on a voyage. They will, however, supply you with a hand-line and bait for the day. They leave early, about 4h30, and do not go far offshore. You may keep whatever you catch or sell it at the local fish market with them. Visitors may even be invited to take their fish to one of the fishermen's houses and have it cooked together with the family meal. This is a delightful experience in itself.

On Grande Comore the places to enquire about fishing with the locals are Mitsamiouli, Foumbouni, Singani, Chindini and Bouni. On Anjouan, try asking around Moya, Chiroroni and Domoni. On Mohéli, the best place is Niumashuwa. Iconi and Itsamia also have a fleet of galawa fishing boats. Mayotte has subsistence fishermen at Bandrele and near Kungu.

Pack your own lunch for the day. Remember to take along a hat and lots of liquid to drink, preferably bottled water. You will perspire a great deal. That night make sure to add lots of salt to your food. Fishing with a hand-line is hard work. Most visitors wake up the next day with numerous aches and pains from muscles that are seldom exercised.

4 GETTING THERE

AIR

This is the most common means of transport for tourists to the Comoros.

International flights connect the Comoros (Moroni) with Antananarivo, Dar es Salaam, Johannesburg, Marseille, Mauritius (Mahébourg), Nairobi, Paris and Réunion (St-Denis). International flights connect Mayotte with Mahajanga (Madagascar), Nairobi, Paris and Réunion (St-Denis).

The airlines servicing these routes are listed below, with their addresses and telephone numbers on the Comoros. For their latest flight schedules and fares, contact a travel agent or these airlines' representative in your own country.

Air Austral, Place du Marché, Mamoudzou, Mayotte.

Air France, represented by Air Comores, Iconi Airport, Moroni, tel. 73.95.24.

Air Madagascar, Embassy of Madagascar, Magoudjou Street, Moroni.

Air Mauritius, represented by Air Comores.

Air Tanzania, represented by Air Comores.

Condor, represented by Air Comores.

Réunion Air Service, Place du Marché, Mamoudzou, Mayotte.

South African Airways, represented by Air Comores.

Air Comores used to connect the Comoros with Madagascar and Tanzania, but since its only aircraft had been sold by a general manager who then disappeared with the money, this is no longer possible! There have also recently been problems with Air Mauritius, which has on several occasions been refused landing rights. Check on its status before choosing this airline as your carrier.

All air tickets must be confirmed at least three days before departure; five days ahead is preferable. No matter which airline you are using, the seat confirmation for a flight from the Comoros must be done through the Air Comores office at Iconi Airport in Moroni, tel. 73.95.24. This is quite an experience. Residents at La Galawa Beach Hotel and Itsandra Sun Hotel simply hand their tickets in at reception and a staff member is despatched to make the confirmations. Visitors staying at other places must do this themselves. Make certain to get there by 8h30.

As the doors open there is a mad dash to reach the counter. There are no orderly queues. Do not stand back and be polite, no-one else does. Push and shove your way through. You can expect to spend at least three hours getting your flight reservation confirmed. Holders of Air Madagascar tickets can sometimes avoid the trauma of Iconi by requesting the Air Madagascar representative at the Malagasy Consulate to make the confirmation telephonically. Usually he will agree, but when he is very busy, e.g. on a Friday or Monday, he will refuse and direct you to the Air Comores offices. It is worth trying, though. You could save yourself some valuable time for exploring.

SEA

Most Comorians travel between East Africa or Madagascar and the Comoros by boat. Part of the passage is on ferry, part on freight carriers bringing products to the islands from the industrial ports in Tanzania, Kenya, Zanzibar and Madagascar. Competition for a berth is fierce and visitors are advised to book their place at least three days before intended departure.

From Madagascar, the vessels leave Mahajanga (north-west Madagascar) for either Moroni or Mutsamudu on a Monday, Wednesday and Friday. Contact Auximad on Avenue de France in Mahajanga. Trans Tour Travel Agents, also on Avenue de France, can arrange for a comfortable berth on one of the freighters travelling between Mahajanga and Moroni. Ferry tickets to the Comoros may also be arranged via SCTT, opposite SA Maxime, in Mahajanga. Alternatively, just ask around the docks whether there are any vessels making the crossing to the Comoros. The trip takes about two days, depending on weather and sea conditions. You must take along all your own food and drink. If you have not reserved a cabin make sure to have something warm to wrap up in at night – it can get very cold at sea.

Travellers planning to go from the Comoros to Madagascar by ship should buy their tickets from Agetransmar, between the lighthouse and Friday Mosque, in Moroni. On Anjouan, visit the Socopotram shipping office, near the bibliothèque in Mutsamudu. Agence General Shipping, opposite the container yard at the port, is the local specialist for sea transport to and from Madagascar and Zanzibar. Agence Bon Voyage Comoria, next to the BIC bank in Mutsamudu, cater for passengers who want a berth aboard vessels going to Mahajanga. Most ships taking passengers between Madagascar and Moroni or Anjouan stop for a few hours in the port of Mamoudzou, on Mayotte. I could not find any agencies catering for boat passengers from Mayotte. For details, visitors should contact the Office du Tourisme near the harbour. The staff are very helpful and will go to great lengths to find out departure times, and even arrange a ticket for you.

If hoping to take a ship from Tanzania to the Comoros, you have the option of either leaving from Zanzibar or Dar es Salaam. Tickets are available from the Zanzibar Shipping Corporation on Morogoro Road, Dar es Salaam. The vessels of this company normally leave from Zanzibar for Moroni twice a week. The other company worth contacting for reasonably priced tickets and clean berths aboard cargo ships to Moroni is the Tanzanian Coastal Shipping Line, along Sokoine Drive, Dar es Salaam. There is usually one trip per week to the Comoros and back. The voyage takes about three days.

Although few people travel by boat from Kenya to the Comoros, occasionally a freight vessel makes the crossing from Mombasa. The Tourist Office, on Moi Avenue, is often helpful in this regard. Otherwise speak to the Port Captain at Kilindini Harbour; he will know of any ships planning a passage to the Comoros.

In South Africa, travellers are advised to speak to the Mediterranean Shipping Company (MSC), on Bay Terrace, in Durban. Another place where you may find transport to the Comoros is at the yacht mole in Durban. Look at the notice boards in the Royal Natal Yacht Club and Point Yacht Club.

5 GETTING AROUND

AIR

Having had its only aircraft sold recently, Air Comores can now offer no air transport between the islands of the archipelago, at least until such time as a replacement has been purchased. Tourists who do not mind spending huge amounts of money to enjoy their vacation may be able to charter a private plane from Iconi Airport. Speak to Royal Transit Express tour operators, behind the Friday Mosque in Moroni, or Tourism Services Comoros, at La Galawa Beach Hotel.

SEA

This is the only way of reaching all the islands of the Comoros. You have the choice of ferries and island trading vessels or asking one of the fishermen to take you across.

There is a regular ferry service, aboard a World War II landing craft, between Moroni and Mutsamudu. Buy your ticket in the building to the left of the harbour entrance gate. There is a blackboard outside the office that announces when the ferry will be leaving from Moroni. Make sure to get your ticket as early as possible on the day of departure. The ferry sales office opens at about 7h30. Turn right as you enter the building, and then immediately left. Go through the doorway in the corridor; the ticket counter is behind the grille to the right.

The ferry leaves Moroni in the evening at about 18h00 and arrives in the port of Mutsamudu at around 5h00 the next morning. There are a few cabins available, but most passengers just find themselves a place on the deck or on a bench. Anywhere else one has to avoid people being seasick, children yelling and the general chaos as the vessel rides the large Indian Ocean swells between the islands. Take along something to eat and drink. A useful purchase for any traveller in the Comoros is a chiromani. These versatile lengths of colourful cloth can be used to wrap yourself in or spread out to lie on.

The same ferry departs Mutsamudu from behind the container terminal. You can purchase tickets from Socopotram, opposite the entrance to the port in Mutsamudu. Walk through the clove-sorting area and up the stairs. Turn left at the top, the counter is to the right as you enter.

Reaching Mohéli from Grande Comore can be a problem. Ferries seldom make the crossing. Your best bet for getting to Mohéli is to go to Chindini or Ifoundihe, on the south of Grande Comore. There it is easy to arrange for a fishing boat to take you south-west to Mbatse on Mohéli. The trip will take between four and six hours. These boats are small and not for those who succumb easily to seasickness. You will probably get wet, so cover your pack with a large plastic bag to keep it dry. Pack some food and water for the voyage.

While ferries crossing to Mohéli from Grande Comore are infrequent, there is an island trading vessel, the *Ville de Fomboni*, regularly travelling from Anjouan to Mohéli, then to Grande Comore and back to Anjouan. There is no fixed timetable and you will have to ask around the docks for her sailing times. Details of her routes can be obtained before arrival on the islands by writing to: Mouhmar-Kadaffi Mohamed, 107 Rue de la Mairie, 97610 Pamandze, Mayotte, tel. 60.08.08. This small, wooden boat is always full of passengers and cargo. Tickets are bought from the "pointure", who can be found wandering about in front of the harbour gate looking for clients. If you manage to get a ticket early enough you may be fortunate to be allocated one of the five beds in the cabin behind the wheelhouse of the boat. Otherwise it is the wooden benches and open deck for you. Once again, take along something to wrap up in, and some food. From Anjouan to Mohéli the boat leaves Mutsamudu at 14h00 and takes about five hours.

To go from Mohéli to Grande Comore, get to the beach off Fomboni at about 18h00 on the evening of departure. The "pointure" hangs about on the beach waiting for passengers. The boat waits for the tide to lift her off the beach and usually sails at around midnight. The crossing to Moroni takes roughly seven hours.

To reach Mayotte by boat, get yourself to Anjouan first. There contact one of the shipping agents mentioned in the section on getting to the Comoros by boat in chapter 4. There are regular boat trips to and from Mayotte. These are either on ferry or cargo vessels or tramp steamers. Whichever you use, chances are that you will be assigned a berth. No food or drink is provided during the voyage. Vessels normally depart early evening and arrive in Mamoudzou the next morning.

TAXI

Taxis are expensive on the Comoros. Most of them are Renaults or Peugots in various stages of decay. Those from Hahaya Airport to a hotel usually charge tourists in French francs. There is no law that you must pay them in Ff, and it is much cheaper to pay the fare in CFr. The fee must be negotiated before setting off.

In Moroni, Mutsamudu and Mamoudzou there is a flat rate everywhere in town. The price of trips to other villages or towns must be negotiated. There are few taxis travelling after about 20h00. Those that do have invariably been waiting for a passenger whom they took somewhere to eat, dance or drink earlier that evening, i.e. they have a guaranteed fare.

The longest and most expensive taxi ride that can be taken on Grande Comore is from Moroni to Mitsamiouli. Taxis are loath to drive any further than this. You will need to make use of a bush-taxi (taxi-brousse) to go any further than about 50 km. Another alternative is to ask a taxi driver to attach himself to you for the duration of your visit to the island. Should you decide on this, state clearly what you expect, and fix a price beforehand. There are definite advantages to having a taxi on call, especially at night, after spending several hours in a local nightclub tasting the palm wine and meeting interesting people.

There are no official taxi ranks on the Comoros, you just stick out your arm and flag them down. If they have space they will stop, otherwise they flash their headlights to indicate that they are already full. It is highly amusing seeing just how many people the drivers can cram into a Renault 4. The accepted number of passengers is two in the front (excluding the driver) and at least five on the back seat.

BUSH-TAXI (TAXI-BROUSSE)

Canvas-covered Peugot pick-up trucks, called bush-taxis, are the Comorian answer to public transport. These overcrowded, speeding machines are the fastest, cheapest and most exciting way of getting around the islands. Bush-taxis serve all towns located along tarred roads. This means that travellers have access to most points of interest on each of the islands. Not many tourists use bush-taxis, preferring the courtesy buses laid on by their hotels. One major problem about bush-taxis is the high rate of fatal accidents in which they are involved. This is as much a result of driving too fast as the steep gradients and hairpin bends of Comorian roads. However, for visitors who want to meet Comorian people, this is the quickest way of making their acquaintance.

On Grande Comore, Anjouan and Mayotte, bush-taxis cover specific routes, while on Mohéli the few that speed about usually make any trip on the little island.

Bush-taxis have a fixed price for their particular route. For example, if you take a bush-taxi anywhere between Moroni and Bangoi-Kouni, you will be expected to pay the standard fee. It makes no difference whether you only go a few kilometres or all the way to the end of the route, the price remains the same.

Bush-taxis do not run in the evenings. They start from about 8h00 and make their final return trip home around 16h30. On Grande Comore a few continue travelling up and down the west coast until 19h30.

In Moroni there are two bush-taxi ranks, although a third is quickly developing opposite Volo-volo market for taxis serving the north-western areas. Bush-taxis going south and south-east from the capital leave from the square in the cluster of houses east of the new mosque. Bush-taxis travelling west, north and north-east depart from the old market and the post office. Travellers often walk along the tarred road in the direction they wish to go, and then wait for a bush-taxi to come along. There is the danger of not getting a lift, though. Bush-taxis from Moroni are nearly always full for the first 10 km.

Mutsamudu has a small but very busy bush-taxi depot under the trees near the meat and fish market, opposite the post office and park. You will need to ask the passengers or drivers for their destinations. Bush-taxis on Anjouan always carry a cargo as well. This could be bags of rice or cloves, chickens, the odd goat and a roof-rack piled high with luggage. It results in some tense moments as the weight shifts when rounding corners, worst on the tortuous road from Page to Sima. Travellers of a nervous disposition should not look down into the deep valleys along this route. They are littered with wrecked bush-taxis that missed the sharp corners.

Mamoudzou bush-taxis crowd around the harbour area and the clutter of alleys around the market. Once again, you must determine their destination by asking both passengers and drivers. Bush-taxis on Mayotte are more expensive than on the other islands in the archipelago, and payment must be made in French francs.

HITCHHIKING

In a nutshell: it is virtually impossible to hitchhike on the Comoros. The only people who stop are the drivers of bush-taxis. Private cars that offer a ride always expect payment, often higher than it would have cost you to take a bush-taxi.

CAR HIRE

This is the most expensive way of getting around the islands. Car rental can be arranged through La Galawa Beach Hotel on Grande Comore, the Hotel Al-Amal on Anjouan and the Hotel le Baobab on Mayotte. There are no car hire facilities on Mohéli.

Drivers need to produce an International Driving Permit or French driver's licence. A non-refundable insurance is charged against possible accidents, and a hefty deposit is required. The longer you keep the vehicle, the less you pay per day. It is possible to see an entire island in a day. If you are planning to stop in villages, spend time on the beach and visit points of interest, then not more than two days of car hire are required. The problem with driving about the Comoros in a hired vehicle is that you seldom get to make real contact with the islanders. But if you have limited time and only want to see the sights, then hand over the cash and race about in a Suzuki jeep, Citroen or Toyota.

TOURS

Organised tours is the way 90% of all visitors see the Comoros. There are definite advantages to joining an organised tour, especially if you prefer not to travel to remote areas on your own or in local transport. While numerous unofficial tour guides may approach you at Hahaya or in the harbours, there are only two professional tour operators on the Comoros: Tourism Services Comoros and Royal Transit Express.

Both operators run trips and tours to all of the Comorian islands. If you have reserved a tour with them, they will send transport to fetch you from the airport, take you to your hotel, conduct you on the tour you selected and then drive you back to the airport on your departure. Their efforts to keep clients happy are exemplary.

Their addresses are:
Tourism Services Comoros, PO Box 1226, Moroni, Grande Comore, Comoros, tel. 73.17.40 or 73.17.50. TSC may also be contacted via La Galawa Beach Hotel, north of Mitsamiouli.
Royal Transit Express, PO Box 19, Moroni, Grande Comore, Comoros, tel. 73.00.10.

TSC deals almost exclusively with the top tourist hotels, such as La Galawa Beach Hotel, Itsandra Sun Hotel and the Hotel Al-Amal. Its best option is a full-day tour of Grande Comore. A driver will collect you from your hotel in the air-conditioned bus and drive down the west coast, across the old lava flows, to Moroni. There you will be allowed time to do some shopping at Volo-volo market before proceeding to the museum. From the museum a guide leads tourists through the old market and down narrow alleys to the jewellery shops around the Friday Mosque. Then the tour goes along the south coast to the 17th century capital at Iconi. There is a quick visit to Singani village before stopping for a packed lunch and swim at the seaside village of Chindini. Then up the east coast to Foumbouni. From here the tour continues north to pass Chomoni, on the edge of a volcanic beach. There is time for a quick swim at Bouni, and another stop at the crater lake of Lac Salé before returning to the hotel.

The guides on these tours speak several languages and have extensive knowledge of the history, flora, fauna and geography of their island. If you go on only one organised tour while on the Comoros, this is the one I would recommend.

Royal Transit Express is geared to mid-level budget visitors who do not stay at the top hotels but want to see the islands with an informative guide and provided transport. Should you require detailed information on their offered tours, tariffs and suggested routes before arriving in the Comoros, write to them at least three months before your arrival.

Many of the smaller hotels offer tour packages around the islands. They seldom advertise these and you should make enquiries from their management. If you only want a guide and plan to travel about with him on local transport, ask around the Comorian eateries for assistance. The manager at the Hotel Al-Amal is also helpful in finding guests a private guide.

6 MORONI

Dozing on the west coast of Grande Comore, Moroni, with an estimated population of 40 000, is reminiscent of an ancient Arab port. White mosques, colourful buildings, galawas and people in traditional Arab dress create the unique atmosphere of this 14th century town. Around the old market is a maze of alleys between coral and volcanic-ash houses and it is quite easy to get lost.

Augustus Earle, explorer, author and adventurer, wrote in 1822 that one of the things he wanted to see before he died was a sunset over Moroni. Although he never managed this, any visitor to the Comoros can see how much he missed by watching the sun setting over the bay.

In the long shadows of early morning, streams of people make their way towards the markets at Volo-volo and in the CBD. At midday the harsh glare of the tropical sun paints the capital a startling white. Once the sun has set, a delicate pink glow lingers on the minarets and splashes the forests behind town. Nighttime sees the streets busy with snack sellers, dope peddlers, families, prostitutes, couples and cavorting children.

Although there has been an increase in crime of late – mainly due to a 65% unemployment rate – no reports have yet been received of tourists being attacked. Use common sense while walking around at night, especially in the area east of the Christian church, although it is highly unlikely that anything unpleasant will happen to you while touring Moroni.

TRANSPORT

There are numerous taxis from Hahaya Airport to Moroni. If you find their prices prohibitive, walk out of the airport gate and wait on the main road. Flag down any bush-taxi going south. The driver will drop you in town.

All ferries dock in Moroni harbour, a few hundred metres from the CBD.

If you have arrived at Chindini from Mohéli, you are bound to find a bush-taxi travelling to Moroni. If not, walk north of the village along the main road. Bush-taxis serving the south and south-east coast will stop for you.

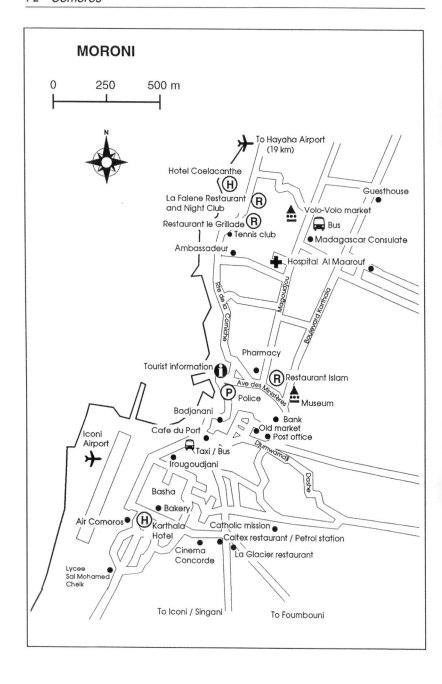

MORONI

0   250   500 m

To Hayaha Airport
(19 km)

Hotel Coelacanthe

La Falene Restaurant
and Night Club

Restaurant le Grillade

Tennis club

Ambassadeur

Guesthouse

Volo-Volo market

Bus

Madagascar Consulate

Hospital Al Maarouf

Rte de la Corniche

Mogoudjou

Boulevard Karthala

Pharmacy

Tourist information

Ave des Ministères

Restaurant Islam

Police

Museum

Badjanani

Bank

Cafe du Port

Old market

Post office

Iconi
Airport

Taxi / Bus

Djumwamdji

Irougoudjani

Dashe

Basha

Bakery

Air Comoros

Karthala
Hotel

Catholic mission

Caltex restaurant / Petrol station

Cinema
Concorde

La Glacier restaurant

Lycee
Sal Mohamed
Cheik

To Iconi / Singani

To Foumbouni

TOURIST INFORMATION

Tourist information in Moroni may be found in four places. The best is Royal Transit Express tour operators, behind the Friday Mosque. If you have the time, much information can be gleaned from the staff at Musée des Comores (CNDRS), behind Caisse Française de Développement, north of the post office. At the Conseil de L'Île de Ngazidja, you will be given a few pamphlets and brochures about the island. The staff speak very little English and seem uncomfortable in dealing with tourists. The least helpful, but offering free city maps, is the Ministère des Transports et du Tourism. Its deserted-looking offices are located directly above Badjanani Bay, opposite the Ministère de Finances et du Budget building. Limited information may also be obtained from the staff of Air Comores at Iconi Airport and the Hotel Karthala across the road.

Banks in Moroni are clustered east of and up the hill from the old market. If coming from the north, you must pass the Musée des Comores to get to the circle around which the banks are clustered.

Banks represented in Moroni are:
Banque Internationale des Comores (BNP)
Banque Pour L'Industrie et le Commerce: Comoros
Banque Central des Comores
Banque de Développement
Caisse Française de Développement

Travel agencies are scarce in Moroni, or anywhere else on the Comoros for that matter. Comoros Services is situated between the headquarters of the police and the Ministry of Immigration. Look for the wrought-iron gate opposite the Ministry of Tourism building. Royal Transit Express can also arrange air tickets, hotel accommodation, sea transport, tours and car hire. Tourism Comoros International has an office at Iconi Airport, is the agent for Europcar car rental and can render the usual services of a general travel agent. Trans-Archipel also serves as a general travel agent. It is still new and has not yet built up a wide client or operator base. As a result, its prices are very competitive and the service is exceptional. The sales office is between the old market and Parfum Baraka.

The post office in Moroni is up the hill from the old market; the entrance is opposite Banque Internationale des Comores (BIC). It is open Monday to Thursday 7h00-12h00 and 15h00-17h00; Friday 7h00-11h30; Saturday 7h00-12h00. International satellite-linked telephone calls can be made from ACTEL, around the corner from the post office and across the road from the Banque Centrale des Comores. (For details of services at the Comoros' main post office see chapter 3.)

There are two newsagents in Moroni; both also sell a few books in French: Nouveautés (Presse), next to the Musée des Comores, north of the post office, and La Maison du Livre, opposite Agence des Musulmans D'Afrique, east of the Hotel Karthala.

Studio Photo Super and Comor Photo, downhill and west of the Caltex filling station, have print film, camera batteries and an odd collection of camera bodies and lenses for sale, and take instant passport photographs. (Visitors may need them to obtain a Madagascar visa.) Although the staff in the shops have some technical expertise in camera repair I would be rather doubtful about giving them expensive equipment to fix.

Free medical services are available at Hôpital Al-Maarouf. The entrance is on Magoudjou Street, a few hundred metres south of Volo-volo market. A little beyond Le Jardin d'Orchidées Restaurant there is a dentist (cabinet dentaire). There are two well-stocked pharmacies: Pharmacie de la Corniche and Pharmacie Wokof, between Al-Watwany newspaper offices and Cinema Concorde. In the CBD near Boulangerie Salimamoud, in the Gobadjou suburb, Pharmacie Ntraleni has a good range of French and South African medicines and can fill most prescriptions from its shelves. The Croissant Rouge Comorien (Comorian Red Crescent) has an office across the lane from Nouveautés bookshop, opposite BIC.

The library in Moroni is housed in the same building as the museum. Enter the Musée des Comores through the main gate, turn left onto the balustrade and the library and archives are in front of you. Anyone is allowed to make reference to the books. Just fill in a request card and all the literature the library has on the topic will be given to you. However, you may not remove any books from the premises – this is not a lending library.

Visas to the Comoros are obtainable from the Ministry of Immigration, north-west of the museum. If coming from the north, you will pass Volo-volo market and then arrive at a T-junction. Directly opposite is the Ministry of Immigration building. In the foyer will be someone to assist you. Visas to Madagascar are obtainable through the Malagasy Embassy, a few metres south of Volo-volo market on Magoudjou Street. For a visa to Réunion or Mayotte you must go to the French Embassy, next to the Hotel Karthala, opposite Iconi Airport.

All airline enquiries should be made through the offices of Air Comores at Iconi Airport, south of the port. For information on Air Madagascar, contact the Malagasy Embassy near Volo-volo market.

Between the Friday Mosque and lighthouse are the shipping offices of Agetransmar, where you can get details of long-distance ocean transport. At the entrance to the harbour, next to a branch of the immigration ministry, are the administrative and sales offices of Socopotram Shipping, which operates the inter-island ferries and has contacts for berths on vessels plying the routes between the Comoros, Madagascar and East Africa.

EXPLORING MORONI

Getting around Moroni is best done on foot. In this way you have the opportunity of exploring the narrow alleys and meeting people. If you must drive from town to Volo-volo market or to one of the hotels along the coast, stop any of the taxis that cruise the streets and ask the price to your destination.

Orientating yourself in Moroni may be difficult. Existing suburbs and new development seem completely haphazard. The most obvious point of reference when touring the CBD is the enormous Friday Mosque, opposite the boatbuilding yard on the harbour. In town, use the church spire as a reference. To the north, Volo-volo market is the best place from which to start a walk. South of the CBD, the traffic-control tower at Iconi Airport is an aid in finding your bearings.

There are several interesting things to do and see in Moroni. The best way of seeing all the sights is by walking. Arguably the best place to start such a stroll is from Volo-volo market, north of the CBD.

Volo-volo market is one of the highlights of any visit to the Comoros. Under the concrete roof, cement trestles are laid out in long rows. Here you may browse among curios, spices, coconut soap, holy Korans, incense and clothing. Outside the covered market are neat rows of fresh fruit and vegetables for sale. In the open courtyard within the market is a bewildering variety of chiromanis in hundreds of colours, designs and lengths. Give yourself at least an hour to explore this marvellous place fully.

Continue south along Magoudjou Street. Tree-lined pavements are cluttered with street vendors and shoppers. Numerous little wooden shops sell various items of clothing, toiletries and snacks. Most foreigners who take the trouble to walk around here will be met with the Arabic greeting "Salaam Aleikum". The shop-owners are friendly and not used to seeing tourists here. They may invite you in for a short conversation and coffee.

Past Cinema Concorde is the entrance to Al-Maarouf hospital. Past the large entrance gates, to the right of the T-junction, is the local football ground; left you will notice a filling station, and directly ahead, on a small hill, is the Ministry of Immigration building. Turn right (west) here, towards the sea. Keep to the left of the road, passing Comoros Services and police headquarters. Opposite the Ministry of Tourism, the tarred road curves and starts a gentle descent. There is a 15th century lighthouse on the left. Although few visitors ever notice this old building, it offers wonderful views over Moroni harbour and across into Badjanani Bay. This is one of the oldest lighthouses in the Indian Ocean. Constructed by Sultan Saïd Moussa in 1487, the lighthouse was vital to guiding his trading vessels into the scalloped bay at night. Now it is dilapidated, a sad place that whispers of history and the age of Persian glory.

Walk along the wall that skirts the boatyard, where wooden vessels are still constructed and repaired by traditional methods. At low tide the shipwrights do most of their work. It is fascinating to watch them using techniques that date back to the early days of Arab sea exploration and have disappeared from the Arab world outside of the Lamu Archipelago, Zanzibar and Yemen.

Proceed along the road, below the small mosque, to Place Badjanani. There are several jewellery shops here. On the western corner stands the beautiful Friday Mosque, where on Fridays between 11h30 and 13h00 hundreds of people gather to recite their ritual prayers to Allah.

Passing the Friday Mosque, the main road curves along the edge of the bay to a large concrete traffic circle. Walk along the road that travels south and to the right of the circle. This will take you past the harbour entrance and further on, the Baumer sports stadium. A few metres south, on the right, are silver-painted fuel storage tanks. Beyond these is the airport of Iconi. No longer used for international flights, Iconi is where you confirm air ticket reservations. There are numerous soldiers in the area and tensions always seem high. Do not try to take any photographs here, nor get near the fuel depot.

Turn left (east) opposite Iconi Airport. With the side entrance to the Hotel Karthala on your right, walk up the busy road, which is a hive of street vendors, Comorian eateries, taxis and people. Off the main road you can also walk between wooden and palm-frond houses by following the gravel paths that connect alleys. At the eastern end of the main road is another, smaller, traffic circle opposite a Caltex filling station. Proceed left (north) from here.

Across the stone bridge lies the old part of Moroni. The streets are narrow, shops have their entrances right on the roadway and cobbled alleys invite exploration. The first road to the right, at Enterprise Elit, will take you to the Roman Catholic church, the only one on Grande Comore.

Returning to the main road, continue north to a junction of four roads. This is where many of the bush-taxis serving the south and south-east can be found. Cross the intersection and follow the lane between the two drivable roads. You will now find yourself in the oldest part of the town. Extraordinary shaped houses emitting the smells of spicy cooking, intricately carved doorways – some fitted with lethal spikes and peepholes – the lilting strains of Arabic music and snack stalls titillate the senses.

At the T-junction opposite the huge, black, brass-spiked door, turn right and continue up the steep stairs back onto the tarred road. Now you are in the old market. Here, laid out alongside the street, you will find fresh produce, textiles, jewellery, food, soap, T-shirts, spices and trinkets. The vendors here cater almost exclusively to the local trade. Therefore prices are lower than at Volo-volo market, but bargaining is still accepted practice.

By going up the hill you exit at the circle around which the post office and banks are clustered. Opposite is the old sultanate palace of the Gouvernorat D'Île Ngazidja. Cross the car-park in front of BIC and follow the road downhill.

On the right is the Musée des Comores (CNDRS). The main entrance is through the iron gates in the white wall. There is a small entrance fee and an ever-changing policy on taking photographs. Ask what the current position is. You have the option of seeing the displays on your own or hiring a guide. Guides are able to speak English, Italian, German and French. Despite being rather small, the museum is certainly worth a visit. There are natural history exhibitions, including hundreds of beautiful butterflies, a coelacanth, birds and fish. Downstairs the museum has created excellent displays of Comorian culture which fully explain local behaviour, rituals, traditions and daily life.

From the museum follow the road back to the T-junction at the Ministry of Immigration and follow the road to the Ministry of Tourism building. Here, take the road going right (north), the Boulevard de la Corniche. This road winds through trees all along the sea. This is an affluent area of luxurious houses, hotels, restaurants, nightclubs and strips of private beach. The French-owned properties are obvious by the graffiti scrawled on their boundary walls, a favourite being "Bas la France". Continue past the tennis club and turn right (east) at the Alliance Franco-Comorienne. This little lane winds uphill and ends outside Volo-volo market, where you started your walk.

To experience all this walk has to offer, allow yourself an entire day for the trip. There are many restaurants and cafés at which you can stop for a meal or drink during the day.

NIGHTLIFE

Moroni offers revellers two recommended night-spots – a dance hall and disco – on Friday and Saturday evenings from about 21h30. The Rose Noire Disco at the Hotel Coelacanthe is popular with foreigners and always busy, but it never gets too crowded or too loud. However, for an experiance of the dancing and partying of Comorians, the only place to go is La Falene. This palm-frond dance hall is deep in the suburbs south-west of Volo-volo market. Take the coastal road north from the Ministry of Tourism. Once past La Grillade Restaurant, and before the Hotel Coelacanthe, take the gravel road going east between traditional houses. About 50 m farther, on the right, is the dance hall. There is no sign outside, but loud music and crowds of locals will be indication enough. There is an entrance fee which includes one free drink. Hand your ticket to the barmaid when placing your order. You are highly unlikely to see another tourist here. Within a matter of minutes you will be joined by a few Comorians who will offer to buy you a drink and encourage you to dance. To find a seat, get there no later than 22h30. Expect a long night of dancing and enjoyment that does not end until the sun creeps over the summit of Karthala volcano.

For those who prefer more sedate pursuits, there are several hotel bars that stay open until midnight. Try those at La Grillade and the Hotel Coelacanthe, along the coast road west of Volo-volo market. Café du Port, opposite the large traffic circle above the port, stays open until about 22h00, has friendly young staff and sells ice-cold beer as well as rum and whisky. Movies are occasionally shown at Cinema Concorde and at another small bioscope just west of Restaurant Caltex.

ACCOMMODATION

Accommodation in Moroni is expensive. Quality and service are not too good, especially when compared to that offered by La Galawa Beach Hotel.

High tariff

The high-tariff hotels all overlook the sea and are located along the coastal road between the Ministry of Tourism and the tennis club.

Hotel les Arcades: A fairly new hotel across the road from the volcanic shoreline. Impressive sea views, friendly staff and close proximity to town will ensure that this hotel becomes popular with tourists. Address: B.P. 33, Moroni, Grande Comore, Comoros, tel. or fax 73.28.47.

Hotel/Restaurant la Grillade: Better known as a restaurant than a hotel, La Grillade does have rooms. Prices are high for what you actually get. The setting is very pleasant, however, and suitable for families who may prefer to do a little self-catering and discover the region for themselves. The staff are attentive, young, and can offer useful tourist information and advice about Grande Comore. Address: B.P. 88, Moroni, Grande Comore, Comoros, tel. or fax 73.30.81.

Hotel Coelacanthe: With accommodation in bungalows, a delightful restaurant, swimming pool and dive centre, this hotel is one of the most reputable in the Comoros. It is right on the sea, has a disco at weekends and is able to arrange island tours, scuba diving and deep-sea fishing. Address: B.P. 404, Moroni, Grande Comore, Comoros, tel. or fax 73.22.55.

Medium tariff

Hotel Karthala: Among the places to stay in Moroni, you will not find a better hotel for price, service, location, ambience and food than the Hotel Karthala. Located across the road from Iconi Airport, this hotel was once a sultan's residence. The 14 rooms are large and clean, and have mosquito nets over the beds. All rooms have bathrooms en suite. Breakfast is included in the reasonable price. The managers speak only French, but staff members are able to communicate in several languages. The Hotel Karthala sends a representative to meet all international flights, but you need to negotiate the transport fare with the tout. Address: B.P. 53, Moroni, Grande Comore, Comoros, tel. 73.00.57, fax 73.02.74.

Low tariff

In the low-tariff category, travellers are well catered for. Take along something on which to sleep, plus some mosquito coils and a pair of plastic sandals to wear while washing. Whatever the drawbacks of this type of accommodation, it is highly recommended for travellers who want to meet and learn about the Comorian people. Despite what tour operators may tell you, it is quite safe and cheap. No reservations are necessary at these places. If they are full, they will do everything they can to arrange for a bed somewhere else for you.

Those tried and suggested are:

Pension de Famille Karibu: In the lane that skirts the northern side of Volo-volo market. If you call from the airport at Hahaya, someone will usually be sent to fetch you: tel. 73.21.47.

Pension Kohinoor: Across the road from the Belgium Embassy, on the road north from Volo-volo market.

Pension Maharajah: Out of town to the south, on the road to Foumbouni, this *pension* is only advised for those who either have their own transport or do not mind using a bush-taxi. The *pension* is in a quiet area on the edge of a lush forest. It is hard to beat for peace, tranquillity and outstanding meals.

Pension Zam-Zam: Situated between La Grillade and Dragon d'Or, this establishment is geared to more well-heeled visitors, but at very reasonable rates. Meals are offered on request, and the management has several contacts for tourist guides, car hire and fishing.

Pension Zilimadjou: Behind the ostentatious Palais du Peuple, south of the Lycée Saïd Mohamed Cheik. This *pension* even has air-conditioned rooms. It is at present being renovated, and the owners are thinking of selling it or turning it into studios, which will cause a dramatic increase in price.

PLACES TO EAT

Moroni has a plethora of restaurants, cafés, bars and snack stalls. Many visitors may be wary of eating anywhere other than in a hotel restaurant. Not only is this unwarranted, it will also cause you to miss out on delicious Comorian cuisine. All the tourist-class hotels in and around Moroni have attached restaurants, which many of them call dining rooms. You do not need to be a hotel resident to eat there, neither is a reservation required. Apart from these, there are numerous local restaurants scattered about the capital. A short walk in any direction from the CBD will bring you to one. Most of the bars also serve a few dishes, normally including eggs and fish.

For extensive à la carte menus or buffets you will have to eat in a hotel restaurant. Prices in hotel dining rooms around Moroni are high, except for the *Hotel Coelacanthe* which twice a week has a buffet that allows you to eat as much as you like for a fixed price. Travellers who have spent several days hiking in the forests and hills of the Comoros should take full advantage of this wonderful opportunity to feast. *La Grillade Restaurant* has an extensive menu of traditional and Continental dishes at reasonable prices. The mixed salads are enormous and more than enough for two people to share. Zebu steaks are another speciality of the house. *Dragon d'Or Restaurant* concentrates on Chinese meals. It is popular with package tours, which frequently stop there for light lunches. All three of these restaurants are on the Boulevard de la Corniche. They are open daily for lunch 11h30-14h30, and for dinner 19h00-22h30.

Restaurant Le Jardin d'Orchidées, near Générales Denrées supermarket, serves enormous plates of Continental food at good prices. The waiters are helpful and will make recommendations about certain meals.

For traditional Comorian food you cannot do better than the tin-shack or wooden stall restaurants.

At *Restaurant Tawakal* diners are offered traditional food accompanied by mountains of white rice from a small menu. *Café Express,* reputed among travellers to be the best local restaurant in Moroni, is a must. Although lunch time is busy, the time to really enjoy this tin-shack café is after about 20h00. Turn east, towards the hills, at the large red and grey warehouse north of the church. A few metres up this road is a row of shanty kiosks. Café Express is unmarked but unmistakeable from the alluring smell of spicy food that wafts from its glassless windows. Only two dishes are served here: either steak or chicken with rice, Comorian sauce and salads. Prices are low, the food is tasty and the evening unforgettable. This is the local haunt of hashish peddlers, palm wine brewers and other intriguing characters.

Restaurant Macym, close to the Collège de Moroni, has a diverse menu that includes Comorian, French and Chinese cooking. The *Café du Port,* on Avenue de la Côte du Port, is the ideal place from which to watch one of those spectacular sunsets over Moroni harbour. More of a bar than restaurant, it has a daily menu written up on a blackboard. *Saraj Restaurant,* a little beyond La Maison du Livre, has the largest servings and the most traditional and cheapest food in Moroni. There is only one dish per day, but it is always tasty and very filling. Opposite the Caltex filling station is *Café-Restaurant le Bon Moment*, a favourite with youths on Friday and Saturday evenings. If you are hoping to get yourself invited to a Comorian house-party, then this is definitely the place to hang out.

Other restaurants worth considering for cheap and authentic local food are:

Le Rishma Restaurant, opposite Dramsee: quincaillerie bricolage

Restaurant Caltex, between the Caltex filling station and Pharmacie des Comores

Restaurant Glacier, on the opposite corner to the Caltex filling station

Restaurant Choidjou, in Zilmadjou suburb, on the road to Foumbouni

Chez Babout, near Volo-volo market on the road north to Mitsamiouli

Restaurant Rahat El-Lahil, across the road from Chez Babout

Snacks are available throughout the day from street vendors and wooden stalls: hot samosas, fried dough-balls, biscuits, roasted peanuts and cups of steaming black coffee. Fresh bread and assorted pastries are offered from a number of bakeries in Moroni. *Salimamoud Boulangerie Patisserie*, across the lane from Volo-volo market, has the largest selection and serves tea or coffee and, infrequently, ice-cream. There is another branch on the same road as the old market, which offers a similar selection, with high-quality bread. *Boulangerie-Patisserie Kalfane*, close to the Caltex Restaurant, has more traditional biscuits and cakes for sale. *Den's Shop*, near the Malagasy Embassy, has daily fresh savoury snacks for sale. *Nassib Boulangerie*, opposite Cinema Concorde, has trays of cakes, biscuits, pies and savoury snacks on offer. You may take your purchase away or sit at one of the little tables and also enjoy a drink. The long loaves of bread, baked early each morning, are perfect for hikers and those doing self-catering. *La Finesse Salon de Thé* offers light meals and delicious snacks from about 7h30-17h00. It is in the same road as the Kalfane bakery.

THINGS TO BUY

Going on a shopping expedition in Moroni requires fortitude, an immense sense of humour and the ability to bargain. *Volo-volo market* has to be visited by all shoppers to the island. On Place Badjanani curio-hunters will discover the bewildering displays at *La Maison de L'Artisanat Msadji-Mwingi*. You could easily spend two or three hours going through all the items offered at this shop. At *Parfum Baraka* you have the opportunity for purchasing small bottles of local perfume, notably ylang-ylang. Among the more exotic concoctions are perfumes made from island flowers and local spices.

A trip into any of the side streets around the old market will expose you to a whole range of local art, carving and clothes. If you desire a piece of the famed Comorian jewellery, then Moroni is the place to visit. Behind the Friday Mosque, in the square, are two jewellery shops worth visiting. *Bijouterie Khodidas*, near Royal Transit Express, works mainly in silver but many pieces incorporate turtle shell, shark's teeth, whalebone and even ivory. Anyone concerned for the environment will therefore want to avoid patronising this shop.

Bijouterie Jogia, across the square, is run by one of only a handful of Hindu families on the Comoros. The speciality is delicate jewellery made in 24-carat Saudi Arabian and Malagasy gold. The animal figurines and charms are exquisite, prices are reasonable and bargaining is possible. You can also have a custom-made piece crafted here.

Bijouterie Essak, on the arcade below the road of the old market, is small, cheap and busy. There is a fine selection of silver jewellery, often incorporating black, yellow and pink coral in the pieces. *Bijouterie Omar* is in the same road as the new mosque. Because it is tucked away, few visitors ever discover this treasure trove of local craftsmanship. Using gold, silver and precious stones, the jeweller produces stunning works of art.

7 GRANDE COMORE (NGAZIDJA)

Officially known as Ngazidja, Grande Comore is the largest island in the Comoros archipelago. Over 250 000 people, out of a total population of about 600 000, live on Grande Comore. It is the island on which most visitors to the Comoros spend their vacation. Youngest of the islands to have surfaced above the sea, Grande Comore is home to Karthala volcano, the largest active volcanic crater in the world. Rainforests, white beaches, remote villages and the island's capital, Moroni, offer tourists a wealth of things to see, do and experience. An excellent road network and good public transport make Grande Comore ideal for travellers and visitors who want to immerse themselves in a Comorian adventure.

The international airport, **Hahaya**, is located on the west coast of Grande Comore. Comore's top tourist hotel, La Galawa Beach, is situated on the northern coast of the island. Karthala volcano is in the south of the island. While the west coast is the part of the island most visited by tourists, it is on the wild east coast that you will encounter isolated villages and that strange mixture of African and Arabic culture that makes the Comoros such a fascinating destination.

According to the Ministry of Tourism in Moroni, over 87% of all foreign visitors spend their first few days at La Galawa Beach Hotel about 1 km east of the village of **Bangoi-Kouni**. There is not much to see in the village. Two small shops sell a few groceries and tepid drinks – there is no electricity here yet.

Lac Salé, on the north-eastern edge of Grande Comore, is the most popular viewsite within walking distance of La Galawa Beach. The interesting stroll from the hotel will take you through Bangoi-Kouni to the crater lake. You can also flag down a bush-taxi heading east from the hotel's entrance.

Lac Salé lies in an extinct crater above a wide curve of beach fringed by a turquoise sea. The nutrient-rich water of the lake changes colour twice a day: in the morning it is a deep green, while by late afternoon it has become a shimmering blue. Between July and October the colour varies from green to brown and even white. Local legend has it that an entire village is submerged under the deepest part of the lake. A sorcerer once arrived in what was then an ordinary village late at night,

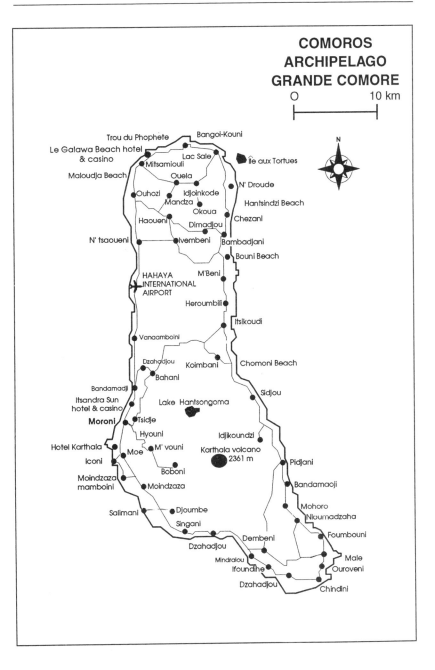

COMOROS
ARCHIPELAGO
GRANDE COMORE

0   10 km

N

Trou du Phophete
Bangoi-Kouni
Le Galawa Beach hotel
& casino
Mitsamiouli
Lac Sale
Île aux Tortues
Maloudja Beach
Ouela
N' Droude
Ouhozi
Idjoinkode
Mandza
Okoua
Hantsindzi Beach
Haoueni
Dimadjou
Chezani
N' tsaoueni
Ivembeni
Bambadjani
Bouni Beach
M'Beni
HAHAYA
INTERNATIONAL
AIRPORT
Heroumbili
Itsikoudi
Vanaamboini
Dzahadjou
Koimbani
Chomoni Beach
Bahani
Bandamadji
Sidjou
Itsandra Sun
hotel & casino
Lake Hantsongoma
Moroni
Tsidje
Hyouni
Idjikoundzi
Hotel Karthala
M' vouni
Karthala volcano
Moe
2361 m
Iconi
Pidjani
Boboni
Moindzaza
mamboini
Moindzaza
Bandamaoji
Djoumbe
Mohoro
Salimani
Nloumadzaha
Singani
Foumbouni
Dzahadjou
Dembeni
Mindralou
Male
Ifoundihe
Ouroveni
Dzahadjou
Chindini

seeking food and shelter from a tropical storm. At every door she was turned away; the villagers were afraid of the stranger. Finally, a woman allowed her in and gave her something to eat. The sorcerer said that she had come to warn the villagers that their homes would be "eaten" by the volcano, and they must flee. But as no-one would help her, she only gave her message to the family who had assisted her. The family packed their belongings and fled that very night with the sorcerer. Two days later, the earth opened and swallowed the entire village and its inhabitants.

The lake is supposed to have curative powers, but it is difficult getting down to the water's edge. Ask the children, who usually appear out of the bush, to guide you down. This descent is not for the faint-hearted or unfit.

In 1986 six Belgian scuba divers rowed a rubber dinghy out onto the lake and dived, hoping to plumb its murky depths. Only five returned. No trace of the sixth diver was ever found. Villagers say that he found the "door to Paradise" and therefore had no reason to return to the suffering world of man.

Clinging precariously to the walls of the crater, a few tall trees are home to a large colony of furry fruit bats. Though not as big as the Livingstone bat on Anjouan island, these Lac Salé bats are not small by any means. You may find the local children throwing stones into the trees to get the bats to fly for tourists' cameras. Do not encourage this; many of the bats are hurt in this way.

Take the path that skirts the crater to the east. This curls around to the northern rim and climbs to the highest point above the lake. Incredible views extend in all directions, over empty beaches, distant craters, forests, hills and villages.

Going west now, proceed through Bangoi-Kouni to **Trou du Prophète Bay**. Once popular with tourists, Trou du Prophète has lost much of its attraction to the beach at La Galawa Beach Hotel. Because of this, visitors will usually find it deserted and peaceful. You will not be bothered by hoards of curio-sellers here. With a white beach backed by black volcanic lava, Trou du Prophète is ideal for those visitors wanting to escape the noisy extravagance of tourist hotels. There is a tiny settlement on the main tarred road above Trou du Prophète Bay. The houses are made of grass, wood and tin. A curio shop offers seashells, pieces of shattered coral and turtle shell products. Remember that none of these items may be exported from the Comoros.

La Galawa Beach Hotel and Casino (high tariff)

This is undeniably the best hotel on the Comoros. Under the jurisdiction of World Leisure Holidays, La Galawa Beach Hotel is the favoured destination of celebrities, aristocracy and the jet set. The five-star luxury hotel has 182 air-conditioned rooms in idyllic surroundings. All rooms have a bathroom en suite, television, telephone and a safe and, arguably, the most beautiful stretch of beach in the archipelago right outside the window.

Attentive reception staff provide all arrivals with a cold fruit cocktail and information on the facilities available. In the foyer you will find Tourism Services Comoros, which can arrange car rental, guides and tours of the island. Downstairs, around the sparkling swimming pool, breakfast and dinner are served. Breakfast is a bountiful buffet of fruit, cereals, pastries, eggs to order and smoked meats. Dinner at La Galawa Beach Hotel is a unique experience. Budget travellers staying at other hotels should definitely make a reservation for dinner here at least once. Theme nights are always a favourite with tourists. They feature set menus and floor shows, and guests are encouraged to take part. Otherwise dinner consists of a sumptuous buffet.

After the meal, many people find themselves drifting into the casino or disco. High rollers are a feature of the casino. Having seen the poverty that plagues the Comoros, you may be disturbed by the amount of money a few local businessmen are able to throw away on gambling. The disco is enjoyable, albeit thoroughly First World.

Visitors wanting to scuba dive should contact the Boat House. Reservations can be made telephonically by non-residents, tel. 73.25.26. Guests have free use of non-motorised water sport equipment.

Reservations to stay at La Galawa Beach Hotel must be made well in advance:
World Leisure Holidays: La Galawa Beach Hotel, Petrob House, 343 Surrey Avenue, Randburg; or PO Box 1474, Randburg, South Africa, tel. (011) 886-9710, fax (011) 886-9709; or B.P. 1027, Moroni, Grande Comore, Comoros, tel. 73.82.51.

Continuing south from the hotel, turn right at the baobab tree and pass an ylang-ylang plantation on the right. Across the road from the plantation is *Mi-Amuse Restaurant and Nightclub*, which is always full of Comorians on Friday and Saturday evenings. You will not see many foreigners here. By midnight any semblance of Arabic influence has vanished, and only African tribal music and abandoned dancing are in evidence.

A few metres south of Mi-Amuse is the *Snack Bar Chez Salim*, which offers huge servings of traditional food at very reasonable prices. Rice, fresh fish and chili sauce are served for lunch. The South African beer is expensive, but chilled palm wine and fresh fruit juice are available. There is a dance here every alternate Saturday night.

Lamaree Restaurant is on the edge of a white beach, north of Mitsamiouli. Seafood is the speciality, but prices are high and the service is poor. Reservations are not necessary, and there do not seem to be any fixed closing or opening times. La Galawa Beach Hotel offers much better value for money.

MITSAMIOULI

This is the second largest settlement on Grande Comore, after the capital Moroni. It is a picturesque village straddling the main west coast road. A stretch of wide, white beach – the longest on Grande Comore – offers safe swimming in view of the busy market. The best swimming area is opposite Mitsamiouli Primary School. Galawa fishing boats lie scattered about the beach. If you get there before sunrise or in the late afternoon you will see the local fishermen putting to sea. Getting a ride with them is easy and highly recommended. They do not go far out, preferring to cast their nets about 100 m offshore.

As women are not deemed strong enough to go out in boats, they fish in the shallows with nets and sticks. Visitors can see them in the morning, off Mitsamiouli, forming a circle in the water, each one holding the end of the net and a stick. Working their way towards one another, they beat the water with their sticks and shout at the fish. Finally the net is closed in the middle and the catch hauled ashore. These fish are not for sale; you must have taken part in the fishing to have a share. Usually, if you ask the day before, the women agree to have you along as part of the team. It is great fun and an opportunity to meet some of the villagers of Mitsamiouli.

The post office is opposite the new mosque and there is a branch of BIC bank near Djema Bonbons. Snacks and tinned food are sold at Chez Zabou. Numerous street vendors offer local food, snacks and fresh bread for sale outside the market. The market in Mitsamiouli really comes to life on Sunday. With a vast array of fresh produce, cloth and trinkets, it makes for an interesting tour. The vendors are used to seeing tourists about. As a result they ask high prices for their wares. It is a good idea first to watch and listen to the locals buying before starting to bargain.

The mosque is off limits to casual visitors. But if you approach one of the "Notables" who spend their days in discussion under the trees opposite the mosque, one of them may take you on a guided tour. You must wash your feet, hands and face and remove your shoes before being allowed inside.

South of Mitsamiouli the road winds through avenues of fragrant frangipani trees and coconut groves before reaching the savanna slopes of the volcano. The volcanic eruption of 1986 spilled molten lava across the road near Hahaya Airport. Already moss and lichens have started to cover the black flow. Closer to the sea, pioneer ferns have found footing in the nutrient-rich lava.

ITSANDRA

The place to stay in Itsandra is the Itsandra Sun Hotel and Casino. Reopened on 4 February 1995, this 23-roomed hotel was once the favourite haunt of Bob Dénard's notorious European "officers".

A mere 15 minute taxi ride from the international airport, and five minutes from the centre of Moroni, the Itsandra Sun Hotel has two suites and 21 standard rooms. Compared to its sister hotel, La Galawa Beach Hotel, the Itsandra is small and intimate. Facilities are limited, but guests are permitted to make use of the extensive tourist facilities at La Galawa Beach, less than an hour's drive to the north, at a price of course. The Itsandra is marketing itself primarily at businessmen, honeymooners and elderly couples.

There is a restaurant with a seating capacity for just 50 people. Breakfast, lunch and dinner are served here. There is a bar near the slot machines. Traveller's cheques, foreign currency and all international credit cards are accepted. Note that the hotel does not accept any children under 12. Make certain to book your reservation at least 30 days in advance. This can be done either directly through Sun International's management: Itsandra Sun Hotel and Casino, PO Box 1027, Moroni, Grande Comore, Comoros, tel. (269) 73-8118, fax (269) 73-8251, or through World Leisure Holidays, PO Box 1474, Randburg, South Africa, tel. (011) 886-9710, fax (011) 886-9709.

The beach at Itsandra is perfect for swimming and sunbathing. Enclosed by a shallow bay, the sea is calm and ideal for windsurfing. Windsurfers and paddle boats can be hired from outside *Le Tiboulen Snack Bar,* on the beach. This snack bar is popular with tourists throughout the day. Le Tiboulen has a good menu which includes Continental and American-style dishes. The food is delicious and the setting marvellous.

To the north of Itsandra are crumbling guard-boxes (pill-boxes) built by the French during the war. Today they are used by local couples in search of privacy.

Across the road from the beach are the ruins of a 16th century sultan's fort. Built of crushed volcanic rock and coral, the grey fort is difficult to see in the thick vegetation. There are three entrances to the five-sided fort. The easiest to reach is along the southern wall. People seldom stop to visit here, and you will be quite alone in the silence of the bastille.

On the road past the President's residence is the Comorian restaurant *Lima.* The tasty local dishes always include baked fish, grilled steak or roasted chicken. The meals are filling and hardly anyone manages to finish all the rice served. It can get very busy on Saturday nights, and you are advised to get there by at least 20h00 if you want a table.

Between Itsandra and Iconi is the capital, Moroni (see chapter 6).

ICONI

South of Moroni lies Iconi village, the capital of Grande Comore in the 17th century. It was off Iconi that the first recorded catch of a live coelacanth was made.

The tall cliff over the sea has a tragic story attached to it. In the 14th century the local sultan built a refuge on the summit of this cliff to protect his people from marauding Sakalava pirates. There was only one route to the top, and the sultan and his subjects thought they were safe. Sadly, a traitor showed the pirates the route. Rather than be taken to Madagascar, over 200 women threw themselves off the cliff onto the rocks and into the sea below. Known as the Cliff of the Faithful Wives, this site has become a proud landmark to Grande Comorians. Today, visitors can struggle up the slippery path to the summit. Little more than the walls of the fort remain but there are good views of Moroni and the west coast beaches.

On the southern side of Iconi, bolted to a crumbling, bullet-marked wall, is a plaque honouring the men of Iconi who were murdered by Ali Solih's Jeunesse Révolutionnaire in 1978. It was against this very wall that the 15 and 16-year-old youths slaughtered the villagers who refused to work as slaves in the infamous "modiria" work gangs.

Continuing south of Iconi the road enters a region devoted entirely to the production of ylang-ylang, coffee, nutmeg, cloves and vanilla. In the 19th century the Comoros displaced Indonesia as the spice islands. However, it was only for a short time, until political instability devastated the country, from which it has still not recovered.

The steep volcanic slopes around ancient craters show a rainbow of colours that change shades and hues as the sun moves across the sky, not unlike the Coloured Earths on Mauritius.

On the south-western corner of Grande Comore is the village of **Singani**. Partially destroyed by the violent volcanic eruption of Karthala in 1977, Singani is split by lava flows that ran through the village to the sea. Most of the residents rebuilt their houses in exactly the same places as before because they believe that lava never flows twice over the same place. Therefore, even if the volcano does boil over again, their homes will be safe. Interested visitors can walk up the mountainside on the lava flows, to the young forest.

All along this wild coast there are deep caves in the volcanic cliffs. Blow holes have been formed through years of battering by the ocean. There are several between Singani and Chindini.

The villages along this remote stretch of coastline are seldom, if ever, visited by tourists. The inhabitants are friendly, curious and amazingly hospitable. Their religion is a mixture of animism and Islam.

On the south-east tip of Grande Comore is the village of **Chindini**. This is the lunch stop for organised island tours. The tour operators have put up little palm-frond huts for their clients. There is a splendid swimming beach and a shipwreck offshore that you can paddle to. Most of the wreck has been stripped for scrape-iron. If you walk through the mangroves to the narrow beach on the south-west, you will be able to see the island of Mohéli.

FOUMBOUNI

Proceeding up the east coast, travellers arrive at the third largest settlement on Grande Comore: Foumbouni. Like the majority of south-east coast beaches, this one consists of volcanic pebbles and grey ash.

There is a post office next to the basketball courts. A badly neglected late 17th century fort is to be found on the outskirts of Foumbouni. From its walls visitors have a good view of the surrounding countryside and black beaches. By walking west, onto the slopes of the hill behind town, you will come to several small craft shops. These cater for Comorian trade and you will not find the tapesteries, art, pottery and carvings of the curio shops of Moroni. Prices are low and the workmanship is high.

Near the point on the east coast where the tarred road that crosses the island back to Itsandra branches west, lies the hamlet of **Chomoni**. Blessed with a smidgen of fine coral beach, and hemmed in by cliffs, Chomoni is a clutter of palm-frond huts, coconut trees and amicable locals. This is another of the stops for tour groups, and the villagers have set up curio stalls.

Continuing up the east coast, follow the signs for Bouni. Between Chomoni and Mtsamdou is the largest baobab tree on Grande Comore, allegedly over 500 years old. Most of the tree is now dead, but the attraction is that its large hollowed-out trunk was once used as the local prison.

Bouni beach is difficult to reach, but worth the effort. The white coral beach is beautiful and ringed by a young reef that offers safe swimming. Take any of the steep paths that drop through the bushes and trees to the beach. On weekends you will probably meet Comorians enjoying themselves with a picnic on Bouni beach.

Toto Island is visible from the road north of Bouni. There are three coconut palms growing on Toto. Locals say that there used to be four – representing the four islands of the Comoros archipelago – but that when Mayotte refused to join the federation one of the trees, apparently without any sign of disease, simply died overnight! There is a small beach on the north side of Toto. To reach the islet, ask the fishermen in Bouni to ferry you across for the day. If you are looking for the experience of being alone on a deserted tropical island, then Toto is the place. Turtles come ashore here to lay their eggs and leave their flipper marks in the white sand. Be sure to visit Toto if you are here between early September and mid-November, and you may be one of the extremely fortunate few to witness the amazing scene of baby turtles scrambling for the sea.

A few kilometres to the north is Lac Salé, where this island tour commenced.

Visitors interested in exploring the highland forests, meadows and hills should return along the coast to the tarred road which crosses the island from Chomoni to Itsandra, and turn west on it. At **Koimbani** there are ruins of a 15th century Arab mansion and abandoned flower and vegetable gardens. Koimbani is blessed with cool breezes that rush up the hillsides, making it a great place from which to escape the heat of the coast. There is no tourist accommodation in the village, but if you speak to the local mullah, he will arrange a bed for you with a villager.

From here walkers can arrange for local guides to take them through the forests or along the mountain ridges to see ancient craters and settlements that cannot be reached by road. Travellers must be careful to minimise their effect on locals and the environment. This is a highly threatened region. The forests are being cut back and modernisation has already started pushing forest-dwelling creatures into an ever-shrinking habitat. You may want to write to the World Wildlife Fund, expressing concern over the vanishing forests and endangered culture on Grande Comore: WWF, PO Box 738, Antananarivo, Madagascar, tel. 348-85.

8 ANJOUAN (NDZUANI)

Officially known as Ndzuani, Anjouan is the most scenic of all the islands in the Comoros archipelago. Although not as blessed with beaches as Mohéli and Grande Comore, what it has to offer those visitors who enjoy mountains, forests, waterfalls, traditional villages and rivers is unsurpassed on the Comoros. Not that there are no swimming beaches on Anjouan; on the south-west coast, bathers will find Moya and Chiroroni beaches more than adequate.

Anjouan is also the most densely populated of all the islands, with 420 people per square km. Here you can see people roped to steep hillsides while cutting terraces and trying to cultivate mountain rice. Despite the overpopulation, there are still areas of this magnificent island where visitors can find tranquillity and silence. No visit to the island can be called complete without at least one walking tour of the forests and mountains of the interior. Many of the villages in the hills can be reached by visitors only with the help of a guide who will lead you along footpaths through the woods. From the summit of Col de Patsi (650 m) or Ntingui (1 590 m) walkers are offered spectacular views of the island, and on clear days you can see across to all the other islands in the Comoros archipelago.

Anjouan is the centre for the production of ylang-ylang, vanilla and cloves. In many of the villages you will see cloves being dried on sacking in the narrow streets. There are French-owned ylang-ylang distilleries and vanilla-drying trestle tables.

The first settlers on Anjouan were Shiraz Arabs from Persia. In the village of Domoni you can see their original houses near the beach. Soon after the Shirazis came a wave of Southwest Asians from the eastern Indian Ocean and western Pacific. Their intermarriage has resulted in Anjouan having the most attractive people on the Comoros. Not only are they physically beautiful, but their warmth and hospitality will be a delight to all visitors. It is said that when a man reaches marrying age on the Comoros, he will inevitably first travel to Anjouan to look for a wife.

Anjouan was home to the late Ahmed Abdallah, the president who was assassinated in 1989. His ostentatious tomb is in his home town of Domoni, on the east coast. Although not geologically the oldest

Comorian island, Anjouan has the longest history. It was on Anjouan that the first settlers to the archipelago arrived. The island has several points of historical interest which include forts, palaces, Shiraz dwellings and mosques. If there is one other island that you must visit, aside from Grande Comore, it is Anjouan.

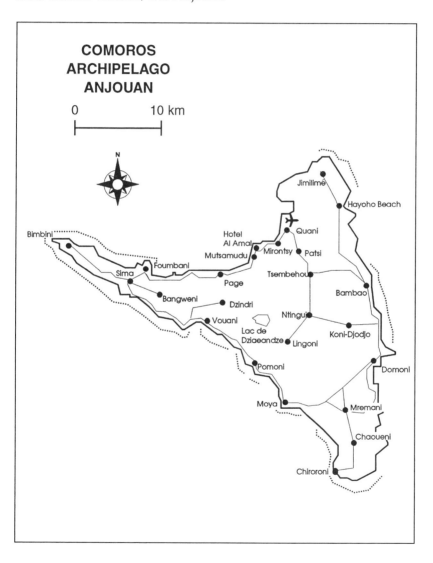

COMOROS
ARCHIPELAGO
ANJOUAN

0   10 km

N

Jimilime
Hayoho Beach
Bimbini
Hotel
Al Amal
Quani
Mutsamudu
Mirontsy
Patsi
Foumbani
Sima
Tsembehou
Page
Bangweni
Bambao
Dzindri
Ntingui
Vouani
Lac de
Dziaeandze
Lingoni
Koni-Djodjo
Pomoni
Domoni
Moya
Mremani
Chaoueni
Chiroroni

MUTSAMUDU

Built in 1482, Mutsamudu is wedged between the sea and steep forested hills, on the north of Anjouan. It is the usual arrival point for visitors coming by ferry from the other islands of the Comoros. As the island's capital, Mutsamudu has the densest concentration of people on Anjouan. Exploring Mutsamudu on foot is a highlight of any visit to Anjouan. Houses are clustered together in a maze of narrow alleys that link the various quarters together. Unlike in Moroni, crime is virtually unheard of in Mutsamudu, and visitors will be quite safe wandering about on their own, even at night.

The main post office is opposite the fountain and park, near the taxi rank and port. There is also an annex post office next to the telecommunication aerials, east of the port and not far from the bibliothèque. There is a BIC (BNP) bank opposite the bush-taxi rank in downtown Mutsamudu. Several shipping offices are situated within a few metres of the harbour entrance gate. Socopotram is directly opposite the Customs building, with another branch near EAF, east of the harbour. Agence Bon Voyage Comoria is next to BIC bank. AGS (Agence General Shipping) is close to Restaurant du Port.

Tourist information is available from the Hotel Al-Amal, east of Restaurant la Phalène, and also at ATS (Agence Touristique de Service), next to Mnadzi Oumoja Shop. ATS is able to arrange Anjouan island tours and book airline and ferry tickets for tourists.

Taxis and bush-taxis line up under the trees between the small park and the meat and fish market, behind the Customs building.

There are several sites worth visiting in Mutsamudu. A wide, volcanic black pebble beach stretches along the coast either side of the harbour. No-one swims off these polluted beaches, but it is the ideal place to see galawas putting to sea in the early morning and late afternoon. For a real treat, arrange to go out with one of the fishermen. Anjouan Bay regularly sees whales (called "baleen" by Comorians). Not hunted by the locals, they are rather tame and will allow a boat or diver to approach quite close before sounding.

It was in Anjouan Bay that the famed Indian Ocean pirate, Olivier le Vasseur, made his first attack on a British merchantman, the *Indian Queen*, after he changed from French corsair into free-booting pirate.

Above the town, to the south, is the Citadel. Built by the Portuguese, the fortress has at various times been manned by the soldiers of an Arab sultan, France and Great Britain. To reach the citadel, walk east past the busy covered market. Then turn south and climb the stairs to the top of the hill. There is a locked, wrought-iron gate at the entrance to the fort. The key is available from the small shop to the right, at the top of the stairs.

The woman who runs the shop is the local traditional healer. She makes strange concoctions and potions for the islanders. One, made of flower essences, herbs and spices, is a favourite with courting couples. They rub the potion onto their hair before going out, to make them attractive to the opposite sex. It has such a good reputation that not only do people travel from the other islands to buy it, but several international cosmetic firms have recently also shown an interest.

Once through the gate, you will immediately see that the site was a sound military choice. Below the cannons lie the entire town of Mutsamudu and the harbour. The cannons have now been embedded in concrete blocks, but their markings are still clearly visible. Look for the fleur-de-lis ensign on the French cannons and the crown on the British ones.

Behind the citadel is a French Roman Catholic church built in the early 1900s. Its doors are usually only open for services on Sundays and Christian holidays.

By walking south-east of the covered market, visitors reach the banks of the Mutsamudu river. All along the viaduct that flows above the river grows a strange variety of plant whose leaves close when touched. In the pools below the waterfalls children splash about. Further up the river, in the depths of the forest, are numerous species of orchids, including wild vanilla.

Opposite the entrance to the port and on the veranda of Socopotram Shipping are the local clove warehouses. When stepping off the ferry visitors can immediately smell the mountains of cloves spread out on sacking to dry. Sorters spend all day separating the various grades and bagging them for export. Paid by the bag, the sorters are not very communicative while working, but do not mind being photographed.

The meat and fish market, across the bridge and behind the Customs building, is chaotic. The main Mutsamudu market is covered, and is reached by going along the main road from the port to the upper part of town. The spice selection is visually and aromatically astounding. Here you are able to purchase fresh produce, clothing, shoes and a variety of local handicrafts, including unique Anjouan raffia dolls.

By speaking to the staff at CARE (an aid organisation), opposite the Société Ismail Badraly warehouse along the main road east of Mutsamudu, visitors can arrange for a trip to see the ylang-ylang, vanilla, clove, coconut, coffee and pepper plantations on Anjouan.

Accommodation

There is only one tourist-class hotel in Mutsamudu: the Hotel Al-Amal (see below). On the road to Ouani is the somewhat dilapidated *La Guinguette*, tel. 71.05.85. More popular as a watering hole than a place to stay, it has five comfortable rooms. *Les Sept Merveilles* has 10 rooms, but I could not ascertain whether it still accepted tourists or not. The two people who sat in the yard would not sign me in, even though the lodgings were obviously empty. Travellers may try their luck by writing beforehand: B.P. 325, Mutsamudu, Anjouan, Comoros. Please let me now if you are successful in finding accommodation here. Cheaper accommodation, albeit much more basic, is available from *La Phalène*, which has two bungalows for rent.

Hotel Al-Amal (medium tariff)

In need of a great deal of renovation, the Hotel Al-Amal still manages to offer visitors suitable accommodation in 16 air-conditioned rooms, all with balconies overlooking the sea, and bathrooms. Meals are offered in the dining room, which looks east towards the distant minarets of Ouani and high hills of north-eastern Anjouan. The swimming pool is an ideal retreat when the hotel's coralline beach is awash at high tide. The staff are pleasant and attentive, and go out of their way to accommodate tourists. At night the bar fills up quickly and patrons become loud and jovial. Unlike many tourist hotels in the Indian Ocean islands, the Hotel Al-Amal encourages locals to use its facilities. This makes the hotel a good place to meet islanders and make contacts for when touring other parts of Anjouan.

Visitors are able to arrange car hire, guides, airline confirmations and organised tours from the hotel. It even offers courtesy transport to and from the airport in Ouani. A television lounge allows guests to watch the latest news on CNN, and each evening videos are shown. Reservations are seldom necessary, especially as there are now no inter-island flights by Air Comores.

Hotel Al-Amal, B.P. 59, Mutsamudu, Anjouan, Comoros, tel. 71.15.80.

Places to eat

The best traditional Anjouan food is found at *Resto Masulaha,* on the seafront road. Steaming plates of rice, chicken and fish are served at very low prices. *Restaurant du Port,* opposite the container yard at the harbour, is upstairs and offers both good views and a good menu. The staff are somewhat surprised to see a tourist sitting down for a meal here. The price, quality of food and enormous servings make this one of the best low-cost places to eat in Mutsamudu. At the *Café Bar Mroni,* opposite PNAC Medicines, only one dish is served daily. This is more of a bar than an eatery. On Friday evenings it gets very full and festive, especially after midnight when the doors are closed and the remaining patrons are entertained. *La Paillote,* between the covered market and CARE, serves large helpings of Comorian food. At lunch time a *plat du jour* is usually served, which nearly always consists of fish, vegetables, rice and a fiery chili sauce.

For snacks, cakes, bread and pastries, there is little to beat the vast selection available from *Viennoiserie Patisserie,* near the bush-taxi rank. In the market and from numerous street stalls visitors can buy samosas, kebabs, brochettes, grilled fish and roasted chicken.

Occasionally the Hotel Al-Amal puts on a dinner and dance evening. But to meet and mix with islanders, the place to visit for a night on the town is *Café Chiromani.* Every Friday and Saturday evening this usually quiet café in the alley above the beach explodes into life. Reggae music, throngs of traditionally dressed locals and plentiful drinks ensure a vibrant, joyful evening. Chances are that you will be the only tourist there.

At *La Paillote Shop,* near the telecommunications aerial, curio-hunters will find T-shirts, raffia dolls, carvings and pottery for sale. There are no fixed prices and you will need to bargain. The Hotel Al-Amal also has a boutique which sells traditional Anjouan handicrafts.

OUANI

East of Mutsamudu, about 6 km away, is the village of Ouani. Between Mutsamudu and Ouani are the 15th century ruins of an Arabian palace and French colonial fort. Hidden by vines and dense vegetation, these crumbling buildings are difficult to see from the road. Walk east out of Mutsamudu and continue through the villages on the road towards Ouani. Near the Centre Formation des Pêcheurs, and behind a palm-frond fence, are the ruins.

Almost directly opposite these decaying buildings on the volcanic pebble beach is one of the wonders of Anjouan. Within a few metres of the sea are fresh-water springs among the black pebbles. The local villagers have made circular wells around these springs. The water tastes like tonic water and is said to be very healthy and aid digestion. Not many foreigners know of these wells. Ask the permission of bystanders before helping yourself to a drink.

In the houses that line the road to Ouani are reputedly the best palm wine brewers in the Comoros. Ask around for someone to take you to one of their stills. A bakery is also located in a back yard along this road but is difficult to find behind the long lines of bamboo and palm-frond fencing. Speak to the children on the beach, they will gladly take you there. The ancient ovens still bake delicious bread, prepared in the traditional way on the concrete floor.

Surrounded by ylang-ylang estates, coconut groves and mango or-chards, Ouani is the site of Anjouan's airport. Few people ever spend time drifting through this traditional settlement. Opposite the taxi rank is a frenetic covered market. From the volcanic pebble beach, galawas put to sea. If you are interested you can get a place on one of these boats for a day of fishing. You will need to take along your own food and drink, but will be supplied with a hand-line and hooks. Whatever you catch is yours to keep or to sell with the catches of the other fishermen.

There are several mosques. A few of these are specifically for women or men; ask before going inside. The mosque near the beach has a particularly high minaret. Ask the mullah and you will be allowed to climb to the very top for a good view of the village and across to Mutsamudu.

South of Ouani the route climbs into the high hills around Col de Patsi, and the cool forests of the interior. Passing a waterfall, the twist-ing tarred road descends to the ylang-ylang centre at Bambao. On the outskirts of Bambao is a vanilla processing factory. Casual visitors are allowed if they get permission from the manager.

BAMBAO

On the north-western edge of Bambao is the 19th century palace of Sultan Mawana. Leave the main road and turn left (north) to reach the palace. The entrance is guarded by two cannons. Near them is the sultan's tomb, dating from 1889. The palace sits atop a knoll overlooking the sea and is surrounded by bread-fruit and mango trees. Expansive flower and vegetable gardens are terraced down towards the village of Bambao. In the outer walls of the palace are several beautifully carved doors (made in Domoni) and windows etched with the crescent and star of Islam. East of the palace is an empty swimming pool which was built by the French after the sultan's death. The palace is abandoned and neglected, but some of the original furniture stands forlornly in the corners on a mosaic floor. The main hall has a balcony at either side. One housed the old harem, while on the other balcony the sultan would sit and hold court, with his ministers and minions sitting in the hall below. When the French seized the palace they stripped most of the valuables and sent them to Antananarivo in Madagascar. Tourists can see several pieces of this furniture, Koran holders and tooled chests from Bambao in the museum there.

Undoubtedly the main attraction of Bambao is SANOFI ylang-ylang distillery. Built by the British in 1880 the factory is now owned by the French, as are most other large business concerns on the Comoros. The entire process of ylang-ylang production can be seen here. Ask the amiable manager to arrange a guide for you. The tour is free and interesting. Visitors may buy small bottles of pure ylang-ylang oil afterwards.

Scattered about the estates are beautiful examples of plantation mansions. Many of these are uninhabited now, the cost of their upkeep being prohibitive for most Comorians. A few foreigners have expressed interest in purchasing the houses, but the present government is prepared to consider only French nationals.

DOMONI

South of Bambao, past the plunging Tatinga waterfall, is the oldest settlement on Anjouan: Domoni. In the path of Polynesian sailors and Arab merchants, the east coast of Anjouan was surely visited by both these groups. It was frequently also the scene of violent Malagasy pirate attacks. Now considered the second capital of Anjouan, Domoni was home to the former President Ahmed Abdallah.

There is a post office opposite the Abdallah mausoleum, on the main road. BIC (BNP) has an exchange counter not far from the post office. Taxis wait across the road from the bank. The only accommodation available is in the four-roomed *Karima Lodge*, tel. 71.92.83.

The most obvious tourist attraction in Domoni is the exquisite tomb of Ahmed Abdallah. With towering white and gold-topped minarets, the lavish tomb was donated and built by the Chinese government as a gift to Abdallah's family upon his death. Visitors are allowed to walk around the balcony above the green-and-gold-covered funeral casket. Take off your shoes before climbing the spiral staircases in the minarets. To the sides of the tomb are separate mosques for women and men. To the left of the mausoleum is the residence of the late president's family. Much of the mansion is now available for rent, but a section is still home to his daughter and her family.

Where the tarred road curves west, continue straight down the narrow alley. About 100 m farther, on the right, is a woodworker's yard where intricately carved doorways, caskets, furniture and curios are made. The woodcarvers and carpenters of Domoni are regarded as the best in the Comoros. This is one place that all curio-hunters must visit.

On the seafront is the beautifully crafted minaret of the Domoni Friday Mosque. From the circular veranda of this mosque, visitors can see across to the island of Mayotte. The first mosque built by the Shiraz Arabs is on the edge of the sea, below the ruined walls which once defended the town against pirates. If you walk directly across the road from the ancient mosque, and then along the alley into the square, you will see the oldest house in Domoni. Also built by Shiraz people, this sheer, white-walled house has tiny windows and diamond-shaped air vents. It is still inhabited, but the residents do not mind allowing you a walk around inside.

SIMA

West of Mutsamudu is the palm-frond village of Sima, above Foumbani beach. Situated high on a hill covered in palm trees, above the reefed sea, Sima rates as one of the most picturesque settlements on Anjouan. It is the second oldest settlement on the island, after Domoni, and the centre of Anjouan's clove production. The cloves are laid out to dry all over the streets of Sima and their scent permanently blankets the village. Visitors cannot walk anywhere without stumbling upon the drying seeds. On the hills around Sima, clove trees grow in wild profusion, bearing their little red-and-yellow blossoms.

Bush-taxis travel between Mutsamudu and Sima about once every hour. They can be taken from the T-junction where the road either goes south to Vouani or further west to Bimbini.

There are three mosques in Sima. The main mosque, with its finely chiselled doorway, is near the market. It was built on the ruins of a previous mosque that had been razed in the early 14th century.

Simamerica Bazar is small but interesting. The selection of spices is really good, and prices are very low.

The only place to stay in Sima is the *Hotel Lagachon* (low tariff). It is cheap, basic and thoroughly Comorian. Finding something to eat is easy. Simply wander up to the bazaar or along the main road where street vendors sell snacks, pastries, bread and local food in paper plates. There are also a few stores in the village that sell tinned goods and packed groceries.

On the unattractive beach at **Foumbani** are the bungalows of the *Relais Hotel*. Few visitors stop here, so there is no need to make reservations. There is only one staff member on duty, who can arrange to have meals cooked for you at the bungalows.

Further south, at **Moya beach**, the *Relais de Tourisme* has nine bungalows and a restaurant. This is the best beach on Anjouan and is popular with islanders as well. The restaurant has a good menu and specialises in seafood. Prices at the restaurant are reasonable, but the bungalows are very expensive for the standard of accommodation they provide. If you have a tent, rather walk into the hills between Moya and Pomoni and camp there. Alternatively, take a bush-taxi to **Kangani** or **Mremani** hamlets. The hospitable inhabitants of these settlements are unused to seeing tourists and you are likely to be offered accommodation.

9 MOHÉLI (MWALI)

Known to Comorians as Mwali, this is the smallest and least developed of all the islands in the Comoros. There are however rumours that NATO and the EU are putting in tenders to build large hotels, military barracks, a proper harbour and an airport here. Until that happens, this tiny island, only 48 km by 18 km, is a wonderland for those who enjoy the wilderness.

The islanders on Mohéli are noticeably negroid in appearance. There seems to have been very little intermarriage between the African slaves, Arab masters and French plantation owners on Mohéli. There is also a lack of adherence to Koranic injunctions on Mohéli. You can buy alcohol quite openly in the shops, many women go about with their heads uncovered, and parties held in the coconut groves and on the beaches are decidedly liberated by Islamic standards. The people of Mohéli are boisterous and often crude, but very hospitable.

Mohéli is the most neglected of the Comorian islands. These islanders have always offered the strongest opposition to dictatorial governments, and as such are ignored as much as possible. It is on Mohéli that you will hear the strongest anti-government and anti-French rhetoric. While the other islands are developed and supported, Mohéli struggles to provide its inhabitants with running water, medical facilities, electricity and schooling. There is only one bakery on the entire island. The marketing and sale of ylang-ylang, fruit, coffee and spices are strictly controlled by agents from Grande Comore. Unless something is done soon to appease the population of Mohéli, the idiosyncratic government of Saïd Mohamed Djohar on Grande Comore will be facing open rebellion from the inhabitants of Mohéli.

Mohéli was the favoured island base of Indian Ocean pirates in the 16th and 17th century, until the British decided to rid the seas of the pirate scourge. They sent a flotilla to the south-western Indian Ocean, under the leadership of Commodore William Quaid. Surprisingly he too considered Mohéli the best place to set up his base. Some of the ruined buildings from that era can be seen on the seaward side of the village of Mbatse. As to whether there is treasure buried on the island, no-one seems to know for sure. But in a letter in May 1800 to his

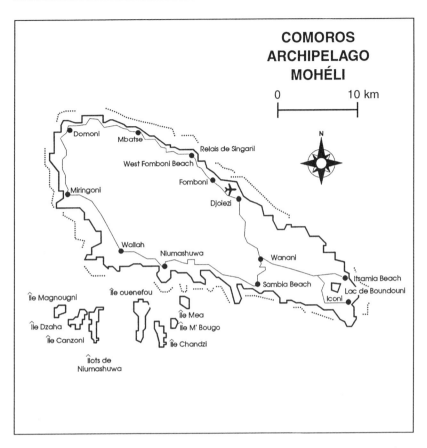

COMOROS
ARCHIPELAGO
MOHÉLI

0   10 km

N

Domoni
Mbatse
Relais de Singani
West Fomboni Beach
Fomboni
Miringoni
Djoiezi
Wallah
Niumashuwa
Wanani
Itsamia Beach
Sambia Beach
Lac de Boundouni
Iconi
Île Magnougni
Île ouenefou
Île Mea
Île Dzaha
Île M' Bougo
Île Canzoni
Île Chandzi
Îlots de
Niumashuwa

nephew, the French corsair Bernadin Nageon de L'Estang seemed to be describing Mohéli as the site where he had buried one of his three treasure seizures.

FOMBONI

Fomboni, the capital of Mohéli, is situated on the north coast of the island. Visitors who travel to Mohéli by ferry will be dropped off on the beach at Fomboni. There are no tall buildings in the town, and there is a pleasant mix of coralline brick houses and palm-frond huts, built in no particular order along narrow lanes and on the beach. Mzekukule peak (787 m), the highest point on the island, can be seen from Fomboni.

The post office is located beneath the red-and-white striped tele-communications aerial, on the south side of town. BIC (Comoros Groupe BNPI) bank is on the corner opposite the post office. Tourist information is obtainable from the Directeur Regional du Tourisme, not far from the beach. However, the best practical tourist information can be had from the Comoros' main opposition party leader, Mr Mohamed. His house is north of the post office. If you have trouble finding him or his equally capable son, Mouhmar, ask in any of the local stores for directions.

For accommodation on Mohéli it is suggested that visitors either arrive with a tent or stay with villagers.

There are no star-graded hotels in Fomboni, but finding lodgings is seldom a problem if you are prepared to rough it somewhat. Ask at the store behind the market for suggestions as to accommodation. The assistants in the shop opposite the beach landing site can also arrange for a few nights' board with a local family. The closest tourist-class accommodation is at the *Relais de Cingani* (medium tariff) north of Fomboni. The hotel has 10 rooms and offers a few water sport facilities, but has an awful beach and very apathetic staff. The hotel does provide all meals and is able to arrange short island tours of Mohéli. Address: Relais de Cingani, B.P. Fomboni, Mohéli, Comoros, tel. 72.02.49.

Bush-taxis wait for custom at the northern side of Fomboni, where the main road through town forks to go along the north coast or inland along the Wamlembeni river. Otherwise just flag a bush-taxi down in town.

On the beach, opposite the school at the north-western side of Fomboni, are a few tombs of early Shiraz Arabs. Not unlike those found on Réunion, these graves are mute testimony to the adventurous souls who sailed their frail dhows in these treacherous waters. On the edge of the beach, opposite the Christian cemetery, visitors are able to see wooden galawas and trading vessels being built according to traditional methods. There is no drawn plan anywhere in sight. The craftsmen work to the plans in their head. The finished result is a craft of the type that has sailed the southern and eastern Indian Ocean for centuries.

In Fomboni visit the local market, opposite the Palais de Justice de Fomboni. There is an excellent selection of fresh produce, plus numerous hot and cold snacks for sale. South-east of the administrative, police and military offices lies the empty mansion of Ahmed Abdallah. The house has been left as it was, and although it is locked, you can sneak inside through the front veranda window. It is a big rambling house that was used as much for private visits as entertaining international diplomats. If totally stuck for a place to sleep, consider these empty rooms for a night.

Near to where you are put ashore from the ferry are the ruins of the palace of Sultan Ramanetaka. They blend in with the other houses and you may have to spend a while searching to find the crumbling entrance. This is to the south-east of the main palace wall. Used by local fishermen for their gear, the decaying palace must have been a luxurious place of cool breezes and magnificent views.

Once across the river mouth, south of the Customs shack, visitors will find themselves among dense coconut groves.

By taking any of the paths that lead west, and uphill, from Fomboni, walkers will find themselves in shanty villages. As overpopulation on Anjouan has become worse, numerous islanders have moved to Mohéli. Many of their fragile-looking homes are dwarfed by huge baobab trees. In the jumble of hills beyond these houses, you will walk through coconut groves and then into forests, where you may be fortunate enough to catch a glimpse of the rare crowned lemur, an exotic species brought to the island years ago from Madagascar as pets. During the day you will probably encounter plantation workers harvesting coconuts. Ask them to open a fresh coconut for you; the water inside is delicious to drink.

East of Fomboni the tarred road passes several villages and the airport at **Djoiézi**. From here the road climbs into lush vegetation of clove trees, forests and fruit orchards. At the fork in the road, near the settlement of **Wanani**, you have the choice of going further east or turning south for the marine reserve and beautiful beaches of the south coast. It is recommended that you first turn left (east), following the signs for Itsamia and Iconi. Where the road forks again, one to the village of Iconi and the other climbing into the hills, take the road into the hills. About 1 km along this road you will come to an enormous wooden and palm-frond house. Walk a little along the road to where a track enters the ylang-ylang plantation. Proceed along this steep track, over the hills and then down to the edge of the crater lake, **Lac de Boundouni**. Tranquil and deep blue, this isolated lake is surrounded by indigenous rainforest, palm trees and ylang-ylang estates.

There is a safe swimming beach at **Itsamia**, but the sand is a dirty grey colour and the water full of volcanic silt. At **Iconi**, the main attraction is not the beach, but rather the village at its edge. The people here are very friendly and encourage foreign visitors to spend the night and enjoy their seafood cuisine. Get there on a Friday and you are in for a night of revelry unequalled anywhere else on Mohéli.

Returning to the fork in the road from Fomboni, turn left and head south for **Sambia** and the best beach on the island. A shallow reef extends for some 100 m off the beach and offers snorkellers a great opportunity for seeing the diverse sea life that flourishes in these protected waters.

There are more Arab ruins, this time of walls that had been erected as a deterrent to pirates, at **Niumashuwa**. Niumashuwa is also the main entrance to the marine reserve off the south coast of Mohéli. From the little beach south of the hamlet, visitors are able to arrange for a boat to ferry them into the wonderland of the reserve or to the three **Îlots de Niumashuwa** where tourists are allowed to land: Kanzani, Ouenefou and Shandzi. Visits to Magnougni are allowed on weekdays only.

The forests behind Niumashuwa are ideal for hiking, and several waterfalls may be seen in the jungle. There is only a rough road from Niumashuwa to **Miringoni**. This stretch of coast is untouched by modernisation and is a must for travellers who want to experience the heady euphoria of exploring a remote tropical island. At Miringoni the tarred road commences again. It rounds the western point of Mohéli at the happy village of **Domoni**, before edging the coast through **Mbatse** and thence back to Fomboni.

10 MAYOTTE (MAORÉ)

Oldest of the islands in the Comoros archipelago, Mayotte – called Maoré by its inhabitants – retained its allegiance to France when Abdallah declared unilateral independence in July 1975. Although Mayotte lacks an active volcano and mist-shrouded peaks, it has the best snorkelling sites in the Comoros. Because it is much older than the other islands, an encircling reef has had time to develop, and has turned the offshore waters of Mayotte into a paradise for divers.

In spite of Mayotte's connection to France, the amount of aid and infrastructure from the French has been less than encouraging. It seems that their prime interest in this island is a military one. Wherever you go on the island you are bound to encounter French soldiers and members of the elite French Foreign Legion. This makes taking photographs a problem. Be very aware of everything included in your frame and keep away from military buildings, telecommunications and radar installations. Even photographing the port in Mamoudzou should be done with caution.

The islanders, known as Mahorais, are very similar in physical appearance, dress, religion and traditions to other Comorians. The major difference is among the youth: they are much more Western in their dress, manner of speech and ambitions. Mayotte has not reached the same standard of living experienced by the Creoles on the other French-owned Indian Ocean island: Réunion.

Despite a fair amount of dissatisfaction at being so neglected, the Mahorais are generally happy people, and quite used to seeing foreign visitors wandering about the streets. As a result, it can sometimes be difficult to get to know locals. Even in the remote villages around Benara and Choungui, the people have had lots of exposure to tourists.

Unlike their Réunionnais cousins, the Mahorais have not often intermarried with French colonials. You will not see many children from mixed Comorian-French marriages, nor Europeans fraternising with islanders.

Mayotte actually consists of two main islands: the large island known as La Grande Terre and the small eastern island of Pamandzi or La Petite Terre. While La Grande Terre is the main island, housing the

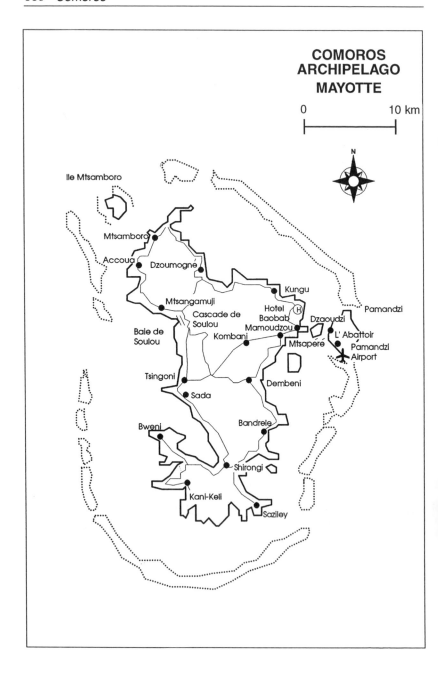

capital of Mamoudzou, La Petite Terre is the base of the French military, notably at Dzaoudzi, a rocky outcrop linked to the rest of La Petite Terre by the Boulevard des Crabes.

MAMOUDZOU

Although the capital of Mayotte is Mamoudzou, visitors arriving by air land at Pamandzi Airport on La Petite Terre. There is a regular, free ferry service from Dzaoudzi to Mamoudzou. The first ferry usually departs at about 5h30. Ferries travel between the two towns throughout the day, leaving every 30 minutes. On Sundays, however, the ferries only start operating around 7h00. If arriving by boat from the other islands of the Comoros or Madagascar, you will be dropped off at Mamoudzou.

Taxis to all parts of La Grande Terre wait near the Mamoudzou ferry terminal. Many have their destinations written across their sides, but if not just ask the driver and a few passengers where they are headed. The first taxi leaves from the ferry pier at about 7h30, the last one at around 20h00.

The post office is near the police station, about 100 m south-west of the port. Tourist information is available from the Office du Tourisme, opposite the ferry quay. Some tourist information is also available from Air France, near SNIE Supermarket, and Air Mayotte, opposite the market. Information about entertainment, culture, events and traditional programmes may be obtained from the Centre Culturel (CMAC), close to the Tribunal building. The BFC (Banque Française Commerciale) is between Air Mayotte and Le Reflet des Îles Restaurant, across the road from the market. Vehicle hire can be arranged from Maki-Loc, on the road behind the BFC. Motorcycles and bicycles are available for hire from the small shop at the end of the ferry pier. Film, batteries and basic camera repairs are offered at Tropicolor 2000, in the same street as the cinema.

Accommodation

Accommodation on Mayotte is expensive, criminally so. Budget travellers are unlikely to afford a long sojourn here. All hotels are in the medium-high tariff category. Cheap accommodation is best located by speaking to the managers of local eateries. They are usually able to arrange a bed with a local family. This is not too easy in Mamoudzou.

Rather head out into the villages where you will find people more hospitable and prepared to assist. Whereas on the other Comorian islands a contribution of food or drink is acceptable, note that in most villages on Mayotte you are expected to pay for private accommodation. The cost is seldom very high, but make sure to get an exact figure before settling in.

Suggested tourist accommodation in Mamoudzou:

Hotel la Tortue Bigotu (high tariff): Six rooms all with air-conditioning, near Mairie (the town hall). The hotel caters for water sport enthusiasts and arranges boat trips for scuba diving and big-game fishing. This is the most popular tourist hotel on Mayotte, and reservations are advised. Address: B.P. 77, Mamoudzou, Mayotte, tel. 61.11.32.

Hotel/Restaurant le Baobab (medium tariff) has 12 bungalows, a clean swimming pool, busy bar and reasonably priced restaurant. Recommended for a family vacation. The management is able to arrange car hire, guides and boat trips around Mayotte and to some of the neighbouring islets. Reservations are not necessary at Le Baobab; just phone from the post office and the staff will normally send a car to fetch you: tel. 61.11.40.

The cheapest accommodation in Mamoudzou can be obtained by asking the staff in either the Caribou Restaurant or Bar du Rond Point. They are usually able to offer you a bed with a friend, in their home, or at a family member's house. To succeed, it is important that you are able to get your request across in reasonable French. Travellers are nearly always assisted at these places, and it is the perfect way to get to know the often reserved Mahorais. They will not hear of your only staying for one night, it must be at least three. Dinner is always included, as is at least one night out on the weekend.

Things to do

Night-time entertainment in Mamoudzou is offered in the form of dancing, drinking, movies or, on certain occasions, productions put on by the CMAC. The Mahaba Club, north-west of the market, has dancing from Wednesday to Saturday. The doors open at about 21h30. You are advised to get there by 22h30 if you want a seat. Golden Lagoon II, close to Le Baobab, has disco-style dancing on Friday and Saturday evenings from 22h00. The cinema is near La Crêperie Restaurant. You can get details of what is being shown by contacting the CMAC.

Places to eat

Visitors to Mamoudzou will find a number of places in town where they can eat from à la carte menus or buy snacks. For pastries and savoury snacks, there is little to beat the price and quality of the *Patisserie le Pamier*, opposite Golden Lagoon II. There is another boulangerie-patisserie near the administrative offices, west of the cinema, whose fresh bread is especially delicious. Pizzas and light meals can be chosen from a small menu at the *Caribou Pizzeria-Bar*. Prices are reasonable and unusual pizza toppings are available. *Le Reflet des Îles Restaurant*, opposite the market, has a typical French menu, at prices similar to those charged in hotel dining rooms. Service is excellent, the staff are very friendly and eating here is thoroughly enjoyable, although somewhat costly. *Restaurant L'Agachon,* on the beach road south of the port, has tasty seafood dishes, attentive employees, good prices and an idyllic setting. The breakfast is enormous and highly recommended to all budget travellers. Where you branch south to reach L'Agachon is the *Bar du Rond Point.* A favourite with locals, this is arguably the best place in Mamoudzou to meet Mohorais. At *La Crêperie Restaurant,* near the cinema, diners can choose from a traditional Comorian or Continental menu. The helpings of Comorian food are large, while the Continental meals are more artistically presented than filling. There is a large difference in price between the traditional and Continental food. If you have previously been hesitant about eating local food, this is the best, and cleanest, place to try a dish of rice, fish, bananas and hot sauce.

Going south from Mamoudzou visitors pass **Mtsapéré**, from where a track leads into the forest and to the summit of Mt Mtsapéré (see the hiking section in chapter 3). Further south, at **Bandrele**, is a splendid little beach known as **Musical Plage**. Visitors can arrange for a galawa to take them out to the reefs from this village. The locals are accustomed to taking tourists on boating trips, and even include a lunch of fruit, cold rice, fish and fresh coconut juice.

A few kilometres south-west of Bandrele is a fork in the road. To the south is the trail down to the remote and beautiful **Saziley**. If going to this isolated settlement you will have to walk from here – about 4 km. Not many foreigners visit Saziley, and it is one of the few places on Mayotte where you can be certain of an immediate welcome from the locals.

Continuing west, past the turn-off to Shirongi, the road goes to Bweni or turns south for Kani-Kéli and **Ngoudja**, the best-known beach on

Mayotte. The 12 bungalows of the *Hotel Ngouja* and restaurant are located here: B.P. 7, Dzaoudzi, tel. 60.14.19. The hotel is able to arrange boat trips to the reef and also hires out snorkelling gear. It has some water sport equipment, which is free to guests. Residents of the hotel are also offered a ride into the rough interior of Mayotte. Transport to and from Mamoudzou can be provided on request. Many of the French package tour groups stay here, and the beach is nearly always crowded with topless bathers, curio vendors and would-be guides.

Kani-Kéli is the place from which to start the three-hour hike to the top of Choungui crater (591 m). The views from the summit rim are remarkable.

Returning to **Shirongi**, turn left (north) and continue to the beach at **Bougainville**. At the northern tip of the beach is **Mtsangachehi**, where you will find the eight bungalows of the *Mtsanga Beach Hotel*, tel. 60.19.72. This beach has excellent snorkelling opportunities in a protected lagoon, and is a quiet haven after the crowds on Ngoudja beach.

Proceeding up the west coast, travellers arrive at the quaint village of **Tsingoni**, on the southern edge of a white, empty beach. The remains of a ruined fort are hidden in the thick bush north-east of the settlement. Locals claim that it was once a refuge for the sultan and his subjects when Malagasy pirates raided this coast. They say that during the full moon in the month of October, you can still hear the screams of women and children who were dragged away by the pirates.

Further north is the most picturesque beach on Mayotte: **Baie de Soulou**. The magnificent waterfall near the bay has a deep pool at its base in which it is great to cool off after the walk to reach Baie de Soulou. The tarred road does not extend all the way to the bay, and visitors must leave the taxi where it turns for Dzoumogue, and take the path to the west of the main road. Apart from curious children, most visitors will find themselves quite alone in this beautiful bay.

There is no proper road from **Mtsangamuji** north to **Accoua**. You must walk from here. Alternatively, catch a taxi across the island to **Dzoumogné**, on the north-east coast. On the eastern edge of the peninsula that projects from the northern tip of Mayotte are a few secluded stretches of white coral beach. Walking is the only way to reach them, but their loneliness is a great attraction to many. At **Mtsamboro**, too, there is a fine beach, and the chance to get a boat to carry you to some of the small offshore islands to the west.

Going back down the east coast, you will come to the renowned **Longoni beach**. Some guides claim that this is the best beach at which to snorkel. The submerged rocks in the wide bay offer protection to many colourful fish. There is a large school of parrotfish, which are tame enough to feed with bread. A shoal of squid lives between the submarine boulders to the east. It is easy to spend an entire day with your head buried in the sea off Longoni beach.

Trévani Holiday Village, south-east of **Kungu**, has its own little beach. This 20-roomed hotel is a favourite of package tours, and you must book early to avoid disappointment. The hotel has water sport facilities and a restaurant, and can arrange island tours, scuba diving and deep-sea fishing excursions. Address: B.P. 235, Mamoudzou, Mayotte.

PAMANDZI (LA PETITE TERRE)

East of Mamoudzou is the island of Pamandzi or La Petite Terre. The capital is **Dzaoudzi**. The post office is on Boulevard des Crabes close to Air France. There is a BFC bank, between the Customs building and police station, on the west side of Dzaoudzi. The CMAC offices are behind the austere French Foreign Legion barracks.

When visiting Pamandzi, be sure to take a trip to **Lac Dziani**, in the north-east of the island. This crater lake has recuperative and tonic waters. Take the path that descends to the lake edge. You may swim in the blue waters, which are too deep to have ever been measured.

Moya beach is the most attractive on Pamandzi. It tends to get crowded with local families on Sundays but the rest of the week you will be alone. The back-line waves at Moya are ideal for bodysurfing, while the edges of the cove offer protected swimming in the shallows. West of Lac Dziani is **Badamiers beach**. Although better for swimming than Moya, the beach is exposed to the prying eyes of military personnel and offers depressing views of fuel tanks and naval dockyards.

Accommodation in Dzaoudzi is limited to *Le Rocher Hotel* (high tariff), which has 14 rooms. The tariff includes breakfast and dinner. The restaurant is open also to non-residents, and the management can arrange car hire and boating trips around the island. Address: B.P. 42, Dzaoudzi, Mayotte, tel. 60.15.05.

The best restaurant on Pamandzi is *Chez Gaston*, which offers an extensive à la carte menu and several daily specials. Prices are moderate, the service is excellent and the quality of the food is high. The view from the dining terrace, over the ocean, is inspiring. The restaurant is popular and you should get there by 12h00 for lunch and by 19h30 for dinner. At the *Ylang-ylang Restaurant* you may choose from a menu of mainly Eastern cuisine. Prices are good and the servings of food gigantic. This restaurant has friendly, smiling staff who hover around patrons constantly, making each diner feel special.

Other restaurants about which good reports have been received are *Moya Restaurant* (popular with French government staff) and *Kamoula Restaurant* (a favourite with Legionnaires).

PART 2

SEYCHELLES

11 FACTS ABOUT THE COUNTRY

"Forever Eden" is what Seychellois call their islands. Lying just south of the equator, the Seychelles have the reputation of being the most beautiful tropical islands on earth. Like most ex-colonial outposts the Seychelles have had their share of revolts, coups d'état and subversion, but now seem to be on their way towards permanent stability.

Tourism to the Seychelles is burgeoning. Each year a growing number of visitors come to enjoy the beauty of these idyllic tropical islands. On the inner islands, granite boulders and dense forests entice the explorer inside, opening new worlds. The outer islands are coral, their hues exquisite and their variety rich. Solitude and unspoilt nature are their main attractions.

HISTORY

While most historians think that Arab sea traders were the first to visit the Seychelles islands early in the 7th century, a breakaway group is adamant that it was Polynesian explorers who first landed. Support for the former theory comes from the typical Islamic circular stone graves found on many of the islands, notably Mahé, Praslin and Moyenne. Backing the Polynesian theorists are several intriguing and obviously Polynesian ceremonial sites in the remote forests of Mahé, Praslin and La Digue.

Whoever the first visitors to the Seychelles were, it is generally accepted that the first Europeans to sight the islands were the sailors of Cabral, the famed Portuguese navigator, in 1499. Landing to replenish water supplies, the Portuguese neither claimed nor settled the scattered coral and granitic islands. Then, in 1502, Vasco da Gama sailed to the islands. Landing in a protected cove on Praslin, Da Gama named the islands *As Sete Irmas* (the Seven Sisters – often mistakenly translated as the Seven Brothers). But it was left to the adventuring English, who arrived almost 107 years later, in 1609, to set about exploring the many islands.

Under the auspices of the British East India Company, John Jourdain led a group of sailors into the thickly vegetated interior of the larger islands. But like earlier visitors he made no formal claim to the islands.

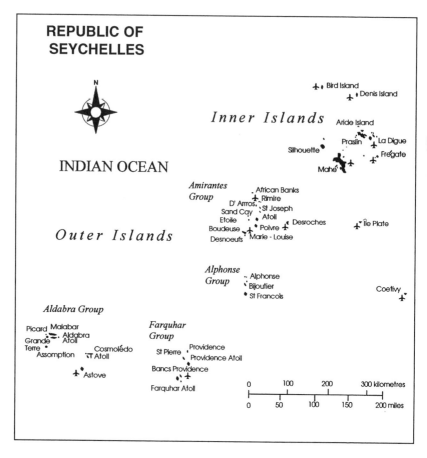

REPUBLIC OF
SEYCHELLES

N

Inner Islands

INDIAN OCEAN

Outer Islands

Bird Island
Denis Island
Aride Island
Praslin   La Digue
Silhouette   Frégate
Mahé

Amirantes Group   African Banks
Rimire
D' Arrros.   St Joseph
Sand Cay   Atoll
Etoile   Desroches   Île Plate
Boudeuse   Poivre
Desnoeufs   Marie - Louise

Alphonse Group   Alphonse
Bijoutier
St Francois   Coetivy

Aldabra Group

Picard   Malabar   *Farquhar Group*
Grande   Aldabra Atoll
Terre   Cosmolédo   St Pierre   Providence
Assomption   T Atoll   Providence Atoll
Astove   Bancs Providence
Farquhar Atoll

| 0 | 100 | 200 | 300 kilometres |
| 0 | 50 | 100 | 150 | 200 miles |

His report lay forgotten in archival records until discovered and published in 1905, 296 years later.

French teams landed at Baie Lazare to map and explore Mahé and
the surrounding islands between 1742 and 1769. Between the departure
of the British expedition and the arrival of the French, pirates and
corsairs were regular visitors. Making landfalls to replenish food and
water supplies, many of them are reputed to have hidden their sizeable
treasures on Mahé and the smaller surrounding islands. Stalking the
great ocean trade routes from India and Persia to Europe from about
1685, the two most famous of all these swashbuckling adventurers were
Olivier le Vasseur (La Buse), pirate and capturer of the greatest treasure

ever seized, and, a little later, Jean François Hodoul, spice planter and corsair extraordinaire.

With war between Britain and France worsening, the French began worrying about the safety of their vessels and immigrants to India. To strengthen their position and at the same time provide a supply depot for their numerous slave ships, they decided to claim and settle the islands in the south-western Indian Ocean. Led by Brayer du Barre, the first settlers arrived on Ste Anne island on 27 August 1770 and named the islands the Seychelles, in honour of Louis XV's minister of finance, Viscount Jean Moreau de Séchelles. It would be two years before these pioneers would be joined by other arrivals. Then, in 1772, Charles Routier de Romainville landed on the largest island in the Seychelles, present-day Mahé. The site of the landing was called Établissement, which was changed in 1841 to Victoria – the modern capital of the Seychelles.

With him, Charles Routier de Romainville brought one of France's foremost botanists, Pierre Poivre, who was to lead these islands into the forefront of world spice production. They were to remain suppliers of the highest quality spices throughout both French and British occupations and until independence. Then minimum wages were raised and planters could no longer compete with other, less affluent countries and were forced to sell their estates.

In 1800 the French Revolution ousted the king. War continued to rage between France and Britain, and France was forced to relinquish control of the Seychelles on 21 April 1811. The Treaty of Paris of 30 May 1812 put the Seychelles securely under British control. Bartholomew Sullivan was given jurisdiction and governed the Seychelles as part of Mauritius.

In power on the Seychelles for 160 years, the British built on what the French had begun. Spices, fruit, copra, vanilla and sugar were all cultivated by a succession of English planters. Britain was, however, never really interested in developing the scattered islands of the Seychelles. They were valued only for their strategic position. By ruling these Indian Ocean islands, the British could effectively control all major sea routes to the east, extend territorial rights and have a base from which to keep an eye on shipping movements. No large colony was ever established as in the Americas or Africa. Even the importance of the islands' agriculture began to wane when the British government decreed that all slaves be freed in 1835. Most of the nearly 5 000 slaves employed in agriculture on the Seychelles left their masters and the plantations to seek employment in the villages.

Another result of the abolition of slavery was marriages across the colour line, which had been frowned upon earlier. Although the British, on the whole, did not intermarry, the French who had remained on the islands were quick to do so. What resulted was the Seychellois Creoles of today with their rich cultural heritage of French, Malagasy and African, and their peculiar language.

In 1853 English authorities allowed the Roman Catholic Church to commence setting up missions, schools and clinics on the islands. This introduction of mass eduction was to result in the continuing high level of literacy on the Seychelles. Where previously education had only been provided for the English, now everyone had the opportunity to learn to read and write.

During both world wars the British enforced conscription. Fighting in the desert in the North African Campaign, members of the Seychelles Pioneer Corps received several medals for gallantry and bravery. A small memorial to the men who died so far from home, in defence of a foreign crown, has been erected at the Mont Fleuri cemetery on Mahé.

GOVERNMENT

Despite having taken over government of the Seychelles in mid-1811, it was not until 1872 that the British finally agreed to some degree of representation for the islanders. Creating the Board of Civil Commissioners to manage Seychellois finances, they allowed one Creole on the board. In the 1888 legislative and executive council meetings, three Seychellois were permitted seats. From 1944 this was increased to six seats. After a long struggle to gain autonomy, the Seychelles received its independence from Mauritius on 31 August 1904.

The first legislative elections were held in 1948, with one major problem: only taxpayers were allowed to vote. This restricted the voting Seychellois to a mere 10% of the population. Already the first murmurs of dissent could be heard from the islanders. In the low chambers of government, the locals were about to enter a period of internal strife. Frans Albert René founded the Seychelles People's United Party (SPUP) in 1964, which put continued pressure on Britain to elect an independent council that would work towards giving the Seychelles full autonomy. In opposition, the Seychelles Democratic Party (SDP), also founded in 1964, was determined that the Seychelles should remain a colony of the British Empire, albeit with greater representation.

Eager to solve what was seen as a petty problem, Britain granted a general election in 1967. The results showed the population split down the middle in their support of the two main parties. In 1970 the Seychelles were given a ministerial government based on the Westminster system of legislative assembly. Five years later, with Britain having little vested interest in the islands, the Seychelles became autonomous, but still under the Union Jack. Just one year later, in 1976, the islands received their independence.

Leading them was one of the Seychelles' more ebullient characters, James Mancham. Aware of the split loyalties of the population he chose the middle road and formed a coalition government with the SPUP. Disregarding reports of general discontent among the islanders, Mancham continued globetrotting in an effort to lure tourists to what he called "the islands of heaven". On a sunny June day in the winter of 1977, Frans Albert René staged a dramatic coup d'état and ensconced himself in power. Mancham was exiled to England and a period of austerity started for the Seychelles.

René led a one-party communist-leaning government that was initially supported by the majority of Seychellois. Following the writing of a new constitution in 1979, René's spies started reporting growing displeasure among the masses. In view of several failed coup d'état plots and attempts, René eventually decided to allow a multi-party government, which came into effect on 3 December 1991. The constitution was again rewritten to include other parties in the governing of the Seychelles.

Today, after almost 17 years, Frans Albert René is still President. There are 11 ministers, an Attorney-General and a Chief Justice. The government is based on a cabinet system of national assembly.

GEOGRAPHY

Scattered across about 950 000 square km of ocean between 4-10° latitude south and 46-56° longitude east, the 117 islands of the Seychelles have a combined land area of only 453 square km. They are of two distinct types: granitic islands and coralline islands.

It is the granitic islands that most visitors get to see. The largest, Mahé, and her satellites are the peaks of a submarine mountain range.

Morne Seychellois, the highest point on the Seychelles at 905 m, is on Mahé and is a favourite hiking destination for tourists.

Bird and Denis islands to the north of Mahé are coral islands, but are more closely related to the Maldives than to the Seychelles.

The granitic islands, called the inner islands, can be divided roughly into four groups: Mahé and the islands immediately surrounding it, Praslin with 10 nearby islands, Frégate and Îlot Frégate to the east, Silhouette and North Island in the west.

The coralline islands, excluding Bird and Denis to the north, make up the outer islands. These too can be separated into four groups: the Amirantes, Alphonse, Farquhar and remote Aldabra groups of islands.

According to geographers, notably Dr Rasheed Setra of New Delhi University, the granitic islands of the Seychelles were originally part of India. Splitting and drifting loose some 400 million years ago when Gondwanaland started to tear apart, these castaway islands are now slowly being eroded away until, it is predicted by one researcher, the granitic islands will have disappeared below the surface of the sea sometime in the mid-23rd century.

Unique for Indian Ocean islands, the granitic groups are composed predominantly of continental rock of Pre-Cambrian age. There have been slight differences in the various islands' formation, the results of which are still visible today. Mahé and its surrounding islands are of a gneissic granite with a grey hue. Praslin and La Digue consist of red granite, which gives the pink shade to many of their boulders. Frégate, to the east, consists of paler aplitic granite. Silhouette and North Island, consisting of syenitic rock veined with microsyenite, rose from the sea about 50 million years ago in the Tertiary Period. All crisscrossed by dolerite dykes, many of the granitic islands were volcanic until about 40 million years ago.

As subsiding mountains and volcanic craters sink back into the sea, coral builds on them. Growing upwards towards the light, this coral has created some of the most beautiful islands on earth: the coral atolls of the Seychelles. Not all the coral islands however grew from sub-merged mountains, a few were pushed up from the bottom of the sea long after the formation of the mountains. This has resulted in two distinct types of coral island:

• Sand cays with coral sand. Usually less than 3 000 years old, with a profusion of marine life, these include the islands of the Amirantes, Alphonse and Farquhar groups.

- Uplifted reefs. Over 150 000 years old, they have unique ecosystems, flora and fauna. Most famous of these uplifted reefs is Aldabra atoll.

Whatever their category, the coral islands are growing. Their landscapes are affected by changing weather patterns and the sea; their veneer of soil is derived from living coral. Their flora and fauna, especially the prolific birdlife, are fascinating.

CLIMATE

One word effectively sums up the climate of the Seychelles: tropical. There are two seasons, but visitors may be forgiven for finding it difficult to notice the difference between them.

The Seychelles can be visited throughout the year. Seasonal variations are insignificant. The climate is warm and pleasant, if somewhat humid, all year long.

Stretching from November to May, the Seychellois summer has warm north-west trade winds which bring high heat, high humidity and increased rainfall. The hottest months are March and April when the thermometer rises from 22 °C at sunrise to 34 °C. Humidity hovers between 70% and 80% throughout summer, rising higher when it rains. The wettest month is January.

In winter, June to October, the winds change direction and bring the cool breezes of the south-east monsoon, which lower humidity and make this the ideal time to visit the Seychelles. July and August are the coolest months, with the average temperature ranging between 21 °C and 30 °C. July is also the month of lowest rainfall. This does not, however, mean that there is no rain. The typical short, warm showers of the tropics can be expected all year.

Sunshine is a fairly constant seven hours per day. Because the Seychelles are so close to the equator, daylight lasts 12 hours throughout the year. There are no long sunsets; darkness comes suddenly, as does dawn. There is no warning: one minute it is dark and the next the sun is up over the eastern horizon and climbing rapidly into an astonishingly blue sky.

Storms are a rarity, cyclones even more so. Whatever cyclones do touch the Seychelles usually affect only the southern coral islands. Tropical rain, however, is usual. Short, torrential and warm, these pleasurable downpours will have you steaming once the sun returns.

POPULATION

Among a population of about 72 000 people, the Seychelles have more women than men: an estimated ratio of 3:1. The Seychellois are a happy mixture of French, African, Asian, Arab and Malagasy. Today, after decades of intermarriage, mostly between French and African, Seychellois are simply called Creoles. Their different features testify to this polyglot of races: from ebony skin and tight curly hair common to central Africa, through all the shades to Nordic white skin and straight blond hair.

Most of the population live on the granitic islands of Mahé and Praslin and their satellites. A few, fishermen and rangers, live out on the coral atolls for a certain number of months per year.

The birth rate is exceedingly high and the famed promiscuity of the Seychellois continues to result in over 50% of the population being under the age of 16.

There is a definite hierarchy in Seychellois society. No matter what Frans Albert René promised after his coup d'état in 1977, there are still large differences between the rich, middle class and poor. Franco-Seychellois, in general, are at the top of the pyramid. Holding high office and key positions in business, industry and government, they form an elite class that lives in the mansions of Bel Air and along the north-west coast of Mahé. Indo-Seychellois own most of the cafés and trading stores scattered around the islands. They are Hindus, keep to themselves and live in tight groups excluding other Seychellois. Sino-Seychellois are involved in textiles and have a few trading stores. They are in the minority on the islands and have formed a small clique to preserve their identity. Muslims are the true entrepreneurs of the Seychelles. Their shops and businesses are arguably the most lucrative on the islands. They faithfully attend their mosque and follow the laws of Islam, but their religious fervour is constantly monitored by the Seychelles secret service. Afro-Seychellois noticeably belong to the lowest class. They work as employees in shops or as junior civil servants and live in the worst conditions on the Seychelles. Being conservative they tend to support the outdated socialist gospel of René. And as they are the largest segment of the total population, they keep him firmly in office at each election. Finally, the pure-blooded French and few English live in fading colonial grandeur. Old family histories continue to lend these gracious people an air of nobility and timelessness. Visitors will see their plantation houses set in magnificent gardens along the east coast of Mahé and at Anse à la Mouche in the west. On Praslin and La Digue their estates, now neglected, still hint at a bygone era.

The Seychellois who live in and around the major urban settlements such as Victoria and Grande Anse are mainly involved in office jobs. Coastal families mostly earn their living from the tourism trade and fishing. The few rapidly disappearing groups of forest dwellers earn their living from cinnamon, cassava and subsistence farming. Their way of life is threatened by development and deforestation.

CULTURE

Cultural influences are as diverse as the origins of the Seychellois Creoles. There is little segregation and no one culture predominates. Government policy is to be thanked for this. The government has instigated several plans to integrate all the people of the islands and to promote cultural development. The Kreol Institute near Anse aux Pins is one such facility. Not only does it keep a dynamic record of Creole history and progress, it also holds workshops and social activities to encourage the mingling of cultures. The ultimate aim is to have one homogenised nation.

Recently, together with a change in political direction, the government has allowed the study of art, drama and literature at schools and the polytechnic. Music is also encouraged, with several wealthy patrons donating funds for a music school. The written word, however, despite a slight slackening of the rules, is still heavily censored and controlled. Visitors may notice this especially in the style of reporting in the popular press.

Theatre and dance

Plays are not high on the list of entertainment for the Seychellois, although troupes from France or Réunion occasionally visit. With the introduction of drama in educational institutions there is a possibility that theatre will become more popular.

Dancing displays are something else altogether. The Seychellois love to dance. Formal dance exhibitions are always well attended, and young children are encouraged to dance and learn intricate movements. Many of the large hotels put on traditional dancing displays for their guests. Unlike the other Indian Ocean islands, the Seychelles' national dance is not the sega, but rather the moutia. Although not as sensual as the sega, the moutia combines the abandoned tempo of African music with the control of European ballrooms.

The younger generation has turned to the politically and religiously motivated music of the Caribbean. Reggae is popular wherever youths gather. Their style of dance, known as skanking, is relaxed and natural, with movements that resemble ritual shamanic dancing.

Art

Numerous Seychellois artists exhibit their works at local curio shops and hotels. Strangely it is the foreign artists who have made the biggest impact on Seychelles' art forms. Michael Adams is without question the most famous artist on the islands. His works adorn galleries and shops in the Seychelles, and several pieces are on display overseas in international galleries. Busy and indigenous, his art has a compelling attraction that forces people to stop and examine each piece carefully. He has a studio at Anse aux Poules Bleues, less than 2 km north of the Baie Lazare police station, on Mahé's south-west coast. A friendly and talkative man, he welcomes visitors and may even offer to paint something specifically for you.

The large, government-controlled Codevar artists' shops and village showcase young talent. Codevar tourist shops in urban centres are expensive but tax-free to foreigners. However, it is much better to visit the artists at the Codevar Craft Village (tel. 376100), near Anse aux Pins on Mahé. The village is built around an 18th century plantation house; small wooden bungalows have been constructed in which each artist works. During the week this makes for a fascinating tour. Potters, sculptors, craftsmen and painters produce the most colourful and professional work in the Indian Ocean.

Seychelles' top sculptor is Italian immigrant Lorenzo Appiani. His studio is on Mahé at Mare Anglaise (tel. 261432). He is the sculptor of the two most visible pieces on Mahé: the independence sculpture and the revolution sculpture, both in Victoria.

Art galleries

Christine Harter, Côte d'Or, Praslin, tel. 232131
Zimaz Kreol Art Gallery, La Digue, tel. 234322
Sculpture Studio Antonio, Beau Vallon, Mahé, tel. 247658
Pottery at Seychelles Potters Co-op, Les Mamelles, Mahé, tel. 344080

Music

The Seychellois are natural singers and musicians. Their excellent voices and repertoire of songs from the sad days of slavery will touch the hearts of many visitors. Most village dances and festivities feature balladeers who lend a nostalgic touch. Telling stories in many of their songs, the singers follow an African beat not dissimilar to that of the West Indies. With the new National Music School has come a renewed interest in traditional music and the playing of almost forgotten instruments.

Foreign musicians occasionally tour the Seychelles. In recent years the most popular of these has been the South African reggae star, Lucky Dube, who consistently played to capacity crowds. Sometimes, unused to the conservative attitude of the people and ignorant of local customs and laws, visiting musicians experience difficulties. Supergroup UB40 were deported within hours of giving a concert in a packed stadium. They had publicly made derogatory comments about the government and flaunted controlled substance laws.

If you want a memento of traditional Seychelles music, wander along the road and alleys around Sir Selwyn Clarke market in Victoria. Usually pirated copies, the cassettes are cheap but well recorded.

Literature

Subjected to years of censorship and media blackouts, there are very few outspoken writers on the Seychelles. Those who feel strongly about their message usually have their works published overseas. Over the last couple of years there has been a slight relaxation of restrictions and increased tolerance of liberal writing. Essay and poetry competitions are now held at schools and the once small, clandestine Seychelles Authors Association is receiving new applications regularly.

The toppled first president of the independent Seychelles, James Mancham, published a collection of poems entitled *Reflections and echoes.* This can be bought at one of three bookshops in Victoria: Space, Huteau Lane, tel. 224531; Jivan Imports, Albert Street, tel. 322310); and Librairie Ste Fidèle, Olivier Maradam Street, tel. 323463. The present premier, Frans Albert René, has also written a book, *The torch of freedom,* which is readily available at local bookshops and tourist outlets.

ECONOMY

The economy of the Seychelles is not strong. Taxes are high, inflation is high and prices are exorbitant. The Seychelles rupee is floated from an international basket of currencies that includes the US dollar, sterling and French franc. Still heavily dependent on imports – over 60% of all food comes from South Africa – the Seychelles is working towards self-sufficiency. Youths are encouraged to study abroad for tertiary qualifications and scholarships are freely available. Studying in Cuba, Tunisia, Russia and occasionally the USA, students then return to work on the islands under contract.

Among younger people there is a growing tendency to steer away from primary production and enter jobs in the tertiary market. Although the standard of living is not high, a sheltered minimum income encourages youngsters to return from abroad and settle on the islands. Older people are still mainly small-scale fishermen, subsistence farmers, artisans and share-croppers.

The Democratic Party has denounced the selling of the Seychelles' islands. In the past, islands were frequently sold to private individuals. South African, British and lately Russian investors, as well as the World Wildlife Fund, bought islands and turned them into private kingdoms. This generated millions for the economy, but was also a finite source of income. This has virtually stopped now, and non-Seychellois citizens are no longer free to purchase land.

The Seychelles is a country in transition. Hovering between the Third and First World, it already has the infrastructure of a modern society. With most of the foreign revenue and employment coming from tourism, there is a drive to train locals in customer service and public relations. Over 70% of all gross domestic income is from tourism, and 32% of all Seychellois work in this industry.

Second to tourism is the fishing industry. As old as the history of the islands, fishing has always played an important role in both the subsistence of the people and in earning foreign currency.

Until 1991 the socialist government worked on a cycle of five-year plans, not unlike those of the erstwhile USSR. But that has now been forgone in favour of a more free-enterprise and market-related system. However, the government, through the Seychelles Marketing Board (SMB) remains directly responsible for all the production, manufacturing and marketing of primary products such as tea, coffee, fish and other agricultural produce.

Following the coup of 1977, greater emphasis was placed on improving social services, especially education and health. Foreign aid has poured in over the last few years, with funds going mainly to the development of tourism, fishing and agriculture. Most of the financial aid has come from the African Development Bank, World Bank and EU. Skills training has also received a boost in recent years with several European experts contracted to the Seychelles on training programmes in agriculture, fishing and manufacturing.

Agriculture

Before independence the biggest earner of foreign revenue was agriculture. Production of cinnamon and copra was the largest employer, and estates were found on even the smallest habitable islands. Since then, there has been a drastic decrease in the number of agricultural workers and economically viable plantations. With a rapidly growing population, land shortages have become inevitable. Minimum wages have forced many planters to sell their plantations. The youth have little interest in working on farms today, and visitors will only see elderly people on the few working estates.

On the smaller, outer islands, visitors will still find estates involved in the production of copra, coconut oil, coconut milk and cream, and tourism. One of the best working coconut plantations to visit is L'Union estate on La Digue, south of La Digue Island Lodge.

Along the west coast of Mahé, large experimental farms have been established. Here agricultural training programmes are conducted and research into alternative crops for the region is carried out. A few state-owned crop and livestock farms are run in an effort to reduce the Seychelles' reliance on South Africa for food.

In the misty highlands of Mahé, tea and coffee are grown, mostly for export. A modern tea factory has been constructed west of Sans Souci and is open to visitors. Although the plantations are small, their production per hectare is consistently high. Tea and coffee cultivation has become a major earner of foreign revenue.

Fishing

Fish are the islands' major natural resource. Commercial fishing, initiated by the British and French, has become a lucrative business in the Seychelles. Until recently, Russian and Japanese trawlers harvested the seas around the islands, but now the government has imposed a 200 nautical mile territorial limit and built its own fish processing factories. This has encouraged the locals to venture into large-scale fishing.

Tuna and squid are the main catches around the islands. A modern, efficient fleet scours the offshore reefs and deep water for these species. Sardines, barracuda, shark and sailfish are caught by smaller boats in day trips to the fishing grounds.

In Victoria, visitors may notice a decidedly fishy odour from the tuna cannery in the harbour. Tours of the facility can be arranged by contacting the Seychelles Marketing Board, tel. 22-4444. Day trips on small fishing vessels can be had by asking the skippers at the fishing wharf. You will need to be there by 4h30.

Manufacturing

Various goods are processed in the Seychelles, including beer, furniture, soap and plastics. The large Seybrew factory south of Mont Fleuri is particularly impressive. You can book an interesting tour of the facility by contacting Seychelles Breweries, PO Box 273, O'Brien House, Le Rocher, tel. 34-4555.

Furniture is made in numerous small workshops throughout the islands. The ones along the east coast of Mahé, near the airport and National Archives, are worth a visit. Model shipbuilding, while not as big as in Mauritius, is gaining popularity in the Seychelles. Small model-making shops can be seen at Codevar near Anse aux Pins, at Beau Vallon and on Praslin near Côte d'Or.

RELIGION, FESTIVALS AND HOLIDAYS

Although over 90% of the population are Roman Catholics and another 7% Protestants, the animism of tribal Africa is still strong. In the remote forest settlements on Mahé, Praslin and La Digue ancient ceremonies are still practised on full-moon nights and at the change of seasons.

Hindu, Buddhist and sectarian beliefs are also practised on the Seychelles, which allows freedom of worship. A magnificent Hindu Vishnu temple has recently been completed in Victoria, near the Sir Selwyn Clarke market. Churches can be found in even the smallest villages, and there are cathedrals in Victoria and large east coast towns. There is a mosque in the long alley opposite the sports stadium in Victoria.

There are 13 official holidays in the Seychelles' calendar.

Public holidays

New Year – 1 and 2 January
Good Friday – March/April
Easter Saturday and Sunday – March/April
Labour Day – 1 May
Corpus Christi – May/June
Liberation Day – 5 June
Independence Day – 29 June
Assumption Day and La Digue Festival Day – 15 August
All Saints' Day – 1 November
Immaculate Conception – 8 December
Christmas Day – 25 December
Other holidays are Family Day and Sports Day. These always fall on
a weekend, usually a Sunday.

All shops, government offices and banks are closed on public holidays. Even cafés and restaurants close, and apart from hotel meals you will find nothing on the streets to eat. Buses, however, run according to schedule, and taxis can usually be found at the inter-island harbour and international airport. Do not try to carry out any official business either side of a public holiday: there are always long queues. Buy any supplies you may need in good time, at least two days before the holiday.

WILDLIFE

Three distinct ecological bio-environments exist on the Seychelles: elevated coral and rock reefs, sand cays and granitic islands. Each of these has a diverse flora and fauna that make a visit to any of the islands a naturalist's dream.

Elevated coral and rock reefs exhibit a similar ecology to that found along the coasts and littoral zones of Madagascar and the Galapagos. Most famous, and spectacular, of these is Aldabra atoll. Among the oldest of the coral islands, Aldabra's remoteness and age have made it a wonderland of natural evolution. The ecosystem is still unspoiled. Over 150 000 giant tortoises, sea feeding reptiles, unique robber crabs and a multitude of sea birds delight visitors.

The sand cays of the deeper sea are home to bird colonies, coconuts and magnificent flowers. They provide the ideal breeding ground for flocks of sooty terns and other migrating birds. Turtles frequently lay their eggs on the sand cays. It is not unusual for a visitor to find the flipper marks of turtles leading from a hole in the sand to the ocean.

The granitic islands are related to the rock parent material of East Africa and Southeast Asia – testimony to a prehistoric supercontinent. Seychelles' granitic islands mark the western limit of the Oriental Biographical Region.

The government is playing a vital role in the protection of the environment. All construction is subject to strictly enforced regulations; penalties are severe. Two regions have been declared World Heritage Sites by UNESCO: Aldabra atoll and the Vallée de Mai on Praslin.

Flora

There are 208 indigenous plant species on the Seychelles. Most famous is the *Lodoicea maldivica* (coco de mer). The only place in the world where these trees grow in their natural habitat is in the Vallée de Mai on Praslin and on Curieuse.

Shaped like a female pelvis, the coco de mer nut was first described by an Arab naturalist, Ishtar Farrokhzad, in about 1322. It came to the attention of the European world in 1520, when the adventurer Arturo del Milla returned to Italy with one. According to folklore in India and Persia, the nuts came from enormous trees that grew on the bottom of the sea. Hence the name, meaning nut of the sea. It was only in 1743 that explorers found the palm growing in the hidden valleys on Praslin. Legend has it that during tropical storms the sighing and creaking heard is in fact the male and female coco de mer trees mating, but that anyone who sees this is doomed.

The largest seed in the plant kingdom, the coco de mer nut has a mass of up to 25 kg at maturity, reached about seven years after germination. Germination, in turn, can take up to two years. Initially the husk is orange and quite delicious to eat. After a year the husk begins to harden into a tough woody exterior, protecting the developing seed inside.

Other unique plants are found on the islands: the *lyann potao* (a pitcher plant), which is carnivorous and feasts on insects; *vya tangue* (dumb cane), the sap of which is intoxicating and poisonous, and causes one's mouth and throat to swell – hence the name; and the spectacular *Ravinala madagascariensis* (traveller's tree). Ferns, palms, wild vanilla, bread-fruit, mango, coconuts, dates, cocoa, frangipani, orchids and flamboyants all grow in profusion on the Seychelles. Among the rare species are the tropical bird orchid and jellyfish tree. Wright's gardenia flowers on the remote island of Aride, while the mystical Medusa tree is hidden in the forests of Mahé. Oddly out of place in such verdant tropical surroundings, the rhipsalis cactus, once thought to exist only in Central America, grows wild in the hills of Port Launay. Takamaka trees, used in boat building, are found everywhere on the granitic islands. Even the legendary medicinal plant *bois chauve-souris* is at home here. The most beautiful plant on the islands is the *batatran blanc*, which blooms only at night.

Cultivated flora include citrus, coconut, vanilla and the unusual jamalaque.

Fauna

Birds occur on the islands in multitudes. Cave swiftlets, fairy terns, seagulls and sooty terns are the most common species. But there are also birds unique to the Seychelles: the Seychelles grey white-eye, black paradise flycatcher, sunbird, bulbul, black parrot, and extremely rare magpie robin, to name a few of the 13 endemic species. The best place to go for those particularly interested in avifauna is Bird Island, especially in April and May when thousands of sea birds arrive to nest. It is an unforgettable experience to stand on the raised platform at sunset when clouds of birds circle and then land all around you at their nests in the tussocky grass.

Four islands in the Seychelles have been declared bird sanctuaries: Bird, Cousin, Aride and Frégate.

Animals, by comparison, are scarce on the Seychelles. The most widespread is the flying fox or fruit bat which defies usual bat norms and flies around during the day. Occasionally you may be fortunate enough to spot a shrew or mole in the thickly vegetated valleys of Praslin or Mahé.

Reptiles are quite numerous and will be seen visiting most hotel and inn rooms on the islands. They include the bronze gecko, green tree frog and chameleon. By far the most fascinating of all island reptiles are the giant tortoises. The largest, and oldest, lives on Bird Island and in the *Guinness book of records* goes by the name of Esmeralda – despite being a male. Many hotels keep a few in enclosures, but little can beat seeing them in their natural habitat. They are gentle creatures with old faces and weepy eyes. Scratch their long leathery necks, they love the attention and will move about contentedly.

Insects, as is typical in the tropics, are many. They include mosquitoes, red centipedes and wicked-looking scorpion spiders that can inflict nasty bites on the unsuspecting.

Marine life

A few metres beneath the surface of the sea lies an enchanted garden of plants, reefs and creatures: over 210 fish and 280 coral species. Dolphins, parrotfish, scorpionfish, white-tipped reef sharks, butterflyfish, angelfish and turtles are just some of the inhabitants of the waters around the Seychelles. In an effort to preserve the islands' natural heritage, the government has declared several national parks: Ste Anne Marine National Park off Victoria, Aldabra Nature Reserve, Curieuse Marine National Park, Port Launay Marine National Park and Baie Ternay Marine National Park.

Snorkelling is a must in the Seychelles. Popular snorkelling spots are often overcrowded; instead, be prepared to swim to where the undersea beauty can be viewed in peace and alone. The top spot off Praslin is undoubtedly around the point off the lighthouse, near La Reserve Hotel. To sight white-tipped reef sharks and shoals of parrotfish, swim to the rocks off Petite Anse Kerlan. Snorkelling north of Moyenne Island is also good. Those not inclined to dive should at least take a day trip with Mason's Travel to Ste Anne Marine National Park in a submerged glass-windowed boat which affords an amazing vista into the ocean – without getting wet.

Visitors can charter a deep-sea fishing boat to hunt marlin, sailfish, barracuda or shark. These trips usually go beyond the marine plateau to the deep water where the seafloor plunges a staggering 2 km. The government requires that all game fish caught must either be released or sold to a hotel or restaurant.

LANGUAGE

The official language of the Seychelles is Creole. English is spoken and understood in even the most isolated settlements. Most signs and billboards on the islands are in Creole and English; occasionally French. Among the older people there is a reluctance to speak English. Most of them speak good French and are much more comfortable using that.

Creole is difficult to master. You will, however, be accepted far more readily if you at least make an attempt at speaking the language. The trick is to start a conversation in Creole, no matter how terrible it may sound. Expect a few laughs from the Seychellois, who will then switch to either English or French to accommodate you. Practise a few basic sentences before you arrive on the islands; there it will be fairly easy finding someone to teach you more.

Good day, hello	Bonzour (note the "z" instead of the usual French "j")
Good evening	Bonswa
How are you?	Comman sava/komman ou sava?
I am well	Mon byen
Goodbye	Orevwar
What is your name?	Ki mannyer ou apele?
My name is . . .	Mon apel . . .
Where is . . .?	Ol i/cote ou . . .?
What does it cost?	Konbyen sa/konbyeni i vann?
Beach	Lanse/anse

12 FACTS FOR THE VISITOR

VISAS

No visa is necessary prior to arrival. A valid passport is all you will need. Children under 16 may be entered on their parents' passport. Upon arrival, visitors will be required either to produce an onward ticket or have proof of sufficient funds to buy one. Having produced the ticket or funds, your passport will be stamped with the date of arrival and a 30-day permit. The entry stamp will specify the date on which the visitor has to depart. This date will be scrutinised when you leave the Seychelles, and the exit stamp will be placed alongside the entry stamp. The injunction beneath the entry date, "Holder is not to engage in any employment paid or otherwise or in any business or profession", also applies to journalists and photographers, but a press card can be obtained from the Ministry of Finance, Information and Defence, Central Bank Building, Central Information Services Division, Victoria, Mahé, tel. 22-4161.

An extension of up to 12 months on a 30-day visa can be obtained from the Principal Immigration Officer, Independence House, Mahé, tel. 22-5333. Office hours are Monday to Friday 8h00-12h00 and 13h00-16h00.

Visitors arriving from countries where yellow fever and cholera are endemic may be asked to show an International Certificate of Vaccination. These can be obtained from your own country's department of health. Have the injections at least six weeks before departure.

FOREIGN EMBASSIES AND CONSULATES

Several countries have embassies or consulates on the Seychelles. Those countries that do not have are represented by honorary consuls – usually a foreigner married to a Seychellois.

Belgian Consulate
Victoria House, State House Avenue, Victoria, Mahé
PO Box 537, Victoria, Mahé, Seychelles, tel. 22-4434

Danish Royal Consul
Bodco Ltd, New Harbour Trading Estate, Victoria, Mahé
PO Box 231, Victoria, Mahé, Seychelles, tel. 22-4710

Consulat et Chancellerie de la France
Mont Fleuri Road, Mont Fleuri (opposite the Ministry of the Environment, Economics, Planning and External Relations)
PO Box 478, Mont Fleuri, tel. 22-4523

German Honorary Consul
Northolme Hotel, Glacis, Mahé
PO Box 132, Victoria, Mahé, Seychelles, tel. 26-1222

Indian High Commission
Le Chantier (on the Mont Fleuri Road, south of Victoria)
PO Box 488, Victoria, Mahé, Seychelles, tel. 22-4489

Honorary Consul of Madagascar
Plaisance (north of the traffic circle for La Misère)
PO Box 68, Victoria, Mahé, Seychelles, tel. 34-4030

Mauritian Consulate
Anse aux Pins (near the Reef Hotel, Mahé)
PO Anse aux Pins, Mahé, Seychelles, tel. 37-6441

Honorary Consul of the Netherlands
Sunset Beach Hotel, Glacis, Mahé
PO Box 372, Glacis, Mahé, Seychelles, tel. 26-1200

United Kingdom High Commission
Victoria House, State House Avenue, Victoria, Mahé
PO Box 161, Victoria, Mahé, Seychelles, tel. 22-5225

Embassy of the United States of America
Victoria House, State House Avenue, Victoria, Mahé
PO Box 251, Victoria, Mahé, Seychelles, tel. 22-5256

Other nations have representatives who are not permanent government officials. Most of these people have other jobs and are available only in dire circumstances. They rarely accept personal visits and will only do so if a prior appointment has been made.

Cuba, tel. 22-4094
Cyprus, tel. 37-6215
Finland and Sweden, tel. 22-4710
Greece, tel. 37-6216
Italy, tel. 22-4741
Monaco, tel. 23-3316
Norway, tel. 22-5353
Russian Federation, tel. 22-6590
Switzerland, tel. 37-1050

CUSTOMS

Seychellois customs officials are strict. With the events of the abortive Mike Hoare coup attempt still fresh in the memory, South Africans in particular are likely to have their belongings searched.

No fresh produce, plant material (including coral) or meat may be either brought into or taken out of the country. Recently there have been increasing reports of foreigners trying to take seed or plant cuttings out of the country. Punishment is severe and fines are high. To take a coco de mer nut out of the Seychelles you will need a permit, which must be obtained from the vendor. Firearms are forbidden, as are spear guns.

The following items may be brought into or taken out of the country:
200 cigarettes or 250 g of tobacco
250 ml eau de toilette, 125 ml of perfume
1 ℓ of wine, 1 ℓ of spirits

MONEY

The Seychelles are expensive. So, arrive with a lot of money, preferably in traveller's cheques. The Seychelles rupee is in the special drawing fund basket of the IMF. This effectively floats the rupee, keeping it stable and strong. The exchange rate for foreign currency varies daily. The current rates are published in the *Nation* newspaper and are available at all foreign exchange counters.

Both hard foreign cash and traveller's cheques can be exchanged at hotels and guesthouses, at a rate lower than that offered by banks – except at the Manresa Guesthouse, which offers the latest bank exchange rate. In the alleys of Victoria and on the beaches of Beau Vallon visitors may be approached by black marketeers, preferably for pounds sterling exchanges. It is illegal.

There are no restrictions on the amount of foreign cash a visitor may bring into or take out of the Seychelles. There are restrictions on bringing in or taking out Seychelles rupees (Rs): no tourist may take out more than Rs100 in notes or Rs10 in coins. Should you end up with a great deal of Seychelles money on departure, take your currency exchange receipts and the cash to any foreign exchange counter. There the Seychelles money will be changed back into the currency you had initially brought in.

If your traveller's cheques or credit cards are stolen, immediately notify the local police and the company's representative in the Seychelles. American Express is in the offices of Travel Services Ltd, Victoria House, State House Avenue, Victoria, Mahé, tel. 32-2414. Visa and Mastercard: Barclays Bank PLC, Independence Avenue, Victoria, Mahé, tel. 22-4101. Diners Club is also in Victoria House, State House Avenue, Victoria, Mahé, tel. 22-5303.

Money in the Seychelles comes in the following denominations, all based on 100 cents to 1 rupee: notes of Rs100, Rs50, Rs25, Rs10; coins of Rs5, Rs1, 25c, 10c, 5c, 1c.

Credit cards can be used for drawing cash at banks in Victoria, paying for accommodation and meals in tourist class facilities, and for medical expenses at government clinics. While most cards are readily accepted, a few travellers have had Eurocard rejected. Cards commonly used are Diners Club, Mastercard, Visa and American Express.

Although all Seychelles banks deal with foreign currency exchanges, some are more efficient than others. The best bank at which to change hard currency or traveller's cheques, or draw from a credit card, is Banque Française Commerciale, Océan Indien, Albert Street, Victoria, Mahé, tel. 32-3096. The worst, with rude and unhelpful staff, is across the road: Nouvobanq, Victoria House, State House Avenue, Victoria, Mahé. Barclays and Central Bank are located on Independence Avenue, Victoria, Mahé. Most larger settlements have branches or agencies of these banks.

Banking hours are Monday to Friday 8h30-15h30; Saturday 8h30-11h00. Agencies are usually open 9h00-15h00 on weekdays.

On La Digue the small Seychelles Savings Bank, near the clinic, changes foreign currency and allows cash to be drawn on a credit card.

COSTS

As mentioned in the last section, the Seychelles are expensive. Budget travellers are in for a tough time, especially compared to a Third World country or Mauritius. It will be virtually impossible to stay anywhere for less than Rs200 per night (meals excluded). But with carefully planned and controlled expenses, you should be able to visit the islands for about 10 days for around Rs10 000 per person – this includes accommodation and two meals per day, but excludes transport, curios and motorised water sports.

Hotels provide guests with breakfast, while guesthouses seldom do. Eat a big breakfast, have a snack in the day and eat something more substantial for supper. If you are invited to a family for dinner, give them a small token of appreciation. Where possible stay in self-catering accommodation, or at least at a place where breakfast is included in the rate.

Hiring a car is costly. Public transport on Mahé and Praslin is frequent and cheap, and gives tourists the opportunity of mixing with the locals. Hitchhiking is really easy on the Seychelles.

Curios can be expensive, depending on where you buy. Avoid the shops on the tourist trail and go into the remote settlements for cheaper and authentic handicrafts. Bargaining is expected. Do not be shy; unlike other Indian Ocean islands, the standard of living is high and people are relatively affluent. Visitors will, however, frequently hear complaints about prices, even from the locals.

TIPPING

Attitudes towards tipping vary on the Seychelles. You will hear that it demeans the Seychellois and returns them to a patronised subservience. Others expect tips as their right or as a fringe benefit in the tourism industry. Still another group says tips go a long way towards maintaining the standard of living of islanders. Deciding what to do can be difficult.

With the great influx of European tourists the practice of tipping has become customary in many tourist establishments. Despite a service charge being added to all tourist bills, you are expected to give something directly to the attendant. Bellboys, waiters and guides usually receive tips. It is not necessary to give a percentage of the total charge, a few rupees is enough.

Note, however, that at some establishments the habit of tipping is frowned upon. At top-class hotels such as the Sunset Beach on Mahé, L'Archipel and Coco de Mer on Praslin and Bird Island Lodge on Bird Island, visitors are not encouraged to give tips to staff.

TOURIST INFORMATION

Planning is essential for any visit to the Seychelles. The islands themselves may be small, but the distances between them need to be considered. Prospective visitors should get as much information as they
can from the Seychelles Tourist Office, PO Box 92, Victoria, Mahé,
Seychelles, tel. 22-5274, fax 22-5131. Alternatively contact one of the
country's representatives, who will supply travellers with the latest
brochures and information. You can, of course, also get the details once
on the Seychelles. The Seychelles Tourist Office is on the ground floor
of Independence House, Independence Avenue, Victoria, Mahé, tel.
22-5313, and is open Monday to Friday 8h00-12h00 and 13h30-16h00.
There is also an information office at the airport which can assist in
finding accommodation and transport, and has details on tours and
points of interest, tel. 37-3136.

The Seychelles Tourist Office is represented at all Seychelles embassies and missions abroad. You can contact the Tourism Section of
the embassy for information prior to visiting the islands:

Belgium
Honorary Consul of the Seychelles, General Avenue, Molière 301, 1060
Brussels, tel. 345-3423

Denmark
Seychelles Consulate, Vejlesoparken, 16 DK-2840 Holte, Denmark, tel.
42-0701

France
Embassy of the Seychelles, 53 Rue François Ier, 75008 Paris, France,
tel. 472-03966

Germany
Seychelles Consul, Bleichenbenbrucke 9/111, D2000 Hamburg 36,
Germany, tel. 356-0040

Italy
Honorary Consul of the Seychelles, Via del Tritone 46, 00187 Rome,
Italy, tel. 678-0530

Madagascar
Consulate of the Seychelles, PO Box 1071, Antananarivo, Madagascar,
tel. 20-949

Netherlands
Consul to the Seychelles, Flevolaan 69, 1272 PC Huizen, Netherlands, tel. 2159/40904

United Kingdom
Seychelles High Commission, PO Box 4 PE, London W1M 1FE, United Kingdom, tel. 224-1660

United States of America
Embassy of the Seychelles, Suite 927F, 820 Second Avenue, New York, N.Y. 10017, United States of America, tel. 687-9766

To reach the privately owned islands or what is called the Outer Island Territories, visitors must apply directly to the owners or relevant government departments. For the Amirantes group, Aldabra group and Farquhar islands, contact at least six months ahead of arrival: Island Development Company (IDC), PO Box 638, New Port, Victoria, Mahé, Seychelles, tel. 22-4640, fax 22-4467. Bird Island should be contacted for information about 60 days ahead of arrival: Bird Island, PO Box 404, Victoria, Mahé, Seychelles, tel. 22-4925, fax 22-5074. Denis Island: Denis Island Development Company, PO Box 404, Victoria, Mahé, Seychelles, tel. 32-3392, fax 32-4192. Information on other islands that are accessible to the public can be had by contacting an island tour operator. The most helpful and experienced of these are Mason's Travel, PO Box 459, Victoria, Mahé, Seychelles, tel. 32-2642, fax 32-4173, and Bunson's Travel, PO Box 475, Victoria, Mahé, Seychelles, tel. 32-2682, fax 32-1322.

European, Asian and South African travel agents all promote the Seychelles for the Tourist Office. They can usually give you a few brochures and leaflets to whet your appetite.

POST OFFICE

The postal system in the Seychelles is efficient and reliable. There is a post office in virtually every settlement. Although not clearly marked, they can usually be found alongside the local police station. Located on Independence Avenue in Victoria, near the national museum, the main post office provides fast and helpful service and has a poste restante service. Ask at the enquiries counter or ask the postmaster in smaller post offices. Poste restante mail in Victoria is not filed into any particular order and you will have to sort through an enormous cardboard box, which still holds letters postmarked 1968! In Grande Anse on Praslin, however, poste restante letters are put into alphabetical order according to the surname.

While the main post office in Victoria is open Monday to Friday 8h00-16h00 and Saturday 8h00-12h00, smaller postal branches work shorter, but seemingly irregular, hours. Do any posting or collection at about 9h00-11h00. Avoid doing business at any post office on a Saturday or either side of a public holiday, when there are long queues.

A collection of the famous Seychelles stamps can be bought through the Seychelles Philatelic Bureau at the post office on Independence Avenue in Victoria.

TELECOMMUNICATION

The international dialling code for the Seychelles is 248, which must be preceded by your own country's access code.

All emergency services – fire, police and ambulance – can be contacted by dialling 999. The correct time can be ascertained by dialling 140.

Telecommunications in the Seychelles are the responsibility of the Cable and Wireless Company, tel. 32-2221. Hotel tourists can make use of its wake-up service: dial 191 for a wake-up call between midnight and 7h00.

There is no need to pre-book telephone calls; they are all instant, even from the most remote islands of the Seychelles. Visitors who are going to make frequent use of the telephone system in the Seychelles should consider buying a phonecard. The cards are sold at the offices of Cable and Wireless on Francis Rachel Street in Victoria and at the international airport. Phonecards are cheaper and more convenient than coins, and can be used in any of the numerous public telephones around Mahé, Praslin and La Digue.

Visitors who need to contact a vessel at sea or the outer islands will need to make use of the very expensive INMARSAT system. Call 37-5733 and give the vessel's or location's number to the operator.

Telegrams are reliable and rapid. If sent before 12h00, the message will be delivered that same day. For sending a telegram via the telephone, dial 131 and place the message. Faxes are now common on the islands. Even many of the outlying islands have fax machines. You can either use those at hotels or guesthouses – which charge exorbitant handling fees – or at the Bureaufax in the Cable and Wireless offices in Victoria. Telexes are also available. Mostly used by visiting media or government representatives, they are however cheap and easy to use. There is a 24-hour machine in the Cable and Wireless offices in Victoria.

Other services that are available include Infolink (mainly for computers), Dattel (for the use of modems) and reverse charge calls to the United Kingdom, Japan and the United States of America.

TIME

The Seychelles are four hours ahead of Greenwich Mean Time, three hours ahead of France and British Summer Time and two hours ahead of South African time.

ELECTRICITY

Standard electrical voltage throughout the Seychelles is 240 volts alternating current (AC). Most hotels can supply visitors who need it with a small transformer upon request. Shaver plugs are built into hotel and guesthouse bathrooms and are the usual 240 volts, but also have a switch to reduce the current.

BUSINESS HOURS

Government and administrative offices are open Monday to Friday 8h00-12h00 and 13h00-16h00. All government offices are closed on Saturday and Sunday. A few administrative offices are open Saturday 8h30-12h00.

Shops, the informal sector, markets and vendors are open Monday to Friday about 8h00-17h00; Saturday about 8h00-12h00.

Hotels, restaurants, guesthouses and public transport operate daily, including Sunday, about 7h00-0h00. Cafés, bistros and street vendors are open from about 6h00-16h00.

MEDIA

The Seychellois are avid readers. Literacy is high and visitors will notice that even children read newspapers. There are nine local news publications, an informative radio service, a television channel and a network of religious radio broadcasts.

The best place for newspapers and magazines, both local and international, is the newsagent in the Pirate's Arms, on Independence Avenue. All the dailies, weekly magazines, periodicals, as well as international publications such as *Time* and *Le Monde* are available here.

The Seychelles *Nation* newspaper is available daily, excluding Saturday and Sunday, by 9h00. It has coverage in English, Creole and French. Mostly concerned with Seychellois and Indian Ocean topics, it does have a small section on international news events. *L'Echo des Îles*, published twice a month, is edited by the Roman Catholic Mission. Also written in three languages, it covers Christian subjects with occasional forays into broader journalism.

Several Seychelles magazines are printed. *Seychelles Weekly Hebdo* has a broad spectrum of controversial and thought-provoking articles. Another weekly is *Regar* magazine, a glossy which concentrates on scandal and shock subjects, and has little to attract the foreign visitor. On the other hand, *Seychelles Today* magazine, which is published only three times per year in English and French, covers events of particular interest to tourists. *Liberal* magazine, issued twice a month, is political and slanted towards the Seychelles Liberal Party. Another political publication is *The People* magazine. Published by the Seychelles People's Progressive Front in English, French and Creole, it encourages debate on island issues.

Two press agencies issue bulletins available at top-class hotels. Interpress copy is available three times a week and carries the main stories of the day as reported internationally in *The Times, La Repubblica, Seychelles Nation* and *Der Frankfurter*. Seychelles Agence Presse issues copy twice a month, in English and French, meant for the international press. This provides useful information about what is happening on the Seychelles.

As television is not broadcast 24 hours a day, many hotels offer guests a video channel. Details of what is showing are obtained from the hotel's reception desk.

Television broadcast times are Monday to Friday 17h45-22h30; Saturday 15h00-0h00; Sunday 14h00-0h00. Visitors can watch world news on CNN in certain hotels. Seychelles news commentary is broadcast in English at 18h00 and in French at 21h00.

Seychelles Broadcasting Corporation has daily radio broadcasts on 1368 Khz, Monday to Friday 6h00-13h30 and 15h00-22h00; Saturday and Sunday 6h00-22h00. There is in-depth news coverage in English at 19h00 and in French at 17h00, and headline news in English at 7h00 and 11h00 and in French at 7h30 and 21h00.

The Far East Broadcasting Association transmits regular religious programmes to the Middle East, Asia and the Far East. I am yet to meet a tourist who has tuned in to these programmes. Interested visitors should contact the station direct for information, tel. 24-1281.

ACCOMMODATION

All advertised tourist accommodation on the Seychelles is under the jurisdiction of the Ministry of Tourism. Prices are high and budget travellers will be hard-pressed to find accommodation at under Rs200 per night. Camping is illegal everywhere. Houses and apartments may occasionally be rented, but they are usually taken by contractors. But check the Seychelles dailies for advertisements, just in case.

Self-catering is becoming popular with holiday-makers. There are relatively few fully equipped self-catering lodges in the Seychelles, but additional ones seem to be sprouting up everywhere. The major drawback of this accommodation is that at least a 40% non-refundable deposit must be made, at least 30 days before arrival. The best established self-catering lodges are on Mahé, along the west coast. The one with the best reputation, facilities and location is La Résidence, on Anse à la Mouche.

Other accommodation on the islands can be divided into four categories: international hotels, small hotels, guesthouses and private homes.

International hotels

These are the most expensive and luxurious hotels on the islands. Many are owned and managed by international hotel chain groups. The best established are the Paradise Sun on Praslin and the Equator Sun on Mahé. Reservations for international hotels need to be made at least 60 days ahead. Most have central reservations offices in First World countries.

The Seychelles' most luxurious and famous hotel is on Praslin: L'Archipel. Visitors who stay here are just as likely to meet Giorgio Armani as the Duchess of Kent walking along the private beach. The Sunset Beach is the islands' most prestigious hotel, with arguably the best location. Northolme Hotel, along Mahé's north-west coast, is legendary.

The likes of Somerset Maugham, Noel Coward and Ian Fleming have graced its corridors.

Many of these international hotels are used by package tours, so expect groups of vacationers there. While tour groups will have break-fast and dinner included in the rate, solo travellers will usually only have breakfast included. Dinner is extra and is always far more ex-pensive than in local cafés or restaurants.

Some of the advantages of staying at these hotels are that they offer free water sports, arrange excursions, and have bars, nightclubs and restaurants. At the Beau Vallon Bay Hotel and Mahé Beach Hotel, even visitors who are not residents are allowed to use the facilities.

There are distinct high and low seasons at international hotels on the Seychelles. Mid-December to the end of April is considered high season. Make reservations well in advance if you plan to visit the islands during that time. Naturally, the December festive season is extremely busy. Book at least three months prior to arrival. August is also busy: European schools go on holiday and there is a flood of tourists to the Seychelles. It is suggested that you do not visit during this time, unless on an organised tour. Although regarded as the low season, May to July and September to November are the best months to visit and find suitable international hotel accommodation. There is the added bonus of having lower hotel rates. Beaches are fairly deserted, the weather is slightly cooler and there is a general feeling of relaxation and tranquillity.

The new Coco de Mer Hotel on Praslin is one of the best. With its exemplary service and attention to detail, tour operators and agencies will soon be clamouring to get their affluent clients into the hotel.

Small hotels

There are not many small, privately owned hotels, and those available are geared to the well-heeled tourist. Small hotels are, however, popular and visitors must make reservations at least 60 days in advance. Prices are high but the service is not correspondingly good. The one notable exception – and highly recommended – is the Auberge de Bougainville, on Mahé, at Anse Royale. The Mountain Rise Hotel in the hills of Sans Souci, although not well advertised, is also recommended. Its prices are high, but the food is excellent and the views unbeatable.

On the quiet bay of Grande Anse on Praslin is the comfortable and secluded Indian Ocean Lodge. On La Digue, where tourist accommodation is at premium, there is little to compare with Choppy's Bungalows – famous among travellers the world over. Book ahead, though, and confirm telephonically or by telegram at least 15 days before arrival.

Many small or privately owned islands have a lodge for guests. Expect high charges, but good value for what you get in terms of scenery and exclusivity. Considering the distance from Mahé, and transport costs, the tariffs are reasonable. The Bird Island Lodge on Bird Island is the most famous. Make reservations at least four months ahead for the high season and 30 days ahead for the low season.

Tour agencies keep a list of the various small hotels. Prospective visitors can contact either travel agencies or the Seychelles Tourist Board for a copy of the booklet, *Where to stay and where to eat in the Seychelles*.

Guesthouses

Guesthouses are plentiful. Usually managed by their owners, they have the cosiness of a family home with the comforts of tourist-class accommodation. It is advisable to make reservations about three days before your intended arrival.

Top of the list is La Louise Lodge, on La Misère hill, Mahé. To the north, the expensive but rather squalid Manresa Guesthouse lies on the edge of Ste Anne Marine National Park. Among budget travellers La Retraite, about 3 km south of the international airport, is a favourite place to spend the first night.

Guesthouses offer good food at reasonable rates, or the staff will cook meals if you provide the ingredients.

Private homes

Staying with a family, either sharing their home or just using one room, is cheap and the best way of getting to know the Seychellois. This accommodation is never advertised and is not subject to the severe restrictions and taxes imposed by the Tourist Board. Booking ahead is impossible, unless you have visited previously and have the address where you intend to stay.

There are few of these rooms on Mahé, but on Praslin and La Digue they abound. One good place to ask at is the small café at Marine Charter, near the yacht club on Mahé. In the south, visitors should ask at the police station at Quatre Bornes. The police are helpful and know of several options in the area. Private accommodation on Praslin can be found by asking at Steve's Café in Grande Anse or at the First and Last Bar near the pier in Baie Ste Anne. La Digue has the most private homes offering accommodation. Walk inland from the harbour and ask any of the shop owners. Most of them will gladly offer visitors a room, at reasonable rates. No meals are included, but when prices are compared with that of accommodation along the coast road, it hardly matters.

FOOD

Visitors will be delighted by the variety and abundance of Creole cuisine. The locals add the delicate taste of tropical fruit to many of their dishes. White rice, chicken and seafood are the staples, but exotic dishes include palm-heart salad, which contains the "heart" or growth point of a palm tree, flying fox stewed in coconut milk, and Chinese noodles covered in French garlic sauce with roast cassava and banana slices.

In guesthouses, residents are fed spicy Creole meals with such ingredients as octopus, shark or marinated and then grilled chicken.

Hotels cater to a broader taste. Their buffets are always enormous and include at least one Creole dish and seafood platter. Having been trained at the Seychelles Hotel School near Beau Vallon, and apprenticed to European chefs, hotel cooks conjure up some interesting and palate-pleasing dishes.

Tourist-class restaurants – those in hotels or around major tourist areas – are expensive and rarely offer local food. There are Japanese, Italian and several good seafood restaurants on Mahé, French *nouvelle cuisine* at any of the hotels on Praslin and English meals at luxury hotels. The yacht club offers enormous, delicious and reasonably priced meals, and you do not have to be a member to eat there.

Takeaways and snack bars are growing in popularity, especially among the youth. Most offer the usual American-style menus, those on Praslin being the exception. Britz and Steve's on Praslin's west coast offer Creole takeaways. The helpings are large and surprisingly cheap. The octopus curry should not be missed. On Mahé, you can get takeaways in styrofoam containers from the small café next to Marine Charter.

Snacks are a rarity on the Seychelles. Despite the influence of Asian and African cultures, street vendors seldom sell food. At the Sir Selwyn Clarke market in Victoria there are a few women who cook light meals and offer shoppers grilled fish or samosas.

Vegetarians and those who enjoy fresh produce are in for feast. Be warned, though, that the price of imported produce is prohibitively high – at the time of writing a cabbage cost Rs60. Local fruit and vegetables, on the other hand, are cheap and freely available. Victoria's market is the one to visit. Everything from spinach to mangoes are on sale, as well as fresh seafood and spices.

Bread is baked by many small bakeries daily, as are cakes and buns. In Victoria, the bakery on Revolution Avenue has an amazing selection of cookies for sale, and slices of tangy pizza.

Seafood is served in every restaurant, guesthouse, hotel and family home. On the smaller islands, fish are caught daily by a family member. Hotel and guesthouse staff visit the fish markets on the beaches. The ones at Beau Vallon on Mahé and Côte d'Or on Praslin are always busy and certainly worth visiting. Should you be invited to a beach party with the locals, the dinner will inevitably be fresh fish grilled over a fire and accompanied with onions and sweet daube sauce. Another favourite way of cooking seafood is to mix several species of fish and crustaceans into a soup, which is then eaten with wads of nutty brown bread, bought at any Indian café.

There are cafés and supermarkets in all settlements. The SMB supermarkets are well stocked, mostly with South African goods. Supermarket prices are controlled, so it makes little difference where you buy. Mahé, being the largest and most populated island, has several supermarkets. The biggest, with the widest selection, is on Albert Street in Victoria. Other large supermarkets are located on the west coast of Mahé at Grande Anse and Port Glaud. Cafés stock an impressive array of foodstuffs, and you can buy fresh fish from them by placing an order the evening before.

DRINK

Popular drinks on the Seychelles are Seybrew beer and fruit juice. All glass bottles carry a deposit. Seybrew beer, made on Mahé at Le Rocher, has a strong taste of hops and is light. Many tourists quickly take to this local brew. Imported beers on sale include San Miguel, Black Label and Tetley's. Guinness, made locally under licence, is enjoyed by many older Seychellois. Beer is sold nearly everywhere, in cafés, restaurants, supermarkets, hotels and even by street vendors.

Fizzy drinks, such as Coca Cola and Fanta, are losing sales to the recently introduced Liquifruit. Made under contract to a South African firm, this 100% fruit juice is wonderful if drunk ice-cold. Tourists going walking or cycling should take with them a litre of mineral water such as Eau de Val Richi. It is sold wherever bottled drinks are available. However, drinking it in hotel dining rooms or restaurants is expensive: it carries a huge surcharge.

Wine and spirits never really gained a hold on the Seychelles as they did on Réunion. Most wine is from South Africa, and even rum is imported from Barbados. People in the forests and hills make a potent alcoholic brew from coconut palms. A sure sign of this drink being made is strips of wood hammered horizontally up a palm tree. The brew is supposedly illegal, but villagers are quite happy to share it with an interested visitor. You will find it in the forest villages of north-western Mahé, on the Salazie track across Praslin and above Belle Vue in the hills of La Digue.

BOOKS

Visitors interested in the history of the Seychelles would do well to read *Forgotten Eden* by Atholl Thomas (Longman, London, 1968). Although old, it will give readers an enchanting glimpse of historical Seychelles. If you are interested in pirates, buried treasure and riddles, read Roy Nevill's book, *The treasure seeker's treasury* (Hutchinson, London, 1978). It has detailed information regarding the mystery of the treasure of Olivier Le Vasseur, reputedly buried at Bel Ombre.

For further information on the history of these fascinating islands, it is recommended that travellers visit the National Archives just north of Victoria. The Senior Archivist, Jean-Claude Pascal Mahoune, is happy to talk about Seychelles history. Call to arrange an appointment: National Archives, La Bastille, Mahé, tel. 22-4777.

A series of eight little books, the *Seychelles nature handbooks*, cover all facets of Seychelles wildlife, with many photographs and information on each species described. They are cheap and very useful.

Fiction, non-fiction photo books, cookbooks and travel guides can all be bought at SPACE, Bookshop Division, Huteau Lane, Victoria, Mahé, tel. 22-4531, and at Librarie Ste Fidèle, Olivier Maradam Street, Victoria, Mahé, tel. 32-3463. Both the National Archives, at La Bastille, and the National Library, on Francis Rachel Street, keep books relating to the Seychelles. The librarians are initially surprised to see a tourist come in, but will then fall over themselves to help you.

MAPS

Good maps are available free of charge from the Seychelles Tourist Office on Independence Avenue in Victoria. They are, however, too small to use for hiking. The map of Seychelles published by Macmillan in its Traveller's Map series is recommended. It includes basic tourist information and descriptions of the more popular islands. Mahé, at a scale of 1:50 000, is detailed with roads, accommodation, tracks, points of interest, restaurants and the islands of Ste Marie National Park. There is also a street map of Victoria in 100 m linear scale. Overleaf are detailed maps of Praslin and La Digue, plus several of the outer islands and satellite islands.

Topographical maps for hiking routes must be ordered at least 60 days in advance. These maps are complicated and more difficult to hike with than the Macmillan map. They are obtainable, at a fee, from both the Ministry of the Environment, Economics, Planning and External Relations, and the Ministry of Defence. The maps can only be collected upon arrival in the Seychelles. Write to the Ministry of the Environment, Economics, Planning and External Relations, Mont Fleuri, Mahé, Seychelles, tel. 22-4688, or the Ministry of Defence, Defence Headquarters, Bel Eau, Victoria, Mahé, Seychelles, tel. 22-4070.

The National Archives keeps outdated British Ordinance Survey maps. A great deal has changed since these maps were done, and apart from providing an interesting glimpse of what the Seychelles must have been like, they are useless.

THINGS TO BUY

Using the artistic background of their ancestors – African, European, Asian and Malagasy – the Seychellois use the materials around them to create spectacular handicrafts and souvenirs. Shells, coconuts, natural dyes and plants are combined in a delicate art form that is unique. Artists are inspired by the wilderness and the sea to paint and sculpt magnificent pieces. Turtle shell, shark's teeth and bones from big-game fish are hand-worked into jewellery, which while attractive, threatens the survival of rare species.

In rural markets, the villagers use grass and leaves to make hats, baskets and bangles, frequently dyed with earth colours to impart a warm hue to the intricate designs. A favourite among tourists is the coco de mer nut. Locally grown spices and tea are also popular. Model ships are being built more often, and silk-screening is now being taught on the islands.

Visitors in Victoria can find most Seychelles handicrafts for sale at the informal flea market on Independence Avenue, opposite the main post office. Bargaining is expected, and the first asking price will be at least 120% of what the seller expects to be paid. On Buxton Lane can be bought a wide selection of jewellery boxes, games and cigar boxes, all made of indigenous wood. On Beau Vallon (Mahé) and Côte d'Or (Praslin) and near La Digue Island Lodge, there are vendors with tables laden with locally produced crafts.

If you are interested in buying a coco de mer nut to take home it is advisable to visit a registered vendor. Some prior knowledge of what you are looking for is necessary. In their natural state the nuts are unattractive and very heavy. Rather look at those that have been hollowed out and polished. You do, however, need to be aware that wooden replicas are often sold. To avoid any possible problem buy from the curio shop next to the Vallée de Mai national park on Praslin, or the Codevar studio on Albert Street in Victoria. Genuine coco de mer nuts are expensive, and you must get an official, stamped export permit from the shop. The replicas do not require a permit, are cheap and make wonderful small gifts.

Spices are sold at Sir Selwyn Clarke market in Victoria, and also at the tourist shops on La Digue. Framed, biologically named exhibits of local spices can be bought at the Seychelles Museum Shop, in the arcade alongside the Pirate's Arms. Tea is best purchased directly from the Seychelles Marketing Board's tea factory above Port Glaud. Although the selection is small, the quality of tea is high. Indian Ocean Island Tea is the highest grade. Other teas are used mostly for blending with Indian and Ceylon teas.

Silk-screening and batiks have become popular in the Seychelles. On Beau Vallon the country's foremost batik artist, Ron Gerlach, sells an amazing variety of prints and designs. Prices are fixed and high, but good value when you consider the workmanship and effort involved in the batiks' creation. The islands' most famous painter, Michael Adams, offers work direct from his studio, west of Anse à la Mouche. T-shirts are sold at all tourist shops, boutiques, hotel duty-free shops and the Museum Shop. The Pirate's Arms and the Museum Shop, close together on Independence Avenue in Victoria, have the most popular motifs.

In the Home Industries shop on Independence Avenue, opposite the National Museum, crafts from all the islands are offered for sale. The items bought are recorded and then analysed by the government. The shop carries all the curios that would interest a tourist, plus those that will horrify environmentally conscious visitors. To discourage the continued sale of products from threatened wildlife, plants and shells, avoid buying these goods.

THINGS TO DO

Sports and activities on the Seychelles are so popular as to be almost a cult. For tourists this translates into a fairground of outdoor activities, of which the most popular are scuba diving, parasailing, snorkelling, game fishing, rock climbing, hiking and golf.

Scuba diving is offered by several of the large hotels. But once you have seen the reefed lagoons and sheltered bays, you may decide that snorkelling is a much better idea. At the exclusive L'Archipel and Coco de Mer, individual scuba instruction is provided. Resort hotels, such as the Paradise Sun, Equator Sun, Mahé Beach and Beau Vallon Bay, offer resort courses in scuba diving, which allow you to dive only at that resort for a limited time. Certified instructors – usually PADI qualified – offer the whole range of scuba courses from Open-water I to Divemaster. If already qualified, you need to take along your certificate in order to hire equipment. There is no need to cart along loads of scuba equipment. All items can be hired locally. For suggested dive locations contact the Seychelles Underwater Centre: not only is this a five-star training school, staff also gladly give qualified divers helpful local site information. Address: Underwater Centre (Seychelles), PO Box 384, Beau Vallon, c/o Coral Strand, Mahé, Seychelles, tel. 24-7357.

Parasailing is the most expensive pursuit on the islands. Nevertheless, unless you are on a very tight budget, give this a go. The fun and adrenalin rush of being towed into the air over the sea is marvellous.

Paragliding is also available. Beau Vallon Bay Hotel, on Mahé's west coast, allows non-residents to use its facilities. Paragliding can be done only when weather conditions are suitable, so you should phone for confirmation: Beau Vallon Bay Hotel, tel. 24-7141. The hotel also offers waterskiing and windsurfing free of charge.

Big-game fishing is popular among many South African and German tourists. You will need to charter a boat for the day, and pay for tackle, bait and lunch. There is a reduced fee for group bookings of four people or more. Fishing competitions are becoming more frequent. Foreigners are permitted to enter these games, and from October to March, fleets of boats leave Victoria harbour and Beau Vallon Bay in search of prey. The most experienced big-game fishing skippers hang around the Marine Charter Association Building on Badamier Avenue, Victoria. You must book at least 48 hours in advance. Considered to have the best skippers in the Seychelles, Game Fishing Enterprise, PO Box 134, La Misère, Mahé, tel. 34-4266, guarantees each tourist at least one catch. Hotels will also book guests onto a charter, and will usually provide a cold lunch, but they charge a fee for these services.

If keen on line fishing, visitors should consider a day trip with one of the coastal fishermen. They will be surprised when asked to be accompanied by a tourist. Take along your own lunch and something to add to their meagre rations. Negotiate the price and pay in advance: the evening before. You will be given a hand-line of gut, a few hooks and bait. The fishing boats leave early. You will have to be on the beach by 4h00 and will fish until about 10h00. You can either keep your catch or sell your fish with those of the fishermen in the local fish market.

Rock climbing is a fairly new tourist activity on the Seychelles. Granite boulders are a feature of the larger islands. Low in height but technically difficult, the rocks on Mahé in particular offer challenging climbing. A number of South Africans and Britons have scaled the larger walls with specialist equipment and support. On Mahé the best rock climbing is on the vertical cliffs between Victoria and Port Glaud. Praslin has low but difficult 20 m cliffs above the Coco de Mer Hotel and on Anse Kerlan in the far north. Boulder climbing on La Digue and Praslin is fun. There is no great danger from a fall, and on La Digue you are likely to fall into the sea. La Digue is littered with boulders of the famous pink granite, and you will not need to walk or look far for a climb.

There is only one golf course on the Seychelles, the technically easy nine-hole course of the Reef Hotel near Anse aux Pins on Mahé. Few visitors other than hotel residents use the course, and there is no need for a booking. Just turn up, pay the high course fee and carry your own bag to the first tee. Enquiries concerning equipment hire should be made at least 24 hours before arrival with Reef Hotel Golf Course, tel. 37-6251.

Hiking is enjoyed, especially by budget travellers. There are no really arduous hikes, and on most routes visitors will be back in their hotels before sunset. The most scenic hikes are on Mahé and Praslin. Aiming to encourage affluent eco-tourists, the government has created hiking trails through the forests and mountains of Mahé. There are also many other tracks and trails that walkers should consider as an alternative to the busy government routes. Several walks on the coral islands are also possible.

The most fascinating walk on Mahé commences 100 m west of Sans Souci. Follow the Trois Frères Nature Trail signs. Passing south-east to north-west through a dense rainforest and edging the highest mountain on the Seychelles, Morne Seychellois (905 m), this journey into primeval nature is about 3 km long. To learn something about this pristine wilderness, hire the expert guide on these forests, Basil Beaudouin, who has an intimate knowledge of the Seychelles flora and fauna. Book his services well in advance: Basil Beaudouin, PO Machabee, Mahé, Seychelles, tel. 24-1790.

Another government trail is the Anse Major Nature Trail, from Danzilles to Anse Major. About 2,5 km in length, this trail hugs the edge of the sea through coconut groves to the remote beach of Anse Major. You can leave your vehicle at the Auberge Club de Seychelles. A guide can also be arranged there, but you do not really need one.

From the Cable and Wireless Satellite Tracking Station, along the Chemin Montagne Road, the La Reserve and Brulée Nature Trail climbs steeply to three superb viewpoints before exiting on the summit of Mount Brulée (501 m), about 1 km south of the tarred road.

Off the beaten track are a multitude of forest trails, paths and mountains to explore. On northern Mahé, a strenuous walk from the Cable and Wireless Station near the Northolme Hotel, up through the forest settlements to La Gogue Reservoir, requires bundu bashing but brings you to a wondrous lake in the hills. The walk to the lake takes about one hour.

In the west, near Baie Ternay Marine National Park, hikers can go north from Anse Soullac to enter the forest above Ternay Bluff. Going north, follow the 2 km track to Anse Major, where you join the Anse Major Nature Trail going east.

To hike in the central area of Mahé, leave the road near the viewpoint below Souvenir Tea Estate. Turn south-east along the track that climbs through the rainforest below the USAF Tracking Station. Immediately south-east of the tracking station take the path going south, which descends to the Cascade Waterfall before ending on the main road between the airport and Victoria.

In the south, walks are limited and visitors cannot get to the southernmost point, as the area is off limits for security reasons. But a splendid 4 km hike through forests, over hills and down to the sea starts 150 m west of La Résidence lodge. Veering east the path enters thick, dripping forests before climbing the hills of Roche Gratte Fesse coconut plantation and descending to the long white beach at Anse Royale.

Apart from the enchanting walks through the fantasy forest of the Vallée de Mai, Praslin has two other hikes worth trying. From Grande Anse on western Praslin take the road that passes the Britannia Hotel and restaurant. Climbing in a series of sharp curves the road soon becomes a track and then a path until it reaches the Plain Hollandaise. There is a fork in the road, about 1 km from Grande Anse. The right-hand path is called the Salazie track and goes another 3 km over the highlands of Salazie, then down to Anse Volbert and the Paradise Sun Hotel. The left-hand path, the Pasquière track, follows the Pasquière river past Manny New Peak and down to Baie Pasquière, north of Anse Possession.

Each of the islands, irrespective of its size, has walks that take anything from 10 minutes to two hours. There is seldom any need for guides on the tiny islands, and the adventure of exploring them yourself adds to the pleasure.

13 GETTING THERE

The most common way of reaching the Seychelles is by air. Other, less conventional methods are being explored by a number of tour agencies and adventure travellers.

AIR

International flights connect the Seychelles (Victoria) with Bahrain, Dubai, Frankfurt, Johannesburg, London, Madrid, Mauritius (Mahébourg), Moscow, Nairobi, Paris, Réunion (St-Denis), Rome, Singapore and Zurich.

The airlines servicing these routes are listed below, with their addresses and telephone numbers in the Seychelles. For their latest flight schedules and fares, contact a travel agent or these airlines' representative in your own country.

Aeroflot, Pirate's Arms Building, Independence Avenue, Victoria, Mahé, tel. 22-5005

British Airways, Kingsgate House, Independence Avenue, Victoria, Mahé, tel. 22-4910

Condor Airlines, Contact Mason's Travel, Revolution Avenue, Victoria, Mahé, tel. 32-2642

Air France, Kingsgate House, Independence Avenue, Victoria, Mahé, tel. 32-2414

Kenya Airways, Revolution Avenue, Victoria, Mahé, tel. 32-2989

Make reservations well in advance. During the peak season, which is July-August and over the December festive season, flights are fully booked at least 30 days before departure.

Visitors should confirm their return flights at least 72 hours before leaving the islands. This can be done telephonically.

Australasian travellers can fly to the Seychelles via Singapore, Europe or Mauritius. The Singapore flight is the cheapest.

Air Seychelles is the national carrier, and has one of the highest standards of service in the airline industry. Branch offices are scattered around the world. If there is not one in your country, contact the nearest Seychelles Embassy for assistance. As most visitors to the Seychelles are from France, Italy, Great Britain and South Africa, Air Seychelles offices in these countries offer a great deal of information to prospective travellers. Contact them when planning your trip: employees can help you put it together. France: Air Seychelles, 32 Rue de Ponthieu, 75008 Paris, tel. (1) 428-98683, fax (1) 456-38512. Italy: Air Seychelles, Viale Alessandro Magno, 282 Casal Oalocco, 00124 Rome, tel. (6) 509-8413, fax (6) 509-15917. Great Britain: Air Seychelles, Suite 6 Kelvin House, Kelvin Way, Crawley, West Sussex RH10 2SE, England, tel. 53-6313, fax 56-2353. South Africa: Air Seychelles, Suite 113, Time Square, Raleigh Street, Yeoville 2198, tel. (011) 487-3556, fax (011) 487-3635. The headquarters of Air Seychelles are on Francis Rachel Street, in Victoria House, Victoria, Mahé, tel. 22-5220.

SEA

Most people who arrive in the Seychelles by sea do so either on a cruise ship or as crew aboard a yacht. A regular cargo service and cruise line operate between the Seychelles, Africa, Asia and Europe. Cruise ships are usually under charter to a large tour operator or several agencies.

Finding passage aboard a cargo vessel is difficult. However, the shipping manager of Mahé Shipping Company is very helpful and will attempt to place you as a crew member. You will need to be a bona fide independent traveller, and have at least a working knowledge of nautical matters. A number of adventure travellers, with time to spare, have reached the Seychelles aboard Oriental fishing trawlers. Reports indicate that factory boat positions are available on vessels sailing for the Seychellois fishing banks out of Singapore, Surabaya (Indonesia), Manila (Philippines), Nagoya (Japan) and Chilung (Taiwan). You will need to sign on for at least six weeks. The skipper will drop you at Victoria Harbour, Mahé. You will need to prove that you have an onward ticket or passage.

Yachts sail the cruising routes of the Indian Ocean and Pacific all year. Usually ahead of the cyclones and hurricanes, they always include a stop in the Seychelles and Mauritius before sailing to Africa. You will find yachts planning voyages to the Seychelles in India (Goa), Australia (Perth) and Kuwait City (Kuwait). Once the cyclones have passed, crew positions become available on yachts sailing from Durban (South Africa), Mombasa (Kenya) and the Mediterranean into the Indian Ocean.

162

14 GETTING AROUND

Relying heavily on foreign revenue from tourism, the government of the Seychelles has done much to provide visitors with a wide choice of public transport which includes inter-island flights, a reliable and regular bus service, taxis, helicopters, ferries and inter-island schooners. A specific department deals with each means of transport. For up-to-date details on travelling about the islands, contact these departments: Civil Aviation, tel. 37-3001; Land Transport, tel. 22-4701; Marine Services, tel. 22-5333.

AIR

Air Seychelles has several daily flights between the islands. This domestic service is known as Island Air Traffic. Getting to the outer islands may be difficult during the cyclone season which affects the southern atolls. Schedule details of these flights can be obtained from Air Seychelles, Island Air Traffic, PO Box 386 (or Victoria House, Francis Rachel Street), Victoria, Mahé, tel. 37-3051, fax 22-5159.

Made in small fixed-wing aircraft, the trip between islands is magical. The view over the reefs, lagoons, forests and beaches is certainly worth the high airfare. Be at the inter-island terminal at least 30 minutes before departure. This terminal is about 100 m to the north of the departure hall of the international airport. Reservations must be made in advance.

Flights from Mahé to Bird, Denis and Frégate islands are booked through their respective publicity offices in Victoria:

Bird Island, PO Box 404, Victoria (opposite the Seychelles Tourist Office in Independence Avenue), tel. 22-4925, fax 22-5074. The fare to Bird Island incudes a return trip, accommodation and all meals. There is one flight a day lasting 35 minutes.

Denis Island, PO Box 404, Victoria (in St Joseph Street, north of the Hindu temple), tel. 32-3392, fax 32-4192. The office is only open weekdays 8h30-10h00. There are three flights a week lasting 40 minutes. It is possible, however, to make arrangements with Denis Island that you be collected from Bird Island en route.

Frégate Island, PO Box 330, Victoria (in Revolution Avenue, near Bunson's Travel), tel. 32-3123, fax 32-4169. There are two daytime flights lasting 20 minutes.

There are up to five flights a day, depending on the season, between Mahé and Praslin. The flight takes only 15 minutes. Make reservations either through the travel agent represented at your hotel or with Air Seychelles in Victoria.

There are three flights per week between Mahé and Île Desroches, lasting 60 minutes.

For flying to Astove or Île du Nord it is preferable to get a group together and charter a flight, otherwise the airfare is prohibitive. Visitors wanting to visit these or other outer islands should work through a reputable tour operator who will contact the respective island's owners. Mason's Travel has numerous reliable contacts for the more remote islands: Mason's Travel, PO Box 459 (in Revolution Avenue, near Kenya Airways' office), Victoria, Mahé, tel. 32-2642, fax 32-4173.

Offering scenic flights and island transfers, Helicopter Seychelles is the most expensive but spectacular way of getting around the Seychelles. Flights are seldom fully booked and visitors can merely phone the day before for a reservation: Helicopter Seychelles, tel. 37-5400, fax 37-5277. The only time that it is suggested you book 20 days in advance is during May and August, when television crews descend in droves on the islands to make documentaries and travel programmes.

BUS

Far more tourists are using the bus services than in former years, possibly because of their increased frequency and low fares. Buses are under the control of the Seychelles Public Transport Corporation. The main bus depot is just north of Victoria on the corner of 5th June Avenue and Palm Street. Buses to all destinations around Mahé leave from here. Buses on Mahé and Praslin run at least hourly between about 5h30 and 19h00. From 19h30 to around 21h00 there are a few buses on special routes.

On Praslin – the only other island with a regular bus service – most buses leave from Baie Ste Anne, on the south-east coast.

Bus stops are marked on the road itself, but every so often there is a tin bus stop sign on a pole. Look for the white, painted sign and the pull-off block on the road.

Getting around by bus is great fun. This is the means of transport that most locals use. However, along certain routes tourists may find the bus drivers exceedingly unhelpful. The route from Victoria north around Nord d'Est to Glacis and Beau Vallon Bay has the worst reputation. If you ask a driver to drop you off at a specific stop, thank him when getting off.

On Mahé the buses will not stop for passengers other than at a designated bus stop, but on Praslin all you need to do is flag a bus down and it will stop. To stop a bus on which you are travelling, despite there being bells, you have to shout. When nearing your intended stop, call out loudly, "Dévant!"

When first using a bus, sit near the front of the bus or near the conductor. In this way you are certain of being noticed and assisted.

Buses with red and green stripes on the side allow both sitting and standing passengers. Those with no stripes or one colour stripe permit only seated travellers. When boarding a bus everyone rushes headlong for the door, where there is an inevitable jam.

On Mahé, information about bus times and routes can be obtained at the office on the northern side of the main bus depot near Victoria. Although destinations are clearly marked above each bus shelter, ask just to make sure.

The following routes are covered by buses from Victoria:

East coast: Buses run between Victoria and the international airport (the bus stop is opposite the southern gate to the airport terminal), Anse aux Pins, Anse Royale, Takamaka, Anse Étoile and La Gogue.

North-west coast: Buses run between Victoria and Glacis, Beau Vallon Bay and Bel Ombre.

South-west coast and the interior: Buses run between Victoria and Sans Souci, Port Glaud, La Misère, Grande Anse, St Joseph's Church, Anse Boileau and Baie Lazare.

TAXI

Tourists planning to use this expensive method of seeing the Seychelles would do well to contact the Taxi Operators Association for current fares: Taxi Operators Association, Ste Claire's School, Victoria, Mahé, tel. 32-3895. The price list is also posted on the notice board near the foreign exchange counter at the international airport. At the large taxi rank in Victoria, on Albert Street, numerous taxis wait for custom. A fixed rate, controlled by the government, is supposedly in effect, but all foreigners will be asked whether they want the fare meter on or want to negotiate a special price. Taxi drivers at the airport, in particular, often "forget" to switch on their meters. Check that the meter is running, even if you are tired and nervous about arriving in a strange country at night.

Although taxis are costly, if you only have a limited time on the island of Mahé, hire a taxi and driver for a few days. Bargain and fix the price before setting off, and suggest that the driver plan a brief itinerary for you, with accommodation. In this way budget travellers may find themselves living with local families and charged prices way below that of registered establishments.

There is an estimated 153 registered taxis on Mahé and Praslin, but the unofficial ones bring the figure closer to 200. Ask at small stores about local taxi hire. Taxis are available 24 hours a day and can be quickly called from any hotel reception desk.

SEA

Over 117 islands make up the Seychelles. All of them can be reached by boat. Ferries and sailing schooners service the inner islands, while cargo vessels make regular trips to the outer islands.

The inter-island ferry service links the larger granitic islands and leaves from Victoria Harbour, Monday to Friday. Schooners are based on Praslin and La Digue, and leave for Mahé at about 5h00 each weekday morning. If a schooner is carrying fuel or explosive materials, passengers will not be allowed for that voyage. The trip between Mahé and Praslin takes about three hours, and that between Mahé and La Digue about three hours and 15 minutes, depending on sea and weather conditions.

Monday: *La Belle Praslinoise, Cousin* and *La Bellone* depart Praslin for Victoria (Mahé) from Baie Ste Anne at 5h00 and return between 11h00 and 12h00. *La Belle Edma* departs La Digue for Victoria at 5h30 and returns at 13h00.

Tuesday: *Cousin* departs Praslin for Victoria at 6h00. *La Belle Edma* departs La Digue for Victoria also at 6h00. Both vessels return at 12h00.

Wednesday: *La Belle Praslinoise* departs Praslin for Victoria at 5h00. *La Belle Edma* departs La Digue for Victoria at 5h30. Both vessels return at 12h00.

Thursday: *La Belle Praslinoise* and *Cousin* depart Praslin for Victoria at 5h00. *La Belle Edma* departs La Digue for Victoria at 6h00. All three vessels return at 12h00.

Friday: *La Belle Praslinoise* and *Cousin* depart Praslin for Victoria at 5h00. *La Belle Edma* departs La Digue for Victoria at 5h30. All three vessels return at 13h00.

Tickets for the voyage are bought on board. Arrive 30 minutes before departure. Stow your luggage in the passenger lounge, or else it gets thrown into the hold with all the supplies being carried. The trip can get very rough, so if you are prone to seasickness take tablets an hour before sailing. It can also get quite cold on the water.

Several daily ferries ply the narrow straits between Praslin and La Digue. The crossing lasts roughly 30 minutes depending on sea conditions. Monday to Saturday the boats depart Praslin for La Digue at 7h00, 9h30, 10h30, 14h30 and 17h00, and return at 7h45, 10h15, 12h00, 15h30 and 17h45. On Sunday, departure from Praslin to La Digue is at 7h00, 10h30 and 17h00, and return at 7h30, 11h30 and 17h30.

To reach the outer islands by sea, you will need to charter a vessel, which is expensive, or hitch a ride on an island supply ship. The timetable for these ships varies throughout the year and prospective voyagers should contact the agents directly: Island Development Company, PO Box 638, New Port, Victoria, Mahé, tel. 22-4640, fax 22-4467.

The best price for chartering a vessel for a trip to the outer islands can be had by contacting a private charter skipper, who will then arrange for a boat (motorised or sail), supply the vessel and make suggestions as to the best routes and sights to see once there. John Benoiton is arguably the Seychelles' best-known charter skipper. His English is fluent, and he is sensitive to the needs of foreign tourists. Contact him about 60 days before arrival: John Benoiton, c/o PO Box 386, Victoria, Mahé, Seychelles, tel. 32-2126, fax 22-4679.

Glass-bottomed boats are run by many private people and travel agencies. Most go to Ste Anne Marine National Park off Victoria. Even on a tight budget, you should make every attempt to take a trip on one of these boats. Mason's Travel has daily excursions in submersible glass boats with expert guides, lunch, the possibility of snorkelling and a visit to Moyenne Island or Cerf.

Chartering a vessel for a voyage around Mahé, Praslin or the nearby islands of Frégate, Silhouette, Aride and La Digue will be expensive for an individual, but far more affordable if a group of at least four people can be gathered. The luxury yacht *My Way* can be booked through Mason's Travel for trips out of Victoria, but this must be done 60 days before departure. On Praslin speak to Paul Turcotte at Café des Artes, Côte d'Or, tel. 23-2131, about arranging a boat for sightseeing. For cheaper boat hire, just go to the nearest fish market and ask the fishermen if any of them would help, for the appropriately negotiated price of course. Take along your own lunch for the day and be there early, at the latest 6h00.

CAR RENTAL

Hundreds of tourists travel around Mahé and Praslin in hired cars, although Mahé is only 154 square km in size, and Praslin only 40 square km. Not only is it cheaper touring by bus, but also more interesting as you mingle with the local Seychellois.

Driving in the Seychelles is on the left side of the road. The speed limit (which is never enforced) is 40 km/h in urban areas and 60 km/h on national roads. Seychellois usually travel at about 80 km/h outside towns and as low as 20 km/h in developed settlements. Drivers wanting to hire a car must prove that they are over 21 years old and must be in possession of a valid international driver's permit.

Avis, Budget, Europcar and Hertz all have branch offices on Mahé:

Avis: c/o Norman's Car Hire, Riverside, Mount Fleuri, tel. 22-4511

Budget: Beau Vallon Bay Hotel, Bel Ombre Road, tel. 34-4280

Europcar: Beau Vallon Bay or Victoria House, Victoria, tel. 24-7379

Hertz: Revolution Avenue, Victoria, tel. 32-2447

Apart from these international car hire companies, about another 21 smaller firms offer surprisingly good deals on car rental. As with all car hire, the longer you keep the vehicle the lower the daily rate. Cost of hire includes insurance, but not fuel, and you will discover that the vehicle has just enough fuel to reach the nearest garage. Fuel garages are open 6h00-18h00. Mini Mokes are the most commonly hired car, but other makes from Suzuki to Mercedes are also available. If you need a chauffeur, contact Car Hire Operators Association, PO Box 502, Victoria, Mahé, Seychelles, tel. 22-4710.

On Praslin, five companies offer local car hire. Praslin Holiday Car Hire, at Grande Anse, has a good selection of packages: Praslin Holiday Car Hire, Grande Anse, Praslin, Seychelles, tel. 23-3219. Although no official car rental is available on La Digue, you can "borrow" off-road vehicles through La Digue Island Lodge and Choppy's Bungalows.

BICYCLE

Bicycle hire on the granitic islands of the Seychelles is popular and highly recommended. Hotels charge for bicycles per hour, while guest-houses usually charge per day. Pleasant and easy cycling can be had by following the coastal roads on Mahé, Praslin and La Digue. Cycling inland is arduous. Mountain bikes are available and if you venture into the hills you will need every gear on the steep ascents and descents. On Mahé, along the east coast, talk to the owner of La Louise Lodge on La Misère hill, west of Mont Fleuri, tel. 34-4349, for bicycle hire. She even packs sandwiches if you will be away all day. In the west, the receptionist at Auberge Club des Seychelles, Danzilles, tel. 24-7550, will arrange bicycle hire if you let her know 24 hours ahead.

On Praslin, bicycles can be hired from Côte d'Or Bicycle Hire, Côte d'Or (near the Paradise Sun Hotel), Praslin, tel. 23-2071. On La Digue, nearly everyone rides a bicycle. Both guests and casual visitors can hire bicycles from Choppy's Bungalows, Anse Réunion (south of the clinic), La Digue, tel. 23-4224. In better condition are the bicycles for hire at Tarosa Rent-a-Bicycle, La Passe (at the harbour), La Digue, tel. 23-4250.

OX CART

Ox cart rides for pleasure are available on La Digue. They are slow and follow a short route from the pier to La Digue Island Lodge.

HITCHHIKING

Though few visitors try hitchhiking, it is easy, quick and a wonderful experience. However, it is no use trying to hitchhike on islands other than Mahé and Praslin. Anyway, they are small enough to walk around in a few hours. No tourist will stop for a hitchhiker, but almost every islander does. Expect derision from tour groups and a happy reception from locals. Should you choose this way of travelling, expect invitations to meals, bars and family homes. Do not stand at the bus stop, nor simply wait. You must be seen to be making some effort, by walking.

During the week, hitchhikers will find lifts quickly. On weekends it is difficult and time-consuming. You will be offered rides in everything from luxury cars to construction trucks and even empty tour buses. All lifts are free, the only price being that you must answer numerous questions. Certain areas are better for hitchhiking than others. On Mahé, there are two stretches of road to avoid. Along the north-west coast, from North Point to Beau Vallon Bay, is home to the nouveau riches, who look down on tourists carrying backpacks. It is also impossible to hitchhike east from Victoria to Le Rocher: there is nowhere for a vehicle to pull off and the traffic is heavy. Everywhere else on Mahé and Praslin, you will seldom have to wait longer than 10 minutes for a ride. Put your thumb out, smile sweetly and act exhausted.

TOURS

Competition for tourist revenue is fierce in the Seychelles. Tour operators vie with one another to offer the best tours and service at the lowest prices. The Tourist Board frequently receives complaints from tourists who have been conned out of substantial sums of money for a poor quality excursion. Stick to the reputable agencies.

Top of this list is Mason's Travel, which offers visitors the widest choice of excursions in the Seychelles. The highly trained staff speak English, French, Italian, German and Swedish. All clients are collected and returned to their hotels in a luxury coach. Mason's most popular tours, of which every visitor to the islands must experience at least one, are:

Mahé Coach Tour: This enables tourists to see all the main attractions of the island in one day. It includes a trip to the Sir Selwyn Clarke market and souvenir shops in Victoria. Tea is taken beneath the highest peak in the Seychelles, Morne Seychellois, at the island's tea factory. Guides lead travellers through the Botanical Gardens and Craft Village, and to see the building of model ships. Lunch is included and is always at a restaurant serving traditional Creole meals.

Reef Safari Tour: This is the most famous tour. It includes a boat cruise from the Marine Charter Association office in Victoria to the Ste Anne Marine National Park. There you will drift through the magical world of the sea at a depth of 2 m in a specially designed submersible glass boat, directed by professional guides. From the national park you are transferred to Moyenne Island where you are given the opportunity to either relax or be taken snorkelling offshore. Gear is provided and the boat waits while you swim among the parrotfish, angelfish, brightly coloured coral and sometimes even dolphins. A lavish Creole buffet lunch is provided on Moyenne, after which you are free to explore the island with the aid of a detailed map that Mason's provides. Giant tortoises, legends of buried pirate treasure and unspoilt forests will entice even the most jaded of travellers.

Mason's also offers tours to Praslin to visit the lost world of Vallée de Mai, with its rare black parrot and coco de mer trees, and to La Digue to see a working coconut plantation, try for a glimpse of the endangered black paradise flycatcher and have a set lunch beneath the palm-frond roofs of La Digue Island Lodge.

Through Mason's Travel tourists are also able to reach the forested wilderness of Silhouette Island and the millions of birds on Cousin, Aride and Bird islands. There is a special tour to Frégate for visitors hoping to see the rare magpie robin, which is found nowhere else in the world. Creole lunch at the historical Plantation House and plant identification are included in the price.

Contact Mason's Travel when planning your Seychelles trip or visit its offices on Mahé. The staff are attentive and cordial, offer advice and are able to cope with any queries you may have: Mason's Travel, PO Box 459 (or Revolution Avenue), Victoria, Mahé, Seychelles, tel. 32-2642, fax 32-4173.

Orchid Travel and National Travel Agency have most of their tours pre-booked months in advance by international travel agents. It can therefore be difficult finding yourself a place with them. Speak to your local travel agent or write four months in advance for details:

Orchid Travel, PO Box 556, Victoria, Mahé, Seychelles, tel. 22-4953, fax 22-5087

National Travel Agency, PO Box 611, Victoria, Mahé, Seychelles, tel. 22-4900, fax 22-5111

15 VICTORIA

Tucked into the verdant hills of eastern Mahé, Victoria sparkles as the smallest capital city in the world. Originally a fishing village, Victoria rose to prominence during the heady days of the corsairs. It was a frequent stop for the most famous Indian Ocean corsair, Jean François Hodoul. The narrow streets still hint at the era of piracy, treasure and gracious damsels. Victoria is the most attractive capital on all the Indian Ocean islands. Not even the medieval buildings of Antananarivo on Madagascar can capture the imagination as do the alleys and markets of Victoria. The British made Victoria the capital because it has the only port in the Seychelles. The French had initially settled on Ste Anne Island across the bay, but the British saw the military advantage of settling on Mahé. Many of the colonial buildings are still used today, and in the lush forested hills around Victoria there are relics of ancient visitors who stopped here on their now-forgotten voyages.

In the bars and cafés along Independence Avenue, men who would look more at home in the Pirates of Penzance sit drinking chilled beer and whispering over maps. The allure of Victoria is strong; few visitors are ever glad to leave. Many return again and again.

GETTING THERE

The majority of visitors arrive in the Seychelles by air, landing at Seychelles International Airport, about 10 km south of Victoria. You can take a taxi or bus from outside the airport into town or, even better, hitchhike. The taxis line up directly outside the terminal building. Taxi fares are much higher than bus fares. Taxis will drop you in the centre of town, either on Albert Street or Quincy Street. To catch a bus walk out of the terminal building and across the main road. On the western side of the road (remember that vehicles travel on the left side of the road on the Seychelles), about 25 m from the southern exit gate, is the bus stop for the frequent buses between the southern areas of Mahé and Victoria. The buses go to their depot, on the corner of 5th June Avenue and Palm Street, about 100 m to the north of the city centre. To hitchhike from the airport, simply stand at the bus stop and stick your thumb out. This is a quick way of getting into Victoria. In addition to being free, it allows you immediately to meet the locals.

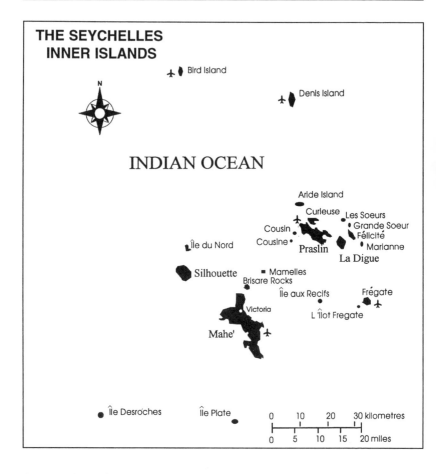

THE SEYCHELLES
INNER ISLANDS

Bird Island

N

Denis Island

INDIAN OCEAN

Aride Island

Curleuse   Les Soeurs
                    Grande Soeur
Cousin   Félicité
Cousine •   Praslin   Marianne
île du Nord   La Digue

Silhouette   ■ Mamelles
Brisare Rocks
          île aux Recifs   Frégate
                        •
Victoria   L 'îlot Fregate

Mahe'

île Desroches   île Plate

0   10   20   30 kilometres

0   5   10   15   20 miles

GETTING AROUND

Getting around Victoria is best done on foot. Tourists arriving from other capitals of the world are inevitably stunned by its miniature size. Within the city centre, known as the Central Ward, visitors will not have to walk more than about 200 m to reach any point of interest. If you plan to see the Bastille or Botanical Gardens you may need transport, but it is much more enjoyable to walk the few kilometres to them.

Taxis for hire in Victoria congregate in the taxi rank outside the public toilets on Albert Street. Another cluster of taxis is found along Quincy Street, opposite the Hindu temple.

1	Victoria House	10	Government Office
2	Bus station	11	Football stadium
3	Sir Selwyn Clarke market	12	Supreme Court
4	Clock tower	13	State House
5	Cathedral of the Immaculate	14	National Library & Museum
	Conception	15	St Paul's Cathedral
6	Freedom Square	16	Botanical Gardens
7	Inner Island ferry harbour	17	Bel Air Cemetery
8	National House	18	Hindu Temple
9	Capuchin Friary		

Hiring a bicycle to explore the city is not a good idea, as traffic is heavy and there are frequent traffic jams.

It is impossible to get lost in Victoria. Arriving from the airport, you travel along the main road, Francis Rachel Street, into the city. At the clock tower, there is a crossing where Francis Rachel becomes Albert Street. To the right is Independence Avenue, where you will find most of the sites of interest to tourists. Left, up State House Avenue, are many of the airlines, banks, the National Library and State House. About 50 m north on Albert Street there is an island which splits the flow of traffic. Vehicles coming from the south must now swing left up Revolution Avenue, where there are numerous travel agencies, tour operators and snack bars. Quincy Street branches right out of Revolution Avenue and passes the Hindu temple. The first road right, after the taxi rank, is Market Street, which has numerous shops and Sir Selwyn Clarke market, and ends in a walkway which takes you back to Albert Street to the east. Victoria's CBD lies between Independence Avenue to the south, Oliver Maradan Street to the north, 5th June Avenue to the east and Harrison Street to the west. The best landmark for orientation is the clock tower or the Cathedral of the Immaculate Conception.

To reach the inter-island ferry harbour, go east on Independence Avenue to Ocean Gate House. Turn left beyond it and continue to the harbour.

TOURIST INFORMATION

The Seychelles Tourist Office is on the ground floor of Independence House in Independence Avenue, tel. 22-5313, fax 22-5131. The staff are capable and helpful. Numerous booklets, pamphlets and maps are available free of charge. Opening hours are Monday to Friday 8h00-12h00 and 13h30-16h00. Both the National Museum on Independence Avenue, opposite the handicraft stalls, and the new Seychelles National Library on Francis Rachel Street, near the Seychelles Cable and Wireless offices, provide excellent information to tourists.

You can also ask anyone on the street for help. The Seychellois are intrigued by tourists who want to meet and mix with them. If you can strike up a friendship with a local, you may be taken to see sites and things that foreigners on tour packages seldom, if ever, get to see. The waitresses at the Pirate's Arms Restaurant on Independence Avenue are particularly helpful in taking a visitor on a tour of the lesser known locations in the forests around Victoria.

Several banks have offices in Victoria. This is the best place to change money in the Seychelles. Many of the larger banks are affiliated to international financial institutions. All banks are required to offer the same exchange rate. Although all banks are also required to have the latest exchange rates easily accessible to tourists, only Banque Française Commerciale (Océan Indien) does this. It has a print-out of the current rates at the foreign exchange counter every day and offers the best service. Banque Française Commerciale (Océan Indien) is on the corner of Albert Street and State House Avenue, tel. 32-3096, fax 32-2676. Nouvobanq, across the road on the corner of State House Avenue and Francis Rachel Street, tel. 22-5011, fax 22-4670, has unhelpful staff. Barclays Bank is efficient but levies high handling charges. There are branches on Albert Street, near the Deepam Cinema, and on Independence Avenue, opposite the National Museum, tel. 22-4101, fax 22-4678. The Bank of Baroda is next door on Albert Street, tel. 32-3038, fax 32-4057. A bank with low handling charges and good service is the Habib Bank on Francis Rachel Street, opposite the fuel station, tel. 22-4371, fax 22-5614. Central Bank is between British Airways and the Bird Island Reservation Centre on Independence Avenue, tel. 22-5200, fax 22-4958.

All the major tour operators and travel agents have their headquarters in Victoria. Most are along Revolution Avenue, a few on State House Avenue and Independence Avenue. The top-rated tour operator on the Seychelles is Mason's Travel. Bunson's Travel is the best place for budget flights and to confirm air tickets:

Mason's Travel (Pty) Ltd, Revolution Avenue, tel. 32-2642, fax 32-4173

Bunson's Travel (Sey) Ltd, Shipping House, Revolution Avenue, tel. 32-2682, fax 32-1322

Other tour operators and travel agents that might be of use to tourists are:

National Travel Agency, Kingsgate House, Independence Avenue, tel. 22-4900, fax 22-5111

Orchid Travel Ltd, Pirate's Arms Building, Independence Avenue, tel. 22-4953, fax 22-5087

Travel Services (Sey) Ltd, Travel Centre, Victoria House, cnr Francis Rachel Street and State House Avenue, tel. 22-2414, fax 32-4010

For Bird, Frégate and Denis islands, visitors must make bookings directly through the relevant promotional offices in Victoria:

Bird Island Reservations, Independence Avenue, tel. 22-4925, fax 22-5074

Frégate Island Reservations, Revolution Avenue, tel. 32-3123, fax 32-4169

Denis Island Reservations, St Joseph Street, tel. 32-3392, fax 32-4192

The main Seychelles post office is on Independence Avenue. To receive poste restante mail, ask at the enquiries counter, to the right as you enter the main door. Queues are common here, and visitors planning to leave Victoria should rather do their postage at one of the village post offices which are just as efficient. The main post office in Victoria is open Monday to Friday 8h00-16h00; Saturday 8h00-12h00.

Long-distance telephone calls, telegrams, telexes and faxes can be sent from the Cable and Wireless offices on Francis Rachel Street, opposite the new National Library building. The office is open 24 hours a day. It is possible to book a call or send a telegram by telephone: tel. 32-2221, fax 32-2777.

There are a number of well-stocked bookshops and newsagents in Victoria. For daily newspapers, periodicals and imported magazines, the best place to visit is the newsstand in the back of the Pirate's Arms Restaurant. You can reach the restaurant by walking down the arcade that leads to the Museum Shop. Other bookshops that stock paperbacks, travel guides and large-format books are:

Librairie Ste Fidèle, Oliver Maradam Street, tel. 32-3463 (the staff can also arrange colour pressing and printing)

Space, Huteau Lane, tel. 22-4531

Jivan Imports (Pty) Ltd, Albert Street, tel. 32-2310

Visitors will also find a number of excellent photo-books for sale at the offices of the Seychelles Tourist Board, at the eastern end of Independence Avenue.

It is not necessary to arrive armed with rolls of colour film, batteries and spares. Photographic shops in the Seychelles are well supplied. They all have a wide range of film, batteries and spares and provide repair and developing facilities. Paul Turcotte on Praslin is the only professional photographer on the islands. Photographers arriving on assignment can contact him for advice and assistance at the Cafés des Arts on Praslin, south of the Paradise Sun Hotel, or at PO Box 698, Côte d'Or, Praslin, Seychelles, tel. 23-2131.

Good photographic shops in Victoria are:

One-hour Photo, Kingsgate House, Independence Avenue, tel. 22-4966

Kim Koon (Pty) Ltd, Kingsgate House, Independence Avenue, tel. 22-4966

Photo and Video Centre, Quincy Street, tel. 32-1542

Only two private doctors are registered in Victoria:

Dr Albert Maurice, Castor Road, tel. 32-3866 (a surgery)

Dr K Chetty, Revolution Avenue, tel. 32-1911 (a private clinic)

Medical attention is also available at any of the many government hospitals scattered about Mahé. The hospital which serves Victoria, located at Mont Fleuri, is modern, with highly trained and motivated medical staff: Victoria Hospital, West of Chemin Mont Fleuri, Mont Fleuri, tel. 22-4400. Go along Chemin Mont Fleuri and take the first road right after passing the French Embassy. The hospital is along the right-hand fork of this road. A 24-hour ambulance service can be summoned by dialling 999 and asking for the control room.

There are also state clinics in the smaller settlements, plus one just outside Victoria: English River Clinic, 5th June Avenue, tel. 22-4400.

Dentists can be contacted via the Victoria Hospital.

There is a well-stocked pharmacy in Victoria House, at the top end of State House Avenue. This is Behram's Pharmacy, but is somewhat difficult to locate. Walk west up State House Avenue. At the old library turn left and go into Passage des Palmes; the chemist is just inside the passage. Most prescription remedies are, however, supplied by the hospital dispensary following a consultation.

State-controlled libraries are extensive and well staffed. Their books on Seychelles topics are freely accessible to tourists, but may not be removed from the premises without written permission. At the old National Library, visitors may borrow books if they put down a small deposit with the Chief Librarian. Both the National Museum and National Archives hold fascinating manuscripts, maps and journals:

National Library, Francis Rachel Street, tel. 32-1072

National Library, State House Avenue, tel. 22-4780

National Museum, Independence Avenue, tel. 22-5253

National Archives (along 5th June Avenue and onto the North-east Point Road), La Bastille, tel. 22-4777

Information on culture is obtainable by visiting the National Arts Council, at Mont Fleuri.

Air ticket reservations must be confirmed several days before departure. You can ask your hotel's reception desk to do this, or personally visit the airline representative in Victoria:

Aeroflot, Pirate's Arms Building, Independence Avenue, tel. 22-5005

British Airways, Kingsgate House, Independence Avenue, tel. 22-4910

Air France, Kingsgate House, Independence Avenue, tel. 32-2414

Kenya Airways, Revolution Avenue, tel. 32-2989

Air Mauritius, Kingsgate House, Independence Avenue, tel. 32-2414

Air Seychelles, Victoria House, Francis Rachel Street, tel. 22-5220

Inter-island flights must be booked via the respective island's reservations office. Arrival and departure times for these island flights can be ascertained via Flight Enquiries, tel. 37-3051.

Daily schooners of the inter-island ferry service ply the passage between Mahé and the smaller islands of Praslin and La Digue. Hiring a boat for fishing or long-distance voyaging must be done either privately or through a reputable agent. Contact Mason's Travel in Revolution Avenue for assistance in this regard. Getting away from the Seychelles aboard a cargo vessel can be difficult unless you have some previous experience.

Inter-island Ferry Service (the schooner *William Rose*), Victoria harbour, ferry terminal (go east on Independence Avenue, round the circle and left to reach the ferry quay), tel. 23-3229

La Belle Edma Ferry Service, Victoria harbour, ferry terminal, tel. 23-4013

La Belle Praslinoise Ferry Service, Victoria harbour, ferry terminal, tel. 23-3238

To try to get a berth aboard an outward-bound commercial vessel, it will be necessary to visit the shipping offices of the various agents. Take along any nautical qualification you have, it will be useful:

Mahé Shipping Company Ltd, Shipping House, tel. 32-2100

Savy Harry and Company, 5th June Avenue Street, tel. 32-2120

Chartering a yacht or motorboat is best done by speaking to the skippers at the Marine Charter Association, on 5th June Avenue, tel. 32-2126. Visitors with yachting experience wanting to cruise the islands should approach the boat owners of the nearby Seychelles Yacht Club, tel. 32-2362.

THINGS TO DO

Because Victoria is so little, it takes less than two hours to complete a comprehensive tour of it on foot. A recommended tour commences at the circle to the south of the city where Francis Rachel Street, 5th June Avenue and Lantanier Road intersect. In the middle of the circle is a sculpture of four sailfish joined together at their swords. Keep left, past the New Apostolic Church sign, and go along Francis Rachel Street towards the city centre. The impressive new building of the Seychelles

National Library is on the right. Continuing north, pass the Cable and Wireless offices before reaching a small alley on the left leading to the Islamic Centre and mosque. Show respect by taking off your shoes before entering and by washing at the taps provided. The mosque is closed on Fridays.

After passing the petrol station and football stadium you will see an old building set in a park of evergreens and flowers. This is the seat of the Seychelles Supreme Court. In the garden edging Francis Rachel Street is a bust of Pierre Poivre, meaning "Peter Pepper". Born in 1719, he spent most of his adult life in the Indian Ocean region, introduced spices to the Seychelles and classified many of the floral species of the islands.

Now you will come to the clock tower, in the middle of the road. This clock is a miniature replica of the famous Big Ben in London. Turn left here and go up State House Avenue. At its top end you will find the enormous gate to State House blocking your way. In the State House gardens lies the tomb of the legendary governor Queau de Quincy. Visitors are not permitted entry unless they have an official government pass or are accompanied by an accredited guide. To the left of the gate is the National Library in a traditional Creole mansion. The library is worth a visit even if just to explore the passages and rooms. Return down State House Avenue and turn left at the clock tower into Albert Street.

Pass the taxi rank and follow the road which curves to the left, Revolution Avenue. On the corner is St Paul's Cathedral and west of the cathedral are the police headquarters. Several airlines and tour agents have their representatives in offices along Revolution Avenue. Continue west as far as Chemin Bel Air. Here turn left and walk along the road to the decaying stone walls of the historical Bel Air cemetery. Now overgrown and neglected, the cemetery is still worth a visit. Take the narrow grass path that leads through the cemetery, up a few steps and ends in a cluster of tombstones beneath tall trees. The long grave to the left is that of the "Giant of Mahé". Said to be over 3 m tall, this man was poisoned by superstitious locals in 1874. Directly beneath the banyan tree is the grave of Jean François Hodoul. The gravestone is decorated with an etching of his ship, the *Apollon*. Next to him is buried his long-suffering wife. (See the section on Anse à la Mouche for more information on Jean François Hodoul.)

Return to Revolution Avenue and turn left into Quincy Street. Another, smaller taxi rank is situated along this road, as is an art gallery and the magnificent Hindu Vishnu Temple. The temple is open to visitors, who should show the proper respect. Remove your shoes before entering and do not walk into the sanctuary.

North of the taxi rank, turn right along Market Street, which threads its way through an alley of ancient shops to the Sir Selwyn Clarke market. Named after a British governor, the market is a chaotic mess of fish, spices, fresh produce and curios. Prices are negotiable, but goods are much cheaper in the rural areas. This is however where most of the locals do their shopping and there is an impressive selection of goods on sale. Turn left from Market Street, where it becomes a promenade, into Church Street. Where Church Street meets Oliver Maradan Street is the Roman Catholic Cathedral of the Immaculate Conception. You will hear its bells ringing every hour as you wander about Victoria. Built in 1933, the cathedral is alongside the beautiful Roman Catholic Mission (Cappucin Friary). Visitors are free to wander about in the quiet gardens and rest in the shade of ancient trees. The grandeur of the mission building is fading now, but there are still brothers working the apiary and occasionally teaching the catechism to children. They enjoy receiving visitors and may even offer you lunch, eaten in the cavernous dining hall.

From the cathedral, go east on Oliver Maradan Street and then turn right into Albert Street, which is busy with cloth vendors, supermarkets, curios shops and banks. A side trip into one of the Indian-owned textile shops is a journey into the pages of history. The material is cheap, colourful and a good buy. Budget travellers might consider buying a length on which to sit, lie or wrap themselves in; the fabric also makes good tablecloths when you return home. Stroll past the taxi rank and turn left down Independence Avenue. On the corner is the colonial Liberty House, home to the post office. Across the road is a large informal market where curios are sold, and Lakaz Home Industries Co-op. Behind these vendors is a small statue of Queen Victoria. On the left is the National Museum, next to the post office.

The National Museum is open Monday to Friday 9h00-17h00; Saturday 9h00-12h00. There are several interesting exhibits, notably of pirate and slave history. At the entrance you will see the Stone of Possession, which claimed the Seychelles for France in 1756. Tourists can also view a host of cultural and art artefacts. The natural history displays contain giant tortoises, robber crabs and the now extinct Seychelles crocodile. The curator has endless stories and anecdotes about Seychellois history, gleaned from her hours of research. She may even agree to take you on a walk through town to the Bel Air cemetery and show you the important graves.

Beyond the museum is the Pirate's Arms Restaurant. Crowded around the popular restaurant are banks, airline offices, curio shops and bars. Upstairs from the Pirate's Arms is the French Cultural Centre, which keeps a great deal of French historical literature about the Seychelles. Beyond the Seychelles Tourist Office Information Centre is a circle in the road. In the middle of the circle, known as Freedom Square, is a sculpture resembling three fishtails. Created by immigrant Italian artist Lorenzo Appiani, it symbolises wings which represent Africa, Asia and Europe, origins of the modern Seychellois nation.

Straight on, Independence Avenue would take you past Ocean Gate House to the fishing port and inter-island ferry harbour. The tuna quay and fishing harbour are on Laurier Avenue, at the end of this road.

Turning right along 5th June Avenue, pass the amusement centre, slot machines and the offices of the Hydrographic and Topographic Centre of the Seychelles. Along the east side of the road is the small-craft port and Marine Charter Association. Opposite the Marine Charter parking lot is a statue commemorating what has become known as Liberation Day, 5 June 1977, the day of René's coup. Resembling a man with arms reaching to the sky while breaking chains, the statue is a bit of a disappointment for such a momentous occasion. The Creole name for the statue is "zonm lib", meaning "free man".

Beyond the trailer office of the Sail Training Scheme, tourists may visit Veuve Recording Studio, adjacent to the fairground. The fairground is hectic over weekends and on Family Day, but is a lot of fun.

This ends the city tour of Victoria, but nearby points of interest extend the tour to about four hours.

To the south, about 1 km along Chemin Mont Fleuri, is the Botanical Gardens (Jardin Botanique), open daily 6h00-18h00. The entrance is opposite the Creole-style building of the Ministry of the Environment, Economics, Planning and External Relations. Trails wind through the carefully tended gardens. Behind the granite boulders are filthy tortoise pens with a few desultory-looking captives. This is the only blight on this otherwise magical garden. There are a few of the almost mythical coco de mer palms and an explosion of colour in the orchid house. Deep in the tranquillity of the gardens, and not easy to find, is the

Sapin Cafeteria. Tucked away behind the flamingoes and lily ponds, it offers a good lunch and light snack menu.

North of Victoria, the road towards remote North-east Point is also good for a walk. Beware of the lunatic drivers though; there is no pavement beyond the housing estates. The National Archives are roughly 2 km from the bus depot on Palm Street, in the old La Bastille building. JLB Smith, of coelacanth fame, stayed in this building while researching the fishes of the Indian Ocean. A small but fascinating traditional craft museum has been established in the gardens. There are displays of sugar cane cultivation, a copra mill, handmade coffee peeler and rope-making machine. Scattered around the lush garden are other historical exhibits: a cinnamon distillery, ships' cannons and a boatyard. Inside, the building is rather austere. On the second floor is the public reading room, staffed with two employees to help researchers.

ACCOMMODATION

Visitors will not find any accommodation in the centre of Victoria. Tour package arrivals will immediately be transferred to their hotels, usually on the western side of Mahé. Independent travellers will find suitable accommodation beyond the city limits. The recommended places are La Louise Lodge to the south, Manresa Guesthouse to the north, and the small Mountain Rise Hotel in the hills of Bel Air.

La Louise Lodge (low tariff)

Located in the hills about 4 km from central Victoria, this family-run establishment is regarded as the best guesthouse on the Seychelles. Take the bus from Palm Street bus depot in Victoria. The Port Glaud bus which goes via La Misère will drop you off at the lane that leads down to the guesthouse. Alternatively, catch any bus that travels to the south of the island: Anse aux Pins, Takamaka, Anse Royale or even Baie Lazare. As you pass the cemetery on the right, shout "Dévant", and get off outside the old age home. Walk to the circle and turn right up La Misère hill. About 1 km up, turn left down a narrow lane. At the bottom is the entrance to La Louise Lodge.

With nine immaculate bedrooms, all with air-conditioners, bathrooms and splendid sea views, this place is a favourite with repeat guests. High season is August-January. The owner does all the cooking, and her chicken Creole is famous among Indian Ocean travellers. A huge breakfast and delicious dinner are included in the rate. The bar is popular with locals. La Louise Lodge can arrange a tour guide for forest walks, as well as deep-sea fishing and excursions. Its marine park tour prices are considerably lower than those of similar packages offered by travel agents. A laundry service is available. La Louise Lodge cashes traveller's cheques and changes hard currency. The owners are friendly people who love mixing with foreign visitors. They provide guests with a free airport tranfer on request. Weddings seem to be their biggest earner, and if you happen to be there when they cater for a local wedding, you will be invited to attend. If this happens, be sure to go, the experience is thoroughly enjoyable.

Bookings must be made at least 60 days in advance:

La Louise Lodge, PO Box 193, La Louise, Mahé, Seychelles, tel. 34-4349.

Manresa Guesthouse *(medium tariff)*

Near the tiny settlement of Anse Étoile, this small, rather untidy guesthouse is perched above the bay within sight of Victoria. Offering bed and breakfast in spartan rooms, this guesthouse is a far cry from the clean and quiet La Louise Lodge. Managed by the owner, who claims to have many years' experience in international hotels, this accommodation is only recommended for hardy travellers. To reach the Manresa, take any bus going north from Victoria to Anse Étoile, La Gogue, North-east Point, Glacis or Beau Vallon via Glacis. Get off where the road branches left to La Gogue and right towards North-east Point. The guesthouse is on the corner to the right. There are five guest rooms, all with bathrooms and sea views. They are mostly used by French and German guests.

The meals reflect the taste of the European clientele. A small outside restaurant offers pleasant views over the bay. During April and May, sandflies plague the Manresa Guesthouse and you will need insect repellant. The nearest swimming beach is a 20-minute walk to the north. Do not expect much assistance in tourist matters, the owner is always too busy.

High season is around Easter, and July and August. Reservations are advisable 30 days in advance. Only Visa or cash is accepted as payment:

Manresa Guesthouse, Anse Étoile, Mahé, Seychelles, tel./fax 24-1388.

Mountain Rise Hotel *(high tariff)*

Tucked into a fold of the hills near Sans Souci, this hotel is a mere five minutes' bus ride from the capital, but 200 m above its heat. It was converted from a private home into a hotel only two years ago. Take the Sans Souci or Port Glaud via Sans Souci bus from Victoria through the dense rainforests. Ask the driver to drop you off at the Mountain Rise Hotel. The first thing that strikes visitors here are the awesome granite cliffs behind the hotel. The views over Victoria are spectacular, as is the swimming pool which perches on the edge of a steep hill. Seven double rooms with bathrooms, fans and excellent views are offered. Included in the price is a small breakfast.

High season is December, April, June, July and August. Prices are high, but the service and comfort are excellent. Aiming at exclusivity, this hotel is well on the way to getting a star classification. Should you decide to eat dinner at the hotel, inform the owner's wife at least five hours before. Vegetarians are well catered for. During summer, evening barbecues are the norm.

Car hire at a preferential rate can be arranged, as can local excursions. Idyllic swimming is available, 10 minutes away at Beau Vallon Bay. There is a cosy, well-stocked bar and videos to watch. Two bus tours per week are arranged by the management.

Credit cards may be used, and both traveller's cheques and cash are accepted forms of payment. Book about 30 days before arriving and confirm via telephone or fax 15 days before:

Mountain Rise Hotel, PO Box 747, Victoria, Mahé, Seychelles, tel. 22-5145, fax 22-5503.

PLACES TO EAT

At the budget end of the market, travellers will find suitable light meals and snacks all over Victoria. There are no top-class restaurants in the capital.

For really tasty and reasonably priced meals, visit the dining room of *La Louise Lodge* on La Misère hill. Phone to book a table, at least 12 hours ahead, tel. 34-4349. A place worth travelling to is the expensive, but exclusive, *Kyoto Japanese Restaurant* on Anse Étoile, near the Anse Étoile police station, tel. 24-1337. The *Pirate's Arms Restaurant* on Independence Avenue has the most reasonably priced lunches and light snacks in town. The varied menu has something for most tastes and even includes dishes for vegetarians. For cheap, tasty and filling meals try lunch at the *Seychelles Yacht Club* on 5th June Avenue.

On Francis Rachel Street is *Bon Appetit Takeaways*, which offers a menu of grilled burgers, fried chips and a few traditional rice dishes.

At the *Marine Charter Association,* a small takeaway offers lavish servings of such delicious delicacies as octopus curry, chicken Creole and shark steaks. The prices are low, and the long queues at lunch time testify to its reputation. *Lovenut Café* on Revolution Avenue serves light lunches. On Quincy Street, the *Moncherry Takeaway* has a limited range of fast foods. On Independence Avenue next to the Seychelles Tourist Office is *L'Amiral Restaurant.* It has a good selection of dishes that are costly but filling.

The market has a great variety of fresh produce. Up each street and down each lane, visitors will find some little restaurant or café selling traditional or Continental food. Simply set off, and you will soon find the diner that suites you.

THINGS TO BUY

All traditional Seychellois crafts and curios can be bought in Victoria: everything from coco de mer nuts through local floral perfumes to printed T-shirts and spices. Apart from the official tourist shops that offer duty-free items at inflated prices, there are also a number of hawkers trading on the streets of Victoria.

Outside the supreme court building, on Independence Avenue and Francis Rachel Street, street vendors have tables laden with curios. Bargaining is the norm, so negotiate hard and compare prices. At Sir Selwyn Clarke market, curios and traditional items for sale are behind the fresh produce stalls.

In the state-controlled tourist shops, visitors will find the same items, but at much higher prices. In addition to the usual array of curios, other more valuable handicrafts are also found. Shops to try for high-quality silk-screening and works of art are:

Codevar, Camion Hall, Albert Street, tel. 32-3161

Antigone Trading, Victoria House, cnr Francis Rachel Street and State House Avenue, tel. 22-5443

Spectra Designs, Hangard Street, tel. 32-2127

The Museum Shop, Pirate's Arms Arcade, Independence Avenue

Lakaz Home Industries Co-op, Independence Avenue

Jivan Imports, cnr Albert and Market Streets, tel. 32-2310

16 NORTH MAHÉ

For ease of reference I have divided Mahé into a northern and a southern section: north Mahé extends south from North Point to an imaginary line that stretches from Grande Anse in the west, across Montagne Planeau (670 m) to the Seychelles International Airport in the east.

Mahé is the largest of the Seychelles islands. It consists of granite and is about 27 km long and 8 km wide. It is to Mahé that most tourists to the Seychelles come. The international airport is situated on the east coast, about 10 km from the world's smallest capital, Victoria. Much of the island is covered in lush forest, granite cliffs and cascading streams. The highest mountain on the Seychelles, Morne Seychellois (905 m), is located on Mahé. Around the coast are an estimated 70 swimming beaches, the most popular of which are Beau Vallon Bay, Anse Royal, Anse à la Mouche and Anse Takamaka.

First named Abundance Island – the reason will immediately be obvious to visitors – Mahé was later renamed in honour of the most famous of French Indian Ocean governors, Mahé de Labourdonnais.

Good tarred roads service the entire length of both the east and west coasts, while six secondary tarred roads cross the island at strategic intervals along its 27 km length. Apart from the wonderful beaches and mountain forests, travels around Mahé will also reveal colonial churches, craft workshops and sites of historical interest. Visitors prepared to shoulder a day-pack and set off into the forests have a choice of 14 trails, at least three of which are a must to experience the beauty and diversity of Mahé.

To explore the coastline of northern Mahé, you have the choice of hiring a car, taking public transport, hitchhiking or walking. Hiring a car is the most expensive; public transport is cheap and reliable. Hitchhiking is easy and the best way of meeting locals, while walking is suitable if you have the time and stamina. If using the bus, take the Glacis or Beau Vallon Bay one from the Palm Street bus depot in Victoria. Hitchhikers should walk north of the bus depot and wait near the pull-off outside the English River School.

Travelling along the north-east coast visitors arrive at the narrow beach of **North-East Point**. The ocean here is rather exposed and sand-

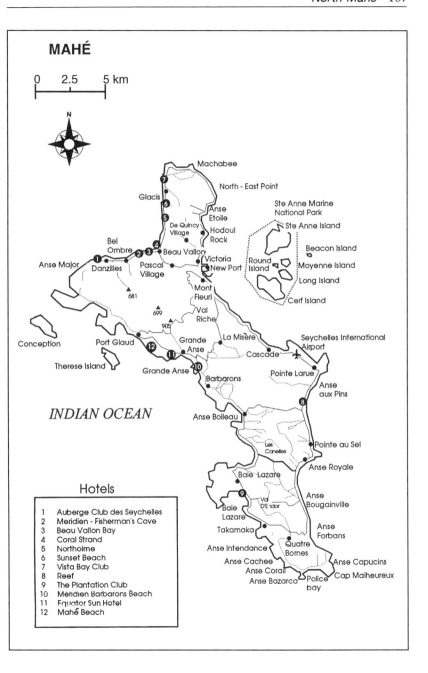

MAHÉ

0   2.5   5 km

N

Machabee

North - East Point

Glacis

Anse
Etoile

Ste Anne Marine
National Park

De Quincy
Village

Hodoul
Rock

Ste Anne Island

Bel
Ombre

Beau Vallon

Beacon Island

Anse Major

Danzilles

Pascal
Village

Victoria
New Port

Round
Island

Moyenne Island

Long Island

681

Mont
Fleuri

Cerf Island

699

Val
Riche

905

La Misère

Seychelles International
Airport

Conception

Port Glaud

Grande
Anse

Cascade

Therese Island

Grande Anse

Pointe Larue

Barbarons

Anse
aux Pins

INDIAN OCEAN

Anse Boileau

Pointe au Sel

Les
Canelles

Baie Lazare

Anse Royale

Anse
Bougainville

Baie
Lazare

Val
D'Endor

Takamaka

Anse
Forbans

Anse Intendance

Quatre
Bornes

Anse Cachee

Anse Capucins

Anse Corail

Cap Maiheureux

Anse Bazarca

Police
bay

Hotels

1	Auberge Club des Seychelles
2	Meridien - Fisherman's Cove
3	Beau Vallon Bay
4	Coral Strand
5	Northolme
6	Sunset Beach
7	Vista Bay Club
8	Reef
9	The Plantation Club
10	Meridien Barbarons Beach
11	Equator Sun Hotel
12	Mahé Beach

flies are a biting nuisance. Stop at Kreol Fleurage Perfumerie. The owner, a German "nose" who once worked for some of the largest fashion houses in Europe, is a delightful man, full of philosophy and amusing anecdotes. The perfumes are made by himself, according to secret recipes that utilise the flowers, spices and trees that abound in the hill forests of Mahé. Those made and sold are Exotic (containing 42 plant extracts), Bwanwar Floral (38 plant extracts), Bambou, Spicy and Ambre Vert (32 plant extracts). Prices are considerably lower than in curio shops.

Around the northern point of Mahé there are numerous secluded little white beaches that are worth visiting. You will need to walk down from the road, but chances are that you will have the beach all to yourself – a real haven on heavily populated Mahé.

The Vista Bay Club Hotel (medium tariff) is located near the northernmost point of the island: PO Box 622, Glacis, Mahé, Seychelles, tel. 26-1333.

Continuing down the west coast, you arrive at Mahé's most exclusive hotel: Sunset Beach Hotel.

Sunset Beach Hotel (high tariff)

This gracious, Dutch-owned hotel with one of the most beautiful locations on Mahé caters to an exclusive set of holiday-makers. The hotel is also home to the Dutch Consul to the Seychelles. A secluded villa offers privacy to the likes of British aristocracy and tennis star Stefan Edberg, who makes an annual trip to the islands. The hotel has 17 sea-facing luxury rooms and six suites, and capable, if demure, staff. All rooms are air-conditioned, with bathrooms en suite, telephones and private patios. The restaurant offers a wide selection of Creole and international dishes, and caters for vegetarians. The owner grows most of the hotel's vegetables and fruit on a plot near the hotel. He is delighted to conduct guests on a short tour of his "farm".

A swimming pool, gym and private beach make the Sunset Beach Hotel highly recommended for the more affluent visitor in search of good service, comfort and style. Do note, however, that no children under the age of 10 are allowed. Also, when booking accommodation, a 30% non-refundable deposit must be made into the hotel's overseas account, and the verification submitted:

Sunset Beach Hotel, PO Box 372, Victoria, Mahé, Seychelles, tel. 26-1111, fax 26-1221.

South of the Sunset Beach Hotel near the Northolme Telephone Exchange is a concrete road going east, inland. Walking along this road is enjoyable and enables visitors to see **La Gogue Reservoir**, forest communities and cinnamon harvesters, and find peace and silence in the hills. Follow the steep concrete road, which later becomes a gravel track and skirts several forest dwellings. The people are unused to seeing foreigners walking here and you are bound to get a warm reception which usually includes a Seybrew beer and something to eat. Where the track loops back down towards the main road, take the path that continues straight on into the trees. This path enters the cool forest and skirts another remote house whose inhabitants are cinnamon gatherers. You will hear their pounding of the bark. Although initially reserved, they quickly respond to smiles. An evening spent with them will be a memorable experience for those fortunate enough to be invited to stay.

Passion fruit grows profusely here, and wild pigs grunt their way through the dense undergrowth. Continue past the concrete water tank to the ridge above La Gogue Reservoir. From the ridge, the grassy trail drops to the very edge of the quiet dam. By skirting north around the dam, walkers arrive at the tarred road near the dam wall. You can take a bus from here to Anse Étoile, and then either south to Victoria or north again, back to where you started.

Back on the west coast – proceeding south – is the legendary Northolme Hotel and restaurant.

Northolme Hotel (high tariff)

Destination of literati, the intelligentsia and the wealthy, Northolme Hotel has been visited by such greats as Somerset Maugham, Ian Fleming, Noel Coward and any number of Europe's jet set. The German Consul is housed here. Yet the hotel has remained largely unaffected by its fame. Its atmosphere is one of serenity and commitment, and although the management can be rather off-handed, the service is of a high standard. There are 20 air-conditioned rooms overlooking the sea, a romantic open-air restaurant and scuba diving facilities. The Marine Divers shop near the reception area caters for all levels of divers. Prices are high, but the opportunity to dive off this coast should not be missed. Reservations for accommodation are seldom necessary, unless you want a specific room, but be assured that you will be better received if you arrive with a letter of confirmation, and in a taxi. Backpackers and budget travellers are not encouraged.

Northolme Hotel, PO Glacis, Mahé, Seychelles, tel. 26-1222, fax 26-1223.

South of Northolme Hotel, one travels alongside the turquoise sea past villas and mansions to the settlement of Beau Vallon Bay. This is Mahé's tourist locale par excellence. You will find more holiday-makers here than locals, prices are higher than anywhere else on the island, and there is a feast of water sports and numerous hotels. The pirate site at Bel Ombre, on the north-west coast, is reached via Beau Vallon Bay.

BEAU VALLON BAY

From Victoria you can reach Beau Vallon Bay by taking the Glacis-Beau Vallon bus, or the one going directly to Beau Vallon-Bel Ombre over the mountains. Both these routes are served by buses departing about every 30 minutes from the Victoria bus depot. Hitchhiking along the road over the mountains is relatively easy and you should not have to wait longer than about 10 minutes for a lift.

There is a branch of Barclays Bank near the police station, at the western end of the main road through the village. Emergency medical and dental treatment is available from the Beau Vallon Clinic, northwest of the police station.

There are quite a few curio shops. Most are worth a look, but remember to negotiate the price, even if there is a price tag. Macouti Souvenirs and Antonio Gallery are on the road going east towards Victoria. Past the Coral Strand Hotel is Papillon Souvenir Boutique, a small shop with a good selection of high-quality products at reasonable prices. The young counter assistants are also an excellent source for finding accommodation with a local family and for information about the Seychellois nightlife in the area. At the northern entrance to Beau Vallon beach is the studio of batik expert Ron Gerlach. He has a variety of interesting batiks and will even print on request a specific item, if given enough time. Across the road is the Boat House, where model ships are sold. Although the selection is not as extensive as in Mauritius, there is a good offering of work. As a guide, bargain at least 30% off the asking price. Your purchase will be packed in protective paper and put into a box marked "fragile", which is acceptable as hand luggage on all airlines.

The nightlife of Beau Vallon is surprisingly quiet. La Perle Noire Restaurant sometimes offers dancing over the weekend and during the high season. Most of the patrons are foreigners and the music is distinctly European. Far more enjoyable, and frequented by the islanders, is the Tropicana Disco. Situated on the beach near the Boat House, this disco is strongly recommended. The doors open around 21h30, and by midnight there is no sitting room. Be assured that you will not be left alone for long. Within minutes some of the Seychellois will approach you and ask that you join them and their friends. Dancing and drinking continues until about 4h30, when people make their way home, onto the beach or into the coconut groves!

Accommodation

Accommodation is easy to find in and around Beau Vallon Bay. Aware of the high demand for lodgings, both international organisations and local people offer rooms. Obviously the tourist hotels are much more expensive, but offer more activities. Private accommodation with a local family can be far more enjoyable, not to mention cheaper, than a hotel. Visitors' own preferences will determine their choice.

Beau Vallon Bay Beach Resort (medium-high tariff)

Once part of the Seychelles Hotels Group, this large hotel has recently been acquired by the Malaysian syndicate, Berjaya. Perched on the edge of a sparkling sea, this hotel is the favoured destination of package tours and families. Free welcome cocktails make tourists feel special and the attention of staff at this hotel is renowned. Residents are issued with a 20% discount "fun card" for all motorised water sports, and have the opportunity to visit the other affiliated hotels: the Mahé Beach, further south-west, and the Praslin Beach on Praslin Island. Water sports are varied at the Beau Vallon Bay Beach Resort. Marine Divers offers guests one free introductory dive, but only unqualified divers may make use of this offer, otherwise you pay the full fee. Glass-bottomed boat excursions are also available, as are windsurfers, paddle boats and dinghies. Parasailing is one of the high-adrenalin, high-expense pursuits on offer at the resort.

There are 183 rooms, all with air-conditioners, television and bathrooms. Although the rooms are quite small, they are comfortable. The major disappointment is that none is sea-facing (odd for a beach resort). The rate normally includes half-board. Special tariffs apply for honeymoon couples. The Chinese or Italian restaurants offer an à la carte menu and Le Grill serves light lunches. Business and conference facilities are available. The hotel staff are able to arrange island tours, car hire, baby-sitting and safe deposit boxes. Traveller's cheques may be cashed, credit cards used for payment and foreign currency exchanged at reception. Reservations are vital, at least 90 days in advance:

Berjaya Beau Vallon Bay Beach Resort, PO Box 550, Victoria, Mahé, Seychelles, tel. 24-7141, fax 24-7606.

Coral Strand Hotel (high tariff)

The Coral Strand Hotel is a far cry from the efficiency and atmosphere of the Beau Vallon Bay Beach Resort. The hotel offers a good selection of water sports, and slightly better currency exchange rates, but this hardly makes up for the often rude staff and apathetic management. Visitors are advised to consider one of the other hotels before selecting the Coral Strand.

Coral Strand Hotel, PO Box 400, Victoria, Mahé, Seychelles, tel. 24-7036, fax 24-7517.

Vacoa Village (medium tariff)

At the northern entrance to the village of Beau Vallon, the recently renovated Vacoa Village is aimed primarily at self-catering visitors. There is, however, a restaurant which offers breakfast, light lunches and delicious dinners. The 11 furnished apartments, each with a private balcony, overlook the wide sweep of Beau Vallon Bay. The hotel has a mini-golf course, swimming pool and caring staff. Book well ahead for this serene accommodation set in a lush tropical garden:

Vacoa Village, PO Box 401, Beau Vallon, Mahé, Seychelles, tel. 26-1130, fax 26-1446.

Other medium-tariff accommodation worth considering in and around Beau Vallon Bay includes:

Beau Vallon Bungalows, PO Beau Vallon, Mahé, Seychelles, tel. 24-7382

Panorama Relais des Îles, PO Beau Vallon, Mahé, Seychelles, tel. 24-7300

Villa Madonna Guesthouse, PO Beau Vallon, Mahé, Seychelles, tel. 24-7403

Locating accommodation with a local family requires legwork. You will need to ask around for assistance. Staff in the curio shops on the road bypassing the police station are usually helpful. Alternatively, ask at the houses along the road in which the Hibiscus Restaurant is. These local families will make every effort to offer you a bed. Included in the budget price is breakfast and dinner, laundry and a wonderful chance to mingle with the Beau Vallon fishing families. Also speak to them if you would rather go out fishing with them than spend hundreds on a resort boat.

Places to eat

Finding a place to eat, outside of the hotel dining rooms, is hardly a problem in Beau Vallon. Top spot is the famous *La Perle Noire Restaurant*. The entrance to the restaurant is near the Coral Strand Hotel on Beau Vallon Beach Road. The menu is extensive, with numerous Creole dishes, and reasonably priced. Reservations are necessary, at least 48 hours in advance, tel. 24-7046.

Nearby, along the same road, is the *Coco d'Or Restaurant*. The speciality is seafood. The biggest attraction to eating at Coco d'Or is that it offers enormous set menus at good rates. The staff are attentive, talkative and able to speak several languages. Reservations are not necessary, but you will have to get there by at least 19h30 if you want a good table.

Overlooking the beautiful Beau Vallon beach is the *Hibiscus Restaurant*. With outside tables on the sand, palm trees and a tranquil view, eating at the Hibiscus is an experience not to be missed. In comparison to the other, more formal, restaurants, prices here are low, the servings huge and the selection good. The seafood and chicken dishes are recommended. At lunch time it is almost impossible to find a seat, but the evenings usually see a few empty tables until about 21h00.

At *La Fontaine Restaurant*, tel. 24-7104, opposite Le Diable des Mers Diving Club, visitors have the choice of takeaways or sit-down meals. There is a big difference in price between the two. The food is the same, but you pay a high price for the rather mediocre service. The menu is, however, exhaustive, and you will always be able to find something suitable to eat.

Next door is a small snack bar, at which you can buy ice-creams, pastries and a few groceries. Self-catering visitors would do well to shop at the *Beau Vallon Supermarket,* near the clinic, which has well-stocked shelves, fresh bread, fruit, vegetables and tinned foods. At the northern end of the village, *M Bamboche Store* has a few tinned goods, fresh fish and an assortment of liquid refreshments.

BEL OMBRE

West of Beau Vallon Bay is the road leading to the mysterious and legendary area of Bel Ombre. From Victoria you can take a Bel Ombre bus, or take the Beau Vallon bus, get off at the police station in Beau Vallon and hitchhike west, past the entrance to the Beau Vallon Bay Beach Resort. The reputation of this region is based on the legends surrounding the last Indian Ocean pirate, Olivier Le Vasseur, nick-named La Buse (the Buzzard).

After a severe tropical storm in 1923, a certain Mrs Savy, who owned a seafront property at Bel Ombre, discovered several unusual markings on the seaward side of granite boulders on her land. Trying to decipher them, she tracked down the cryptogram of La Buse to Réunion, but was never able to break the code of the marks and inscriptions which were believed to indicate where the treasure of La Buse had been hidden. Then, in 1949, a former Coldstream Guardsman, Reginald Cruise-Wilkins, arrived on Mahé from Kenya. While convalescing from a bout of malaria, he developed a keen interest in the code and wanted to search for the treasure. Upon returning to Kenya, Cruise-Wilkins' fascination with finding the enormous treasure of La Buse became an obsession. Using Greek mythology, astronomy and engineering he claimed to have broken the code and immediately returned to live at Bel Ombre.

Using the law that beaches were public property, he started excavating. The evidence of his initial efforts can still be seen along the coast of Bel Ombre. During his dig he discovered pirate coffins, walls, more encoded messages and a few trinkets. Spread over about 60 ha, the diggings are a labyrinth of passages and submerged chambers.

One of Reginald's sons, John Cruise-Wilkins, still lives near the site. John is adamant that he has solved the vital riddle. But, sadly, the government has awarded the contract to an American fortune-hunter, who has three months in which to strike the right chamber. The biggest problem at present is the method that the American treasure-hunter is using to locate the cache. He is simply blasting away existing rock. Subtle clues are being shattered and lost, and still no treasure has been uncovered.

Casual visitors are not permitted onto the site of the present excavations, but you can reach them by walking along the sea. After 17h00 and on weekends the dig is empty, and it makes for a few hours of fascinating exploration to try to read the markings and inscriptions. Interested travellers can contact John Cruise-Wilkins, tel. 24-7152. His house is the first one east of the original excavation ruins.

An interesting forest walk can be taken from outside the Fisherman's Cove Hotel on the way to Bel Ombre. Take the road that turns south past the hotel, and follow this until it becomes a track. This continues over Vingt-cinq Sous and Mare D'Antin before descending through thick vegetation to exit at Port Launay Marine National Park. Give yourself about three hours.

One of the most spectacular routes open to walkers on Mahé starts just west of the Auberge Club des Seychelles, Danzilles. Follow the steep track that climbs to the summit of stark cliffs before dropping to the remote beach at Anse Major. After a refreshing dip, you can either return or proceed further into the forest, across high hills offering wide panoramas and then to the marine national park and youth camp at Baie Ternay. The entire walk should take about two hours.

Bamboo thickets and the looming bulks of Trois Frères (700 m), Le Niol (680 m) and Jasmin (645 m) mountains are features of the Bel Ombre district. The tropical forest extends to the very edge of the road, inviting the adventurous to explore its cool green depths.

Further along this road the *Polytechnic Hotel School* and *La Goelette Restaurant* offer diners the opportunity to taste traditional Seychellois cooking.

High-tariff accommodation is offered at *Le Meridien Fisherman's Cove Hotel,* PO Bel Ombre, Mahé, Seychelles, tel. 24-7247.

Beyond the hotel a boutique, Silk Creations, offers shoppers a wide choice of prints, batiks, T-shirts and locally designed clothing. The impressive St Roch Cathedral is on one side of the Bamboo river and P & P Couture shop is across it. Here, Seychellois creativity is available in a kaleidoscope of clothing, designs and prints. Prices are high, but so is the quality of the goods.

Beyond the soccer field is a splendid stretch of isolated beach. A few fishermen and courting couples use the area, but few tourists stray here from the bustling hotel beaches. A little past the way to the Russian Ambassador's residence is the Bel Ombre fishermen's harbour and fish market. If you manage to get there early enough you are in for a spectacle of auctioneering, bartering, arguments and laughter. The fishermen commence selling their catches around 7h00.

At *Le Corsaire Restaurant* – within site of the Olivier Le Vasseur treasure site – travellers are offered a good, reasonably priced menu. The seafood is especially tasty. The ambience of Le Corsaire is no doubt influenced by its surroundings, and many diners find themselves drifting into a reverie of pirates, romance and adventure. Give yourself over to the dreams while feasting on the excellent food.

At the end of the bus route, where the road climbs to Danzilles, is *La Scala Restaurant*. Specialising in Italian and Continental dishes, La Scala ranks high on the list of tourist restaurants. You will be sadly disappointed if you arrive without a table reservation. The restaurant is nearly always full. Phone a minimum of 48 hours ahead, tel. 24-7535.

West of La Scala the road climbs up a narrow lane past the Danzilles mini-market and ends near one of the Seychelles' most delightful hotels, the Auberge Club des Seychelles.

Auberge Club des Seychelles (medium-high tariff)

Overlooking the beaches of Bel Ombre, this hotel is built on the site where pirates frequently made landfall during the exciting years of the 17th and 18th centuries. With 40 fully equipped rooms, some in chalets, in a wild forest on the edge of the sea, the Auberge Club des Seychelles is one of Mahé's best kept secrets. Be assured of a visit that will tantalise the imagination and make you sad to leave.

Meals may be taken in the hotel's Silhouette Restaurant, which overlooks the bays of Bel Ombre and Beau Vallon, with views all the way to the stark outlines of Silhouette and North islands. On certain evenings theme entertainment is offered with Creole dancing, dishes and shows. Six days per week, the specialist entertainment staff cater for most tastes and offer cabaret, traditional dancing, singing and short story-telling plays. Apart from on-site indoor games, water polo and aerobics, residents are given cards to allow them free access to the water sport facilities at the Beau Vallon Bay Beach Resort. The hotel provides a courtesy bus to the resort.

Credit cards are acceptable, and traveller's cheques and foreign currency may be exchanged. There are safe deposit boxes. The Club is able to arrange sea and land excursions and car hire. Make reservations early, and ask for the chalet right on the edge of the sea:

Auberge Club des Seychelles, PO Box 329, Mahé, Seychelles, tel. 24-7550, fax 24-7703.

The next described route for north Mahé starts a few kilometres south of Victoria and climbs into the forests along the Sans Souci road, over the mountains, and down to Port Glaud, before turning north to end at Cap Ternay Estate and the youth camp.

To travel to **Port Glaud** from Victoria, visitors using public transport have the choice of two buses. One goes via Sans Souci, while the other struggles up the steep La Misère hill to Grande Anse before turning north to Port Glaud. The route described below is the one followed by the Port Glaud bus along the Sans Souci road.

Passing through dappled forests, you exit in a hilly area of tea and coffee plantations. Tea has been cultivated on these slopes for several years, and citronella on the lower, more gentle slopes.

SEYCHELLES TEA AND COFFEE FACTORY

Situated on the foothills of **Morne Blanc** (670 m), the tea and coffee factory and Tea Tavern are a must for visitors travelling this route. A small entrance fee is charged and tourists are taken on an informative guided tour of the facilities. Blanketed by the scents of drying tea and roasting coffee, you will be taken through each step in the tea production process. Used mostly for blending with other teas, Seychelles tea lacks the briskness of tea from Darjeeling and Gangtok. At the SMB tea factory, the local tea is blended with Ceylon teas for teabags, flavoured with vanilla and exported – mainly to Great Britain. Most of the tea around the Port Glaud area is grown and cultivated without artificial chemicals or fertiliser. Known as bio tea, it is finding a ready market among environmentally and health-conscious consumers.

The Colombian-grade coffee, of the Arabica variety, is roasted and vacuum packed at the factory, and the entire crop is exported.

Once the tour is over, spoil yourself with a cup of the local brew at the Tea Tavern. Light meals and scones are also available, as are sachets and boxes of the manufactured tea and coffee. The vanilla flavoured tea and citronella are especially refreshing.

It is possible to walk to the summit of Morne Blanc from the tea factory. The path leads through the tea plantations and a lush rainforest to the summit. From here the views in all directions are breathtaking. Although the walk is rather strenuous, it should not take you more than two hours to reach the top. Take along some water to drink and don't forget your camera.

To reach the summit of the highest mountain on the island, Morne Seychellois (905 m), enquire about a guide at Bunson's Travel in Victoria.

From the tea factory it is a pleasant 30-minute downhill walk through cinnamon and vanilla forests to the coast and Port Glaud. Hitchhiking from the factory is easy, and buses service the route every half-hour or so. On the descent visitors are offered good views of Thérèse and Conception islands to the west.

PORT GLAUD

Apart from a health clinic, police station, two stores and a school, there is not a great deal to the settlement of Port Glaud. The Sans Souci road ends at a T-junction opposite the beach. South takes you along the west coast road, while north the Port Launay road heads towards the marine national parks. Turn right (north) here.

There is a fairly good swimming beach along this road, and a shallow reef has created a tranquil lagoon that extends almost all the way to **Thérèse Island**. You can arrange a trip to the island by speaking to the fishermen who hang about near the Port Glaud district market. The crossing usually takes between 15 and 30 minutes and is worth the occasional drenching and sea spray.

Continuing north up the west coast, you will pass the Cradle of Love President's Village. A little beyond this children's village, local families sit in their shady yards weaving fish traps. The technique is passed down from generation to generation and has hardly changed in the island's history. The locals will patiently pose for photographs and are delighted when a foreigner asks them questions about their work, their lives and history of the area.

Opposite the large cement cross (built in 1950) there is an excellent snorkelling beach with a shallow reef. The hillsides around this beach are covered in wild passion fruit and coconut palms.

Nearby is **L'Islett**, as its name implies a tiny island, with its famous restaurant and basic accommodation. There is a free ferry service from the little bay to L'Islett. Honeymoon couples are frequent here, and on any Saturday and Sunday visitors can see beautiful brides and elegant grooms crossing in a little motorboat for a reception banquet. There are thatched bungalows on the tiny island, but they are seldom used as most visitors only come to try the renowned dishes offered at the restaurant.

Back on the mainland of Mahé, visitors will find Blue Bird Game Fishing charter service, which caters exclusively to tourists wanting to hunt the dwindling numbers of fish species such as marlin, barracuda and shark. Prices are high. The *Sundown Restaurant* offers a small menu of delicious fresh seafood and serves ice-cold beers. Celine Curio Boutique has a selection of local handicrafts, shells and clothing.

At the church, opposite the bay where the ferry to L'Islett leaves, a cement road turns inland. Walk along this road and you will enter more forests and pass deep pools and cascades up to **Sauzier Waterfall**. There is a pool at the bottom of the waterfall: a wonderful place for a dip after the long walk.

North of the church there is a dramatic change in vegetation and terrain. Few tourists ever come this far, which is a pity as the area is unusual. Mangrove swamp is the dominant plant life, and shallow estuaries, tannin-stained rivers and mud flats are obvious features. The locals are not used to seeing foreigners walking here. You may even be invited into their wooden houses for tea and cake.

The main road ends outside the Port Launay National Youth Service Camp. This is also the last stop for the Port Glaud-Victoria bus. Ignore the large stop sign north of the bus depot and continue into the marine park and forest reserve area. Along this road, walkers will see several Christian shrines under overhanging boulders, discover empty white beaches and see enormous bread-fruit trees. Clear views are afforded of Conception Island, across Port Launay Marine National Park. This is a very narrow road, and if you have hired a car, park it and walk from here. Forest takes over again, and wild flowers brighten the greenery. Orchids, hibiscus, jasmine, honeysuckle and tall blossoming trees create an enchanted garden of astounding natural beauty.

At the small huts of fishermen and farmers above the sea, travellers may be fortunate enough to experience some of the local food. Sleeping here at night is an experience not to be missed. As the tide rushes in and huge waves crash against the granite cliffs, the land trembles under the attack, while still basking in the sweet fragrance of forest flowers.

Take a side trip along one of the paths that wind into the woods. Strangely shaped boulders and weird inscriptions on rocks make this a region of mystery. There are isolated coves along the shore all the way to the gates of Cap Ternay National Youth Service Camp. Permission to enter must be obtained prior to arrival, but there is not much to see in the camp.

Returning to Port Glaud, continue south along the west coast road, passing Mrs J Bibi's mini-supermarket. The most striking feature along this tarred road is the massive and stark Mahé Beach Hotel.

Mahé Beach Hotel (medium-high tariff)

The tallest building on Mahé, and indeed on the Seychelles, the Mahé Beach Hotel has recently been acquired by the Berjaya Group, along with the Beau Vallon Bay Beach Resort. (There was once a law that no building was to be taller than a coconut tree. Money does, however, manage to circumvent most obstacles!) There are 173 rooms, all with television, bathrooms en suite, balconies and air-conditioning. One problem is the incessant roar of air-conditioning motors which cause the entire structure to shake all the time.

Daily excursions are provided to Thérèse Island, where there are free water sport facilities and a restaurant. A casino will soon be built and there are already tennis and squash courts. A large swimming pool is the centre for water polo and volleyball for guests. Travel and tour operators have representatives at the hotel, as do three car-hire companies. There is a breakfast restaurant with panoramic views. Light lunches are served around the pool, and candle-lit dinners are taken in the restaurant under the stars. A quaint à la carte restaurant is set in the 20 ha gardens near the beach.

Next to the evening restaurant is a vibrant disco, which really gets going over the weekend. Happily, this is one of the few tourist resorts on the Indian Ocean islands that allows locals to use the facilities. And on Friday and Saturday evenings those who make the effort will soon find themselves ensconced with a group of Seychellois.

A dive centre is also located at the hotel, as are two exorbitantly expensive curio shops. There is an entertainment officer on duty each day, ready to help plan excursions and prepare theme evenings that include traditional dancing and light shows.

Prior reservations for accommodation are essential:

Mahé Beach Hotel, PO Box 540, Port Glaud, Mahé, Seychelles, tel. 37-8451, fax 37-8517.

Proceeding south along the west coast, visitors travel through La Beoliere coconut estate and several agricultural plots before coming to the entrance to the Equator Sun Hotel, just north of the Ministry of Health Clinic (Beoliere).

Equator Sun Hotel (high tariff)

What must once have been a truly grand hotel is now sadly slipping into mediocrity. Not to say that everything is bad at the Equator Sun. If you can put up with the brusque staff and musty rooms, then the location and the quality of food are both pleasant. Catering mainly to package tourists, this hotel is built around granite boulders in fruit orchards, overlooking the sea – where turtles often pass on their way to the remote beaches of Port Launay. A small beach is available during the summer season, and the snorkelling between the cliffs and Île aux Vaches is good all year round.

Although the 56 rooms were initially planned as self-catering units, their cooking facilities no longer function. Coffee and tea can, however, be made in each room. The rooms all have balconies, air-conditioners and bathrooms. A specialist team of entertainment staff arranges daily programmes for tourists. At night, theme evenings are presented in La Palafitte Restaurant. Trips are arranged to Thérèse Island and into Victoria for shopping. Island tours and excursions can be organised through any of the three tour operators represented at the Equator Sun. A walk through the tropical fruit orchards that surround the hotel should not be missed.

Most residents are on half-board, which includes a large buffet breakfast and supper. The restaurant is shaped like a wooden sailing vessel and commands a beautiful vista of the ocean and sweeping south-west coast of Mahé. A coffee shop, open 10h00-17h00, serves light meals, snacks and beverages.

Be certain to book well in advance for this remote hotel:

Equator Sun Hotel, PO Box 526, Mahé, Seychelles, tel. 37-8228, fax 37 8244.

Beyond the Equator Sun Hotel, the road dips through cassava fields to the National Agricultural Documentation Centre. In the same grounds is *La Marie Galante Restaurant*, which has a good menu of Creole and Continental dishes, all at cheap prices and enormous servings. Across the road is one of the best-stocked mini-markets on Mahé: Grande Anse Supermarket. Self-catering visitors staying on the west coast are advised to do their grocery shopping here. Not only are prices lower than in the SMB supermarkets, but the staff are also helpful and can find you cheap lodgings with locals around Grande Anse.

Where the road curves away from the coast, continue straight on, to **Grande Anse** beach, past the school's sports fields. With a long, wide white beach and good rideable waves, Grande Anse is popular with local bodysurfers. The best waves are back-line. It can be a bit of a struggle getting out past the shore break, but once between the sets you are in for a feast of smooth walls and long rides. Over weekends, the beach is popular with Seychellois families who picnic on the sand and among the palm groves. Music is prominent at these times, and those visitors who enjoy reggae will be delighted with the offerings.

From Grande Anse village, walk around the school to the BBC Relay Station and wait for the bus at the T-junction, outside the agricultural projects. The bus back to Victoria travels from this bus stop, up over the misty heights of **La Misère hill**. To the right are the garish white domes of the Satellite Tracking Station, operated by the US Navy. Supposedly used to track orbiting satellites, the general consensus is that the massive radar installations keep watch over warship movements in the Indian Ocean. The station is self-contained, with canteens, accommodation, a bar and entertainment. Where previously casual visitors used to be allowed a cursory visit, this has now been stopped for "security reasons", and unless you are a family member, access to the facilities will be denied.

Once over the mountains, the road plunges into rainforest until reaching the steep descent past La Louise Lodge and down to the east coast. Turning right (south) at the circle at the bottom of La Misère hill, the route goes to the settlement of **Cascade**. An old water mill marks the start of the path up through the forest to the cascades and their pools, in which you can swim.

Beyond Cascade, the north Mahé route ends at the Seychelles International Airport, just south of **Anse Talbot**, opposite the Mont Sebert Estate.

17 SOUTH MAHÉ

South Mahé stretches from Police Bay in the south to a line connecting Anse Cimitière in the west, over Grand Bois to Anse aux Pins in the east.

The southern part of Mahé is still relatively unexplored and is not yet being exploited by luxury hotel chains and organised tour groups. Although Mason's Travel takes visitors on island tours through the southern part of the island, the tours cover only a small part of the region. Adventurous tourists must discover the area for themselves. While forests and mountains are a feature of northern Mahé, the south largely consists of agricultural estates, empty white beaches and traditional Creole villages.

Four roads traverse south Mahé: the Chemin Montagne Posée connects Anse aux Pins on the east coast with Anse Boileau on the west; the Chemin les Cannelles connects Anse Royale with Anse à la Mouche; the Chemin Val d'Endor connects Anse Bougainville with Baie Lazare; and the Chemin Quatre Bornes connects Anse Marie-Louise via Quatre Bornes with Anse Takamaka. All these roads branch out of the national road that extends all the way around the east and west coasts of Mahé.

The best way to travel through the southern part of Mahé is by hitchhiking or using public transport. Hitchhiking is best done from outside the airport, where there is also a bus stop serving the south-east and south-west coasts and the inland villages of Quatre Bornes and Les Cannelles.

South of the international airport are the Seychelles Coast Guard camp and Katiolo Disco, which offers reasonably priced meals from its attached restaurant. This is definitely one disco to visit over the weekend. It is frequented by the islanders, many of whom make the journey all the way from the villages on the northern part of the island. You will find few other tourists here. Expect a long night, lots of dancing and most likely ending up on the beach watching the sunrise with new-found friends.

On the northern edge of **Anse aux Pins** village is *La Retraite Guesthouse* (low tariff), one of the best-known budget guesthouses on the Seychelles. It is recommended to travellers on a shoe-string budget.

Just 4 km from the airport, La Retraite is the ideal place at which to spend the first night if you are travelling independently. Not many people spend long here – hygiene and cleanliness are somewhat lacking. Breakfast is included in the low price. There are four rooms, all with bathrooms and excellent ocean views. For an additional fee, you can have dinner cooked for you. Self-catering is allowed and residents have access to a fully equipped communal kitchen. The owner is something of a character on Mahé, and will often conduct personal tours of the island if you provide a car.

Reservations are necessary at least 14 days in advance:

La Retraite Guesthouse, PO Anse aux Pins, Mahé, Seychelles, tel. 37-5816.

Opposite La Retraite Guesthouse is Labank Sevings (Seychelles Savings Bank) and St Michael's church. Changing foreign currency at this bank is virtually impossible, and traveller's cheques are not accepted. You have the choice of either going north to Victoria or south to the Reef Hotel, which charges a higher handling fee and commission than the capital's banks, but not exorbitantly high. The village of Anse aux Pins has a post office, police station, public phones and bus depot all grouped astride the east coast road. To reach Anse aux Pins from Victoria, travellers can take any bus going to Anse aux Pins, Anse Royale, Anse Boileau, Takamaka, Baie Lazare or Anse à la Mouche.

An interesting walk can be taken from Anse aux Pins to **Cascade**. Take the path west from the golf course opposite the Reef Hotel. This walk goes through coconut plantations and sections of indigenous forest, and follows the Grand Bassin river to where it meets the Cascade river, then past the waterfall and down to the main road near the airport. Allow yourself about two hours to appreciate this walk properly.

A few hundred metres south of the Reef Grocery Store, which has a good selection of fresh fruit and vegetables, is Victoria Car Hire, tel. 37-6314, and the Reef Hotel.

The *Reef Hotel* (high tariff) caters for tourists keen to play golf, laze on the beach and taste traditional cuisine. There are 150 air-conditioned rooms, all with sea views. The hotel regularly puts on evenings of folk dancing. The restaurant is renowned for its excellent Creole menu and late-night dancing. There are water sport facilities, which include a fresh-water pool and boat excursions. Reservations are necessary:

Reef Hotel, PO Box 388, Anse aux Pins, Mahé, Seychelles, tel. 37-6691, fax 37-6296.

There are reefs along this section of coast and the beaches are wonderful for swimming and snorkelling. People not resident at the Reef Hotel may use its water sport facilities if they arrange this with the general manager at least 24 hours in advance.

A site worth visiting is the SMB Hydroponics Project, near the *Lalla Panzi Guesthouse* (low-medium tariff). This three-roomed house, set in a lush tropical garden near the beach, serves expensive but tasty Creole meals, tel. 37-6411.

Several old plantation houses are located on this stretch of road south, and all can be visited. *La Roussette Bungalows* (medium tariff) offers accommodation for guests staying longer than three days. Reservations are necessary during the high season: November-December, March-April and August-September. During low season visitors can usually just phone ahead for lodgings:

La Roussette, PO Anse aux Pins, Mahé, Seychelles, tel. 37-6245.

Next is the *Casuarina Beach Hotel* and restaurant (high tariff). There are 16 rooms and the restaurant specialises in Creole cooking. The hotel is popular with repeat guests, and prior bookings for accommodation and meals are essential:

Casuarina Beach Hotel, PO Box 253, Anse aux Pins, Mahé, Seychelles, tel. 37-6211.

Lenstiti Kreol (Creole Institute for Sport and Culture) is housed in a beautiful old Creole mansion, and is able to provide visitors with a wealth of information about Seychellois culture and history. The staff are pleasant and able to converse in French, English, Italian, German and, of course, Creole. A little further south is Codevar Craft Village, which has 12 stalls where local artists work at their particular speciality. This is the best place at which to do your curio shopping. Prices are all negotiable and well below those in the shops of Victoria or the duty-free shop in the airport. Shoppers may choose from items crafted from bamboo, palm leaves and coconuts.

Take a turn through the coconut grove, west of the east coast road. The Coconut Museum is in a palm-frond building in the grove. The end of the drive will take you to the steps of an 18th century plantation mansion. The house is open to visitors every day of the week and contains original furniture and paintings from the gracious colonial years between 1850 and 1950.

Across Codevar Craft Village at the *Pomme Cannelle Restaurant* diners may select from an extensive menu of both local and international dishes.

The *Ty-Foo Restaurant* is also nearby. Something of a legend among visitors to the south-east coast, this restaurant has a menu of both traditional Creole and Chinese dishes. Prices are rather high, but the food is good and servings are large. To get a table at lunch time, book at least 48 hours ahead, tel. 37-1485.

One of the best beaches on Mahé is at **Anse Royale**. There is a small settlement near the beach which has a BFC bank, post office, church and school. This is also home to a busy theatre group. Details of shows and events are obtainable from the Lenstiti Kreol. The beach at Anse Royale is also popular with locals. Over weekends they descend in droves to swim, picnic and just relax on its 3 km long stretch. You can swim or hire a fishing boat to take you the few hundred metres to the tiny granitic island of **Souris**. A small restaurant on the island serves delicious seafood lunches and snacks at low prices. To find some seclusion, head further south, to **Anse Bougainville** or Pirate Cove (Anse Forbans). At Anse Bougainville is one of the Seychelles's finest guesthouses, the Auberge de Bougainville.

Auberge de Bougainville (medium tariff)

This gracious old Creole mansion overlooking the sea is under the capable management of a husband-and-wife team. Having spent several years in South Africa, they have recently returned to create the most highly recommended guesthouse on the islands. Built to allow a breeze to flow continually through the mansion rooms, this eight-roomed house has had the original kitchen and store converted into an additional four rooms. Original colonial furniture is being installed to add to the atmosphere and authenticity. Almost 30 ha of forest and farm extend up into the hills behind the house. In front, across the road, is a small beach that offers privacy and splendid swimming. Snorkelling equipment and the use of a metal detector (for finding buried treasure!) are available.

Most residents are on half-board and enjoy traditional meals, made by a highly trained Creole chef, from a set menu. There is also an à la carte menu. Prices are good, quality is high and the service attentive. Fish is the speciality, although vegetarians are also catered for. Tropical fruits and vegetables are grown in the grounds. Tour groups use the restaurant on organised island tours – a sure indication of superior service and tasty meals. Traveller's cheques, foreign currency and credit cards can all be used at the guesthouse. A lively bar offers guests the opportunity to mix with locals and the chance to relax in the historical setting. Personal attention is a feature of the Auberge de Bougainville. Guests are met at the airport. Reservations are necessary:

Auberge de Bougainville, PO Box 3010, Anse Royale, Mahé, Seychelles, tel. 37-1788, fax 37-1808.

One of the best walks on Mahé is available from **Anse Bougainville**. It takes about three hours to complete this cross-island stroll. Take the path to the south of the Chemin Val d'Endor road. Passing through several coconut estates, you enter a region of forest and scattered hill dwellings before coming to the source of the Baie Lazare river. Continue along the river through agricultural plots and then down the gentle hills to the west coast bay of Baie Lazare.

At **Anse Forbans** (Pirate Cove), visitors will find a small beach. Local legend has it that pirates and corsairs – notably Jean François Hodoul – obtained water, fuel and food here. Stories of buried treasure in the surrounding hills have lured numerous treasure-hunters to the area. Joel Hoarau, of the Auberge de Bougainville, is convinced that there is some truth to the tales. Interested visitors may borrow a metal detector from him and spend a few fascinating hours combing the beach and forested hills for treasure. Serious diggers are advised to contact John Cruise-Wilkins at Bel Ombre for more details and suggestions, tel. 24-7152.

Between Anse Forbans and Anse Marie-Louise the road turns west, inland, to the hill village of Quatre Bornes, before dropping to the coast at Anse Takamaka. It is difficult to reach the southernmost point of Mahé at **Pointe du Sud** (Cap Malheureux). There is no road, but two tracks run through the coconut estates from Anse Marie-Louise to Pointe Capucins, Pointe Cocos and the southern beach of Petite Boileau. Next to Petite Boileau is **Police Bay**, which is off limits to visitors. It is used as a military, police and correctional facility. By turning west at Pointe Capucins, walkers can get expansive views from the 300 m summit of **Beau Sejour**, midway between the east and west coasts.

The detailed route described below, down the west coast, commences at Anse Boileau.

ANSE BOILEAU

To reach this point from Victoria, travellers using public transport should take the Victoria-Anse Boileau or the Victoria-Port Glaud (via La Misère) bus from the Palm Street bus depot.

Huge Boileau Bay has several beaches offering solitude, privacy and tranquillity. They are not nearly as crowded as the northern Mahé beaches. East of **Anse Polite** are the Indian Ocean Nurseries, where beautiful orchids growing in the open under shade netting are a delight. The horticulturalists seem to enjoy taking interested foreigners on a tour of the nursery. The wide variety and colourful profusion of orchids, all in one place, make this site well worth a visit.

Anse Boileau has a protected beach but no offshore reef. This means that the Indian Ocean rollers come tearing in whenever there is a spring tide or storm. Although ideal for experienced bodysurfers and surfers, this beach is not suitable for swimming or snorkelling. Rips and cross-currents need to be carefully studied before you venture out to ride the magnificent barrel waves which often reach 2 m.

Creole, Chinese and seafood dishes can be ordered from the well-priced menu of *Chez Plume,* on the edge of Anse Boileau. During the holiday season book in advance, tel. 37-5660.

ANSE À LA MOUCHE

At the northern approach to Anse à la Mouche is *Au Capitaine Rouge.* Prices are exorbitant here but the meals lavish. Exclusive candle-lit dinners and cold lunches make this restaurant popular with honeymoon couples and affluent tourists. No reservations are necessary, but you should arrive no later than 20h00 on Friday or Saturday evenings.

Anse à la Mouche has a similar reputation to Bel Ombre, connected to the last and most famous of all Indian Ocean corsairs, Jean François Hodoul, whose descendants still live in the original house built by their scallywag ancestor. Genuinely interested visitors – not casual tourists – may make an appointment to see the spice gardens, ruined distillery, orchids and wooden house. An original portrait of Jean François Hodoul hangs in the living room, which is furnished with pieces brought to Mahé by him during his years as pirate for the French King. Contact Marie-Anne Hodoul, PO Anse à la Mouche, Mahé, Seychelles, tel. 37-1370. You can also make enquiries at Bunson's Travel on Revolution Avenue, Victoria.

Travellers can reach Anse à la Mouche from Victoria on the Anse à la Mouche or Baie Lazare bus.

Anse à la Mouche beaches tend to be shallow and muddy at low tide. Few people ever come here to swim; the surrounding wilderness of hills, rivers, forests and hidden valleys is the main attraction. There are, however, strips of beach opposite the main road, near La Résidence and beyond the palm grove outside the Anchor Café.

The *Anchor Café* offers takeaways and light meals throughout the day and early evening. There is a small but adequate menu at prices that will suit all budget-conscious travellers. Try the seafood; the grilled line fish is excellent.

There are a few places offering low quality accommodation in the area. The best accommodation, for location, price, service and ambience, is at La Résidence.

La Résidence (medium-high tariff)

Situated on a hillside above Anse à la Mouche, La Résidence is one of the few fully equipped self-catering lodgings on the Seychelles. Each of the three villas is built in the style of a plantation house, complete with shutters, patio and estate furniture. There are also four double-storey apartments. All accommodation has bathrooms en suite, fans, telephones, kitchens and exquisite views, plus fridges and gas stoves.

The rates are per unit and may seem high, but depending on the number of people in the unit the rate per person may be very reasonable. By doing your own catering you can keep the total price of your vacation low. Discounts are offered according to season and length of stay. You can do your shopping in either Grande Anse or Victoria. Alternatively, you can give a list of requirements to the staff who will arrange for the purchase of the goods. You can also hire a cook from the lodge.

La Résidence offers airport transfers to guests – something very few of the tourist resorts do. Flights are reconfirmed by the staff. There is a laundry service and baby-sitting service, and each of the rooms is serviced daily. Car hire can be arranged, as can boat excursions and island tours. Guests may use hard currency, traveller's cheques and credit cards.

One of the great attractions of staying at La Résidence is that you are actually staying on the original Jean François Hodoul estate. The corsair's house is located below the apartments. Ask the manager for a short tour.

Reservations are necessary, at least 30 days prior to arrival. A 10% deposit is required when booking, and the balance is due on confirmation:

La Résidence, Marie-Anne Hodoul, Anse à la Mouche, Mahé, Seychelles, tel. 37-1370 or 32-2682, fax 32-2292.

Along the peninsula that juts out west of Anse à la Mouche lies **Anse aux Poules Bleues.** The home of Michael Adams, the most celebrated artist on the Seychelles, is here. His paintings adorn exhibition halls, books, walls and homes. Stop and spend an interesting hour being guided through his studio and gallery, and maybe buying one of his works: tel. 36-1006, fax 36-1200.

Between Anse à la Mouche and Anse aux Poules Bleues is *La Sirène Creole Café.* Noted for its Creole seafood dishes, La Sirène is highly recommended. It does not seem to have definite opening and closing times, and diners will just have to try their luck if in the area.

Once through the little village of **Baie Lazare**, where there is a fuel station, post office, clinic and store, visitors descend to the entrance of the *Plantation Club Hotel and Casino* (definitely high tariff). This 206-room tourist village has a fine section of beach and extensive water sport facilities. There are three restaurants, a disco, casino and nightly theme entertainment. Each room has a television, telephone and mini-bar. Book well ahead:

Plantation Club Hotel and Casino, PO Box 437, Victoria, Mahé, Seychelles, tel. 36-1361, fax 36-1517.

All along Baie Lazare are small coves and beaches, many only accessible at low tide, fringed with filaos and palm trees and backed by imposing grey granite boulders. On the edge of Baie Lazare beach, across the stone bridge, is the turning for Val d'Andorre Pottery, along the Baie Lazare river. This little workshop set amid palm trees turns out wonderful pieces of art. There is a wide variety of glazed and unfired pottery.

South of Baie Lazare is **Anse Gaulette** and the *Anse Gaulette Bar and Restaurant.* A broken reef offers some protection to bathers, but it is better to continue further south to find more idyllic beaches.

Beyond Pointe Maravi is a long downhill through indigenous forest to the spectacular beach of **Anse Takamaka**. The waves are big hereoo, but the beach and forests make for a splendid setting. *Chez Batista's Restaurant,* Italian owned and managed, is right on the beach among coconut palms. Specialising in fresh seafood, this quaint restaurant is a favourite stop for package tours. Lunch time is always hectic, but despite the full tables you should try at least one meal here: the food and setting are worth it. The staff can arrange cheap, basic accommodation with local families.

Along the sand road to the restaurant, a few enterprising Seychellois have set up curio stalls. Avoid the temptation to buy pink, black and white coral pieces. Not only is it illegal to take them out of the country, but it will also encourage the continued destruction of the fragile reefs with their delicate ecosystems.

Further inland, east of the beach, is Takamaka Beach Farm. Here you can buy citrus fruit, find accommodation and eat at the pleasant garden restaurant. Nearby, at **Petite Paradis**, is *Le Reduit Creole Fish Restaurant*. This is the most economical place for lunch or a light snack. The staff speak very little English, but no matter what you choose, it will be cheap, filling and scrumptious.

Campers wanting to pitch their tents in the abandoned coconut groves in this area can get written permission from the police chief in Quatre Bornes.

By either walking past Chez Batista's or taking the turn-off from Quatre Bornes, visitors will arrive at the remote and secluded beach of **Anse Intendance**. This is one of the foremost snorkelling beaches on Mahé. Take along food and drink for the day, which can be bought in Quatre Bornes. Alternatively, a packed cold lunch can be bought from Chez Batista's. In winter and early spring, bathers must be cautious when swimming out to the Roche de L'Intendance. Strong currents and a big back-line can make things difficult. You may well find a no-swimming sign on the beach during this season. It pays to adhere to the warning.

Turning west from Anse Takamaka, visitors enter a district that is still largely unaffected by modernisation and tourism. Those fortunate enough to be invited to spend time with one of the local families may encounter the strange mixture of animist and Christian beliefs they hold. During full moon, ancient rituals are performed deep in the rain-forests around Quatre Bornes and Takamaka.

The farmers who live on the edges of the still pristine forests are friendly, quiet people. Hospitable, they may well invite backpackers in for a meal or offer them a bed for the night. Acceptance is the best way of getting immersed in the southern Creole life style. No payment is expected, but contribute something to the meal.

In the village of **Quatre Bornes**, Ste Marie Madeline church rises proud and solid near Takamaka school. During the school term the afternoons are devoted to choral practices in the vast dome of the church, and the children's voices ring out. Raju Store bakes fresh pastries daily and has a limited supply of imported tinned food. Buses serving this settlement stop at the small bus depot between the school and the Takamaka District Council building. Takamaka Health Centre offers emergency first-aid treatment only. A busy fish and fresh produce market does business daily 7h00-12h00. There is a district post office and a police station.

It is possible to reach Anse Intendance from Quatre Bornes and travel some way along Chemin Grande Police, on the way to the restricted area of Police Bay. Turn west at the market and follow the gravel road through the groves between Mounts Takamaka, Corail and Caghee. There is a deserted plantation house near the beach at **Pointe Golette**. According to the Seychelles Tourist Board this is the most beautiful of all estate mansions on Mahé. It can be difficult to reach, as the path used by walkers is overgrown and barely visible. Budget travellers should consider spending a night in the empty building. Once home to the Roucou family, it is now neglected and rather eerie at night.

Anse Cachée and **Anse Corail** are two strips of white sand west of the road to Police Bay. Beyond this point armed guards will politely but firmly turn you back. Some travellers are permitted to pay a quick visit to and swim at pristine **Anse Bazarca**, but if you are refused permission, don't push. One visitor from Germany was escorted all the way back to Quatre Bornes and physically put on a bus going back to Victoria. Occasionally visitors may be granted permission to visit the lighthouse on the promontory between **Petite Police** and **Police Bay** by asking, in advance, the Commissioner of Police, tel. 32-2011, or the Chief of Staff at Defence Headquarters in Bel Eau, tel. 22-4070, or the Station Commander at Takamaka Police Station, tel. 37-1249.

18 ISLANDS AROUND MAHÉ

SILHOUETTE ISLAND

Lying about 20 km north-west of Mahé, Silhouette is devoted almost entirely to agriculture. There are no more than 220 people living on this granitic island. Protected by a treacherous reef and tidal streams, the island has remained relatively unspoilt. Accommodation is limited, but campers will find it easy to locate a suitable pitch in the dense forest or by asking one of the farming families.

Getting to Silhouette can be difficult. There are no regular ferries making the crossing. You have three options. You can contact the Island Development Company, PO Box 638, Victoria, Mahé, Seychelles, tel. 22-4640, fax 22-4467, which has a ship going to the island every other week. A far more enjoyable way of reaching Silhouette is to ask one of the fishermen at Beau Vallon Bay to take you. For a fee, which is less than half that charged by the Island Development Company, you will be motored across. You should arrange to be collected within a day or two. Pay half the price upon landing; hold the remainder as security that you will indeed be fetched. The third, and most expensive, way of getting to Silhouette is on an organised tour from Victoria. Ask for current rates and itineraries from Mason's Travel (see the section on tours in chapter 14).

Silhouette Island was once home to the Dauban planter family. Visitors can still see the family mausoleum near **Anse la Passe**, in Anse Cimitière, south of Pointe Ramasse Tout. A deserted and reputedly haunted settlement is located near the copra factory at **Grande Barbe**, on the south-west coast. Equally intriguing is the restored plantation house, known as La Gran Kaz, close to La Passe pier. At **Anse Lascars** lie the sea-eroded remains of typical Arab tombs. Other sites to see are the copra-producing areas around **Anse Mondon** and La Passe. Apart from coconuts and patchouli, cinnamon and both tropical and sub-tropical fruits are cultivated.

Three paths cross the island from east to west, and a track skirts the coast on the east, north and west. There is no public transport on Silhouette and tourists must walk to the various sites. One of the best walks is across the island from **Anse la Passe** to **Anse Grande Barbe**.

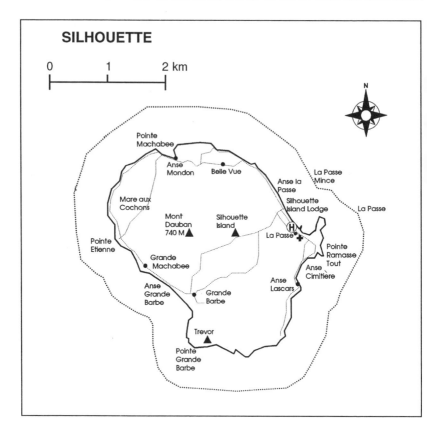

SILHOUETTE

0   1   2 km

Pointe
Machabee

Anse
Mondon   Belle Vue

Anse la
Passe   La Passe
                         Mince

Anse la
Passe

Silhouette
Island Lodge   La Passe

Mare aux
Cochons

Mont   Silhouette
Dauban   Island
740 M   La Passe

Pointe   Pointe
Etienne   Ramasse
                                          Tout
Grande
Machabee   Anse
                                Cimitiere

Anse   Anse
Grande   Grande   Lascars
Barbe   Barbe

Trevor

Pointe
Grande
Barbe

Walk north from Silhouette Island Lodge to the small lake opposite the beach. Turn left here and follow the Rivière Grande upstream onto the 500 m high plateau. Continue through **Jardin Marron** and begin the descent on the southern slopes of the island's highest peak, **Mont Dauban** (740 m). The path runs parallel to Rivière La Glacis and then joins with the Rivière Séme to exit near Grande Barbe. You will need a guide for the walk through the thick jungle, and a machete, plus food and drink for six to eight hours. Guides may be arranged from the Silhouette Island Lodge or by talking to the locals who live along the Rivière Grande.

Silhouette Island Lodge (high tariff) is the only tourist accommodation on the island. It is unashamedly expensive, has 12 rather basic huts and includes all meals in the rate, which varies according to the high and low season. The lodge provides snorkelling gear, windsurfers, canoes, paddle boats and various other water sport activities. Reservations can be made directly with the lodge or via its offices in Victoria: Silhouette Island Lodge, PO Box 608, Victoria, Mahé, Seychelles, tel. 22-4445, 34-4154, fax 22-4897, 34-4178.

Those arriving with their own tents can head into the plateau mountains for a few days of peace and solitude. Some of the best places are along the path connecting **Anse Mondon** via Mare aux Cochons with **Pointe Etienne**, and south of the main cross-island track near **Gratte Fesse**. Along the southern coast, especially at **Pointe Civine** and **Glacis Platte**, are sections of wild coastline just inviting campers to stop for a while. You must carry all your own food for camping.

THÉRÈSE ISLAND

Less than 2 km west of Port Glaud, Thérèse Island is a mecca for water sport enthusiasts. The facilities cater for windsurfers, swimmers, divers, walkers and those who just want to lie in the sun. A daily boat trip, under the direction of the Mahé Beach Hotel, takes guests across to lunch or just relax on Thérèse Island. Visitors not staying at the Mahé Beach Hotel can arrange to use the same boat or ask the fishermen at Port Glaud to take them across. Holiday-makers keen on game fishing should speak to "Speedy" about chartering a boat. You can contact him via the reception desk of the Mahé Beach Hotel or the bar of the Marine Charter Association in Victoria. He has the reputation of being the best game-fishing skipper in the Seychelles.

There is nowhere to stay on Thérèse Island and you will be required to return to Mahé before nightfall. However, if you have a tent and enough food, you may be allowed to spend the night. A discreet chat to either the security guard, who lives with his wife on the island, or "Speedy" usually secures permission. You will be expected to slip away out of sight when the day trippers leave – there could be problems otherwise.

ISLANDS OF THE STE ANNE MARINE NATIONAL PARK

Ste Anne Island

About 5 km east of Mahé, Ste Anne Island is where the first Europeans settled on the Seychelles in 1770. There is an abandoned whaling station on the beach. A youth camp is being either constructed or dismantled on Ste Anne. (I received conflicting stories about it from government officials and nature conservation personnel, and access to the site was denied.) The highest point on Ste Anne is **Mount Ste Anne** (250 m). It is a fairly stiff walk to the summit, which affords magnificent views of Mahé and the other islands of the Ste Anne Marine National Park.

The laws pertaining to landing on Ste Anne are as fickle as the tropical breezes. Sometimes visitors are permitted but charged a "landing fee". At other times no-one is allowed even within swimming distance of the island. The surrounding waters are patrolled by nature conservation guards and occasionally by military personnel. The latest details pertaining to visiting the island should be obtained 24 hours before from the Department of the Environment (in Mont Fleuri, opposite the Botanical Gardens on Mahé), tel. 32-2891.

Moyenne Island

Moyenne has been inhabited since 1850 and is now privately owned by B Grimshaw. He has developed Moyenne Island into a delightful tourist dream exploiting the myths about pirates and buried treasure, and has opened Moyenne to tour operators on certain days of the week. Only those tourists visiting with an organised operator, such as Mason's Travel, are allowed to land. Offshore from Moyenne is an enchanted submarine world, where over 800 species of fish and 150 species of coral have been identified. On shore the aptly named "I Don't Care Beach" lures visitors into a reverie of relaxation. Each visitor is provided with a detailed map of the island, whose paths are all clearly signposted.

There are views to all the neighbouring islands from well-chosen viewpoints. A chapel and graves lie deep in the forest. The chapel was built in 1979, but mystery surrounds two of the graves. The ruins of Julie Melidor's house (1850-1892) stand silent and alone in the forest near the site where Grimshaw believes pirates hid treasure. No treasure has been found on Moyenne, and one look at the shallow reef and tidal rips will convince anyone that a pirate would have been a fool to try to land here.

From **Elephant Rock** look-out point you have clear views of **Coral Cove** and the empty beaches to the south-east. The gloomy Fiapi's Forest is named after Grimshaw's faithful dog. Treasure Peak is a little further up, and then the path under the filao trees turns to Vera's viewpoint. A trail drops to Coral Cove, then climbs up to the House of Dogs, built in 1900. The house's owner was an eccentric Englishwoman who would make forays to Mahé to collect all the stray dogs she could find and bring them back to Moyenne to care for them. Today there are no dogs left on Moyenne.

Lovers' Leap overlooks cliffs and a drop to the ocean and rocks below. Bamboo thickets, granite boulders and the Gold Cavern entice walkers on their way back to the Jolly Roger Bar and Restaurant.

Accommodation on Moyenne is dependent on the whim of the owner and the Jolly Roger manager. Very few visitors stay on the island, but it is apparently possible. It would be best to ask Mason's Travel to arrange the lodgings.

CERF ISLAND

Approximately 5 km east of Victoria, Cerf Island is home to about 40 people. One of the homes of famed South African novelist, Wilbur Smith, is here. Well known for its flying fox bats, Cerf is blanketed by tropical vegetation and rimmed by a broken reef. Scuba divers can explore the area to the north of Cerf, between Cerf and Round islands, but do not stray too far to the east – Long Island is a penal colony. Sites of interest include the Anglican and Roman Catholic churches. Two restaurants cater for day trippers: *Beach Shed Bar and Restaurant* and the *Kapok Tree Restaurant*. Both serve delicious meals with an emphasis on seafood. It is necessary to book ahead to eat at the Kapok Tree Restaurant, tel. 32-2959.

Getting to Cerf from Mahé is a problem. You will need to speak to the Marine Charter skippers or walk around the fishing port and ask the fishermen if they would be prepared to take you across for the day. There is not a great deal of interest on Cerf Island, and as numerous of the properties are large, access to certain areas is forbidden. Rather visit one of the other islands in Ste Anne Marine National Park.

ROUND ISLAND

A mere 150 m in diameter, Round Island is the headquarters of the Marine Park Protection Unit. The crumbling ruins of a former leper colony are among the few buildings on this densely vegetated island. A solitary park ranger lives on Round Island, which is off limits to overnight tourists. While the island itself is virtually closed to visitors, the waters surrounding it are not, and provide excellent snorkelling. You will come face to face with starfish, giant shells, crabs and, if you are really fortunate, green turtles, which lie offshore, waiting for night-fall and the safety of darkness to struggle ashore and lay their eggs.

Chez Gaby is a small restaurant on Round Island catering for the infrequent tourist trade. It has an excellent reputation. Those tourists who consider themselves connoisseurs of gourmet cooking are strongly advised to patronise it. Located in the historical chapel that was once the centre of the leper colony, the restaurant has an extravagant menu which offers the best of Creole seafood dishes. The restaurant is only open for lunch. It is seldom necessary to make reservations. Simply turn up and enjoy the culinary delights. You will, of course, need to arrange a boat from Mahé by speaking to skippers of the Marine Boat Charter Association or local fishermen.

LONG ISLAND

Totally forbidden to tourists, Long Island is the site of the Seychelles' low-security prison. Its security seems rather dubious, though. During a four-week period in the Seychelles, I heard of three escapes: each escapee had simply jumped into the water and swum across to Mahé. Two were later arrested at local night spots, while the third was apprehended while watching television at home! The prisoners appear to have an easy time of it. On weekends they are permitted to fish from little smacks offshore. Tour guides to the other islands seem to think that the prisoners have landed themselves in paradise for a few months!

19 PRASLIN

Praslin, 11 km long and 4 km wide, is the second largest island in the Seychelles. Initially named Île de Palme in 1744, it was later renamed after the French aristocrat, the Duc de Praslin.

Not as mountainous as Mahé, 36 km away to the west, Praslin is the original home of the rare coco de mer palm tree. In the protected Vallée de Mai, visitors can see beautiful specimens of this unique tree. Praslin has some of the best beaches in the Seychelles, and inland walkers will discover hidden valleys and a profusion of plant species endemic to Praslin. In the main settlements of Baie Ste Anne and Grande Anse, the pace of life is at least 20 years behind the "rush" of Mahé. Grande Anse is the capital of Praslin and exudes an atmosphere at once relaxed and businesslike.

Transport around Praslin is in a few dilapidated buses and Peugeot cars. It is really not necessary to hire one of the expensive taxis. Instead, simply set off walking or hitchhiking. If you are travelling north to south, flag down one of the buses that happen along every 40-50 minutes. Avoid the temptation to spend your entire vacation stretched out on one of the glorious coral-reefed beaches. Inland there are forests, waterfalls, rivers, unexplored hills and farming settlements not yet exposed to modernisation.

Offshore, to the west, are two islands: Cousine Island, which is privately owned and off limits to tourists, and Cousin Island, a nature reserve. To the east, Curieuse Island forms part of Curieuse Marine National Park. The small islands of St Pierre and Chauve Souris house luxury hotels and restaurants. Off the south-eastern tip of Pointe La Farine lies another Round Island.

Praslin can be reached from Mahé either by sea or air. The flight takes about 15 minutes. There is one daily flight, and additional flights during the high season. Although it is quicker to go by air it is also considerably more expensive and may be less interesting than taking the daily schooner. These wooden, motorised sailing vessels leave from the inter-island quay in Victoria about noon each day (Sunday excluded). You purchase your ticket aboard and find your own place to sit for the crossing. The schooner voyage takes anything from three to six hours depending on weather and sea conditions. One warning about

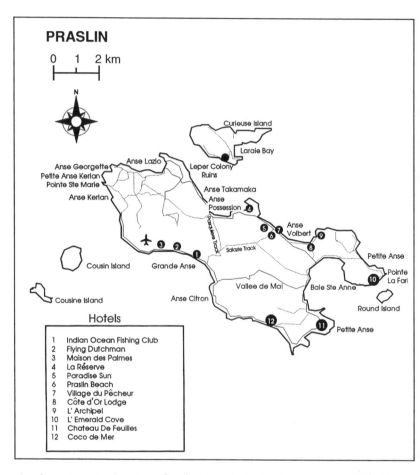

PRASLIN

0   1   2 km

N

Curieuse Island

Laraie Bay

Anse Lazio

Leper Colony
Ruins

Anse Georgette
Petite Anse Kerlan
Pointe Ste Marie

Anse Takamaka

Anse Kerlan

Anse
Possession

Anse
Volbert

Petite Anse

Cousin Island

Grande Anse

Salazie Track

Pointe
La Farl

Cousine Island

Anse Citron

Vallee de Mai

Baie Ste Anne

Round Island

Petite Anse

Hotels

1	Indian Ocean Fishing Club
2	Flying Dutchman
3	Maison des Palmes
4	La Réserve
5	Paradise Sun
6	Praslin Beach
7	Village du Pêcheur
8	Côte d'Or Lodge
9	L' Archipel
10	L' Emerald Cove
11	Chateau De Feuilles
12	Coco de Mer

the ferry terminal: prices for food and drinks here are 30-60% higher than at the shops a few hundreds metres away in the city.

The airport is on the west coast, midway between Grande Anse and Anse Kerlan. Taxis wait at the terminal. There is also a bus stop outside the airport grounds near the entrance gate. Schooners dock at the pier on the south-western side of Baie Ste Anne, a few hundred metres north of Pointe Cabris. Taxis are also available at the pier. Travellers using public transport should walk along the pier, past the First and Last Bar, to the T-junction. Buses going north make a turn outside the bar, while those heading south stop for passengers at the bus stop across the road, at the little beach.

VALLÉE DE MAI NATIONAL PARK

No trip to the Seychelles is complete without at least one visit to the magical Vallée de Mai. To catch a bus or hitchhike there from the west coast, walk through Grande Anse and wait near Praslin Holiday Car Rental, or further on at the fork in the road. Take the Baie Ste Anne bus and ask to be dropped at Vallée de Mai. To get there from the east coast, wait at the T-junction between Anse L'Amour and Cap Samy, or walk west opposite the causeway to the bus stop outside the hospital. All the buses travelling along this road pass the reserve entrance.

Open daily 8h00-17h30, the park attracts bus loads of tourists who somehow fail to overcrowd its majesty and tranquillity. Upon paying the entrance fee, each visitor is given a pamphlet which details trails and describes various sites of interest.

Until the early 1930s the hills and valleys comprising the Vallée de Mai remained largely unexplored wilderness. "Chinese" Gordon, who was later murdered at the siege of Khartoum, visited the area in 1880. True to his philosophical nature, Gordon believed the unique coco de mer palm was the Tree of the Knowledge of Good and Evil described in Genesis. (A walk through this tropical forest easily convinces one that Vallée de Mai is a remnant of the original garden of Eden.) The Vallée's coco de mers had such an effect on him that when he later designed the Seychelles' coat of arms, he incorporated into it a coco de mer tree growing on the back of a Seychelles giant tortoise.

Immediately after entering the park, visitors come upon a thatched shelter in which coco de mer nuts are de-husked, cleaned and polished for sale in the curio shops and stalls of the Seychelles.

There are three main trails in the Vallée de Mai, and it is strongly recommended that you walk all three. The surroundings are beautiful and fascinating, but do not be surprised to find exotics growing in the national park. Since the 1930s, when Europeans first exploited the forest, growers have planted many trees from other countries. The National Parks and Nature Conservancy Commission has now started a programme to eradicate all non-indigenous species.

Visitors will notice the coco de mer "bowls", hollows in the ground where a tree had stood. They can remain for half a century after the coco de mer had died. The trees are long-lived. Some of the coco de mers in the park are reputed to be 800 years old, although some botanists estimate their age at less than half that.

The forests of palms have given botanists an insight into the early vegetation of the Seychelles' granitic islands. It is now believed that during the earth's early evolution, palm forests covered vast tracts of land in the tropics.

Other plants that will capture your attention in the Vallée de Mai are numerous rare ferns, five other varieties of palm, screwpines, bald-patted capucin, once prized bread-fruit, cascades of flowering bou-gainvillaea, prickly pineapples, wild vanilla and dumb cane, from which a toxic drink, to be forced down the throats of recalcitrant slaves, was once made.

Animals are scarce, and apart from occasional lizards, frogs and fresh-water shrimps, the biggest attraction is the highly endangered black parrot (*Coracopsis nigra barklyi*). Very few people are fortunate enough to spot one of these birds, but its high-pitched whistle may sometimes be heard. Colonies of fruit bats fill the tops of trees in the early morning and evening, while chameleons camouflage themselves in a hundred hues.

Take seriously the motto of the Vallée de Mai: "Take only photographs, leave only footprints".

WEST PRASLIN

Starting at Baie Ste Anne and travelling south, visitors arrive at the remote, sea-lashed **Anse Marie-Louise**. A pleasant one-hour walk can be taken through the lush vegetation back to the bus stop at Baie Ste Anne. Take the track that turns north off the main road, opposite Anse Marie-Louise, and follow this along the forested edges of Fond Ferdinand and down to the main road again.

The expensive *Château de Feuilles* (high tariff), located at Petite Anse near Anse Marie-Louise, seems to accept only French tourists. It has 12 rooms, a restaurant, bar and boutique, and caters exclusively for visitors who do not want a beach, nor busy nightlife. You could try booking from countries other than France, but I have no idea how successful you'll be:

Château des Feuilles, PO Baie Ste Anne, Praslin, Seychelles, tel. 23-3316.

Badamier Guesthouse (medium tariff) is also near Anse Marie-Louise. It has a good restaurant and access to a pretty strip of beach. Unless you have booked at least 90 days in advance, forget about finding accommodation here. Popular with European holiday-makers, the Badamier offers comfort, fair service and serenity:

Badamier Guesthouse, Anse Marie-Louise, Praslin, Seychelles, tel. 23-3066.

Further west, at **Anse Consolation**, are a delightful beach and picturesque granite rocks off Pointe Cocos. An overgrown path takes walkers across the green hills to above the road at Anse Marie-Louise. This stroll should take no longer than 30 minutes, and introduces visitors to the luxuriant vegetation of Praslin.

Anse Bois de Rose has one of the best hotels and cleanest beaches on the Seychelles: the Hotel Coco de Mer.

Hotel Coco de Mer (high tariff)

This is one hotel where the service and quality equal the price. Owned and managed by a South African, the Hotel Coco de Mer offers visitors five-star luxury and personal attention. The management has even devised a method of keeping the atrocious seaweed from washing up on the beach. Not dictated to by absent directors, the owner has created a First-World hotel of 40 sumptuous air-conditioned rooms, all with sea views. Silence and tranquillity are characteristic of the Hotel Coco de Mer. Each room has a bathroom en suite, ceiling fan, television, radio and telephone. Arriving guests are greeted with a welcome cocktail and advised of the hotel's facilities. These include water sport equipment, a coco de mer-shaped swimming pool, long palm-fringed beach and, overlooking the sea, the Black Parrot Restaurant. In the Hibiscus Restaurant large buffet breakfasts are served to residents 7h30-10h00. The Mango Pool Bar has a menu for lunches served at the pool. No stay at the Hotel Coco de Mer is complete without a meal in the famed Black Parrot Restaurant. Book your table at reception. This restaurant boasts an expert chef and impressive wine list. Diners have the choice of buffet, carvery or set menu. Dishes range from traditional Creole to Continental. Live entertainment is offered each evening. Non-residents must reserve a table at least two days in advance.

Excursions, car hire and bicycles can all be arranged, as can a guided walk along the Jean Baptiste Nature Trail through the hotel's own nature reserve in the forests and hills behind the hotel. Visitors who want to do game fishing, scuba diving or snorkelling should contact the reception office at least 24 hours in advance. Boat trips around Praslin are also available, and local guides can be arranged.

Book accommodation well in advance. The peak season is between 22 December and 7 January, and accommodation over this period should be confirmed about six months ahead:

Hotel Coco de Mer, Anse Bois de Rose, Praslin, Seychelles, tel. 23-3900, fax 23-3919. In South Africa reservations can be made via La Buschagne-Smith, Suite 43, Groote Schuur Apartments, Erskine Terrace, Durban 4001, tel. (031) 37-4854, 42-7140.

North of the Black Parrot Restaurant, the curved sweep of **Anse Takamaka** is a favourite weekend spot for Praslin Seychellois families. Not many foreigners use this beach, and you are bound to be invited to join a group of Seychellois if you happen to be there on a Saturday or Sunday afternoon.

The road forks a little beyond Anse Citron at Fond de L'Anse. To the right it goes east, past the Vallée de Mai, and descends to Anse L'Amour and back to the village of Baie Ste Anne. Take the left branch, for Grande Anse Village.

Grande Anse

Mason's Travel has an office here. Nearby, next to Praslin Video Rental, is the reasonably priced Praslin Holiday Car Rental. Ivey's Bar is a local hang-out where budget travellers should ask about cheap accommodation with a Grande Anse family. The bar is open from 6h45-22h00. Around the corner is the Parish Church of St Matthew. Rebuilt in 1904, this cool, blue church comes alive with harmonious singing on Sunday mornings. You are likely to be the only foreigner attending the Mass, but can be assured of being invited to tea with a local family after the service.

Behind the church is *Britz Takeaways*, open 8h00-22h00 daily. It offers cheap, filling meals at prices way below those at hotels or tourist restaurants. The seafood dishes are enormous and served with rice, salads and piment sauce.

Following the road south-east of Britz will bring you to the upmarket *Britannia Restaurant, Bar and Guesthouse* (medium tariff). The Britannia has five well-appointed rooms and is about five minutes' walk from the beaches of Grande Anse. The guesthouse is, however, more noted for its restaurant than its accommodation. Specialising in Creole cooking, it offers an extensive menu. The servings are large and the quality of food is excellent. Every visitor to the region should try at least one

Creole meal here. Reservations for accommodation are seldom necessary, but be advised that backpackers are regarded with disdain and may be refused a room:

Britannia, PO Grande Anse, Praslin, Seychelles, tel. 23-3215, fax 23-3944.

Between Britz Takeaways and *Steve's Snack Shop and Takeaway*, across the bridge, is the Independence Monument commemorating the Seychelles' independence on 29 June 1976. It can be difficult to find among the trees. Steve's is probably the best low-cost eatery on Praslin. Scrupulously clean, the shop serves delicious meals, either as takeaways or on a plate, and sells ice-cream and fresh pastries. A sure indication of its calibre is that many islanders travel from the east coast just for its tasty food. Because it is a favourite with Praslinois, visitors here have the opportunity of meeting and mixing with locals.

Near Selvaray Store, where you can buy groceries, cloth and phonecards, is Barclays Bank. A little further up the street is a Seychelles Savings Bank agency. The Banque Française Commerciale (Océan Indien) has counters near the Coco de Mer Boutique, to the north of the village. Traveller's cheques and hard currency can be exchanged here, but to draw cash from credit cards authorisation will have to be obtained from Mahé. The bus stop for Grande Anse is in front of Praslin Trading, opposite the Grande Anse Community Hall. Praslin Trading has a wide range of frozen products, eggs and dairy goods. Do not be put off by the seeming emptiness of the shop, most products are kept in the large deep-freezers.

North of the police station is the post office, next to the Civil Status Office. The National Library is open to visitors and the helpful staff will do their best to find you information that may interest you about Praslin. Instant international telephone calls can be made from the public telephones outside the main gate of the Cable and Wireless buildings.

Curio hunters will be fascinated by the large displays at the Shopping and Collecting Museum and the Coco de Mer Boutique. Locally produced handicrafts are sold here. The quality of workmanship is high.

At *Grande Anse Beach Villa* (high tariff), tel. 23-3445, accommodation is provided in eight palm-thatched chalets. Most guests have been here before and book their next visit when leaving, so there is seldom room available.

A far better place to stay, for price, service and food, is the nearby Indian Ocean Lodge, whose entrance is at a road sign warning of tortoises crossing.

Indian Ocean Lodge (medium-high tariff)

Perched on the very edge of Grande Anse beach and bay, the Indian Ocean Lodge has one of the best locations on Praslin. It is the oldest hotel on Praslin (built in 1937) and has 16 quaint, Creole-style beach bungalows with air-conditioning and bathrooms en suite. The bungalows are spaced between palm trees and all overlook the pale blue waters of the bay. Indian Ocean Lodge offers visitors advice on island tours and can arrange car hire and trips with Mason's Travel. The owner personally meets each new arrival and gives a detailed account of what is available, plus suggestions and recommendations. He is especially good at providing independent travellers with guidelines for seeing the sites on Praslin. Among the hotel restaurants on Praslin, the one at the Indian Ocean Lodge has the reputation of offering the best value for money.

The Indian Ocean Lodge has an armed night-guard and the property will soon be walled in, offering guests exclusivity at an acceptable tariff. It has beautifully landscaped gardens of whispering palm trees, lush lawns and cascades of indigenous flowers. Sitting on the lawn of the Indian Ocean Lodge and watching the sun set must rate as one of the highlights of any visit to Praslin. Even if you are not staying at the lodge, have a quiet cocktail in the garden as evening falls. Another good idea is to take a skinny-dip in the warm shallows, late at night, under a canopy of stars.

Foreign currency and traveller's cheques may be cashed at the hotel, and all international credit cards are accepted. Reservations are always necessary, at least 60 days ahead:

Indian Ocean Lodge, PO Grande Anse, Praslin, Seychelles, tel. 23-3324, fax 23-3911.

Try some of the walks that commence in Grande Anse and cross the island, via forests and valleys, to the east coast. Take a hat, sunscreen, water and something to eat on these walks. Although they are not at all difficult, the high humidity and heat of the interior can dehydrate walkers quickly.

One of the most pleasant walks starts from behind St Matthew's church. Walk along the gravel road, following the signs for Britannia

Restaurant, Bar and Guesthouse. Keep left of the guesthouse and pass Janessa's Boutique. Continue to the fork in the road and go right alongside the ruined Creole house and cemetery. The road is cemented on the steepest sections of this climb into the forested hills. Walkers will see the remnants of sugar cane plantations among the trees and can meet the hill-Seychellois of Praslin, famed for their hospitality. After about an hour you will reach another fork. To the right, the Salazie track follows the Salazie river down to the east coast road on the **Côte d'Or**. The left path, the Pasquière track, swings north and exits opposite **Anse Possession**. Both tracks traverse a pristine wilderness of secluded valleys, granite cliffs, tumbling rivers and montane forests. Magnificent views of both coasts can be had from the rocky summits of the inland cliffs. Irrespective of which track you choose, the entire walk should not take longer than two to three hours.

Another walk worth considering, albeit about an hour longer than the other two and much more strenuous, is along the path from Grande Anse north, then east to **Anse Boudin** on the east coast. Start at St Joseph's chapel and follow the gravel track that turns north through the coconut grove. There is a steep climb to the summit of Grande Fond (342 m), which affords impressive views of the entire northern part of Praslin. From the ridge the path drops steeply through severely damaged and eroded forest land to the gravel road linking Anse Boudin and Anse Lazio.

Buses going north and south stop outside the Indian Ocean Lodge. Going north up the west coast, travellers will pass the Praslin Airport, cross the Mare Baccar river and bypass an aquaculture project before reaching Anse Kerlan.

Anse Kerlan is the beach made famous by the movie *Castaway*. It is seldom busy, and during the week you are quite likely to be the only person visiting. To reach Anse Kerlan from Grande Anse, catch the Anse Kerlan bus opposite the Grande Anse Community Hall. Ask the driver to drop you off at the sand road leading to Anse Kerlan Farm. Follow the road past the estate manager's house and into the large coconut grove. To the left of the plantation is the beach of Anse Kerlan. Swimming off Anse Kerlan is not always pleasant. The sloping beach causes "dumpers" and a strong backwash that may present problems for holiday-makers unused to dealing with currents.

If you continue along the road to where it ends, you will find yourself at Praslin's best-kept secret: **Petite Anse Kerlan**. This small white beach is protected by rocks on one side and forested cliffs on the other, creating a perfect swimming bay. Although the water quickly gets deep, it is seldom rough. Snorkelling around the offshore rocks in the bay is not to be missed. Drift out over the submerged granite boulders, watching the brightly coloured fish and dancing sea plants. Look for the resident white-tipped reef shark. Only about 1 m in size, this small shark seems to delight in appearing unannounced in front of people snorkelling. Of course the initial reaction is one of panic, but remain calm, and after a few cursory circles the white-tip will lazily swim off into the deepening blue, north of the bay. The shark will not attack and is far too small to present any threat, but will fill you with a sense of wonder and heightened appreciation of these mysterious creatures.

On the granite rocks to the west, known as **Pointe Ste Marie**, is a statue of Mother Mary, in both honour and remembrance of those Praslinois who died at sea. There are also good views across to Cousin Island. At high tide, brave youths plunge off these rocks into the deep sea far below. Once you have tried this free fall, it becomes rather addictive, and is certain to get you invited to one of the locals' home for a meal, drink or discussion of this adrenalin-rush activity.

Back in the coconut groves are ruins of the original estate buildings, storehouses and copra factory. These have now been turned into pigsties by the people who live in the little house on the edge of Petite Anse Kerlan. Ask them if you may wander about the crumbling buildings. It must surely once have been a grand plantation. Today it barely operates. The low price of coconuts, the falling demand for copra and severe competition from Southeast Asia have virtually destroyed the Seychelles' coconut industry.

There is a gravel path that goes east between the ruined plantation buildings. This overgrown path follows the northern bank of Rivière Anse Kerlan for about 500 m and then climbs into the hills around Newcome farm. Turn north at the farm buildings and cross through the indigenous forest onto the state land of Savoy, before exiting opposite the stark granite boulders on the palm-lined beach of **Anse Lazio**. It should not take you more than one hour to complete the distance.

EAST PRASLIN

There is little difference between the vegetation and topography of western and eastern Praslin. Although there are far fewer hotels and tourists on east Praslin, two of the best hotels on the Seychelles are on its east coast: L'Archipel and the Paradise Sun.

A regular bus service runs all along the east coast from Baie Ste Anne to Anse Boudin. From there you can walk or hitchhike the few kilometres to Anse Lazio. It is a tiring walk over steep hills. Hitchhiking is a much better option, or hire a bicycle in Anse Boudin for the day.

Baie Ste Anne

Going north from the ferry pier in Baie Ste Anne, visitors pass a small boatbuilding yard, where wooden fishing vessels are still handmade in the traditional fashion. On the left is the *Orange Tree Guesthouse* (medium tariff), a four-roomed guesthouse popular with budget travellers. Breakfast and dinner are included in the reasonable rate, and both meals will leave you comfortably sated. Reservations are necessary, 60 days ahead:

Orange Tree Guesthouse, PO Baie Ste Anne, Praslin, Seychelles, tel. 23-3248.

Nearby is *Seaview Self-catering Accommodation* (low-medium tariff). These spartan rooms are ideal for people travelling through the expensive Seychelles on a shoe-string. Supplies can be bought from nearby Cynthia's General Merchants. Seaview is usually full all year, and bookings are necessary at least 90 days ahead:

Seaview Self-catering Accommodation, PO Baie Ste Anne, Praslin, Seychelles, tel. 23-3250.

Model ships and local curios are available from Atelier de Maquettes. The craftsmen are friendly and enjoy chatting to foreigners. Prices are high but credit cards are accepted, and the quality of workmanship is as high as in Mauritius. Close to the concrete jetty is the post office and police station. If you are stuck for lodgings, the teachers at Baie Ste Anne School will go out of their way to find you a bed. Barclays Bank has a branch opposite the Baie Ste Anne Community Hall and administration offices.

A curious church with a red tin roof is the gathering place for local families on Sunday mornings. They seldom get the chance to mix with a foreign visitor, and will extend their hospitality to those who join them. *Coco Rouge Restaurant and Takeaways* lies between the church and Bassa Tailoring. The cheap menu includes fresh fish, traditional Creole dishes and spiced vegetables. You will not find hotel guests dining here – only the Praslinois – which makes it an ideal place to get to know some of them. *Downtown Takeaways* is a few notches below the Coco Rouge but nevertheless offers excellent cheap meals, cooked in the traditional manner. The octopus curry is frequently recommended by local diners.

A fairly wide choice of clothing and souvenirs is available at Seaside Store. The shop does not appear to have any definite opening times, and you will just have to try if you are in the area. Le Cocotier Boutique and Austral Car Rental have an amazing selection of goods for sale. These range from shells to snacks, film and coco de mer nuts. All prices of curios are negotiable, and hard bargaining is necessary. Remember to get an export permit from the shop if you buy a coco de mer nut.

At the northern edge of Baie Ste Anne village is another self-catering establishment: *My Dream Self-catering*. With young, "hip" staff who play wonderful reggae music, very loudly, all day, this place is recommended for younger travellers. You are bound to be invited to a local house-party if staying here. These go on until the early hours of the morning and are not to be missed.

From Baie Ste Anne north, the road skirts farms and travels through an avenue of trees until forking. To the right, the road continues to **Au Cap** and a little cove also called Anse Takamaka. From here a track leads east across to another beach called Petite Anse and south-east across Au Morne to **Pointe La Farine**, from where you have a clear view across to Round Island. By taking the left fork in the road, travellers cut across the peninsula and reach the exclusive Hotel L'Archipel.

Hotel L'Archipel (high tariff)

Frequent destination of the world's jet set, including the likes of Giorgio Armani, L'Archipel is sheer luxury in the tropics and is definitely for the well-heeled tourist. Owned by Cecile Hodoul (relative of the 18th century corsair, Jean François Hodoul), it has 22 magnificent air-conditioned rooms and two superior suites offering the best in architecture and comfort. All rooms have uncluttered sea views, a lavish bathroom, television, radio, digitally operated safe, veranda with deck chairs and direct dialling telephone. The sumptuous suites also have a spa-bath, walk-in cupboard and tastefully furnished lounge.

Note that no children under three years old are allowed.

The hotel's strip of private beach is raked each morning. Residents can make use of the free water sport facilities. The reception staff are able to arrange boat cruises, deep-sea fishing, scuba diving, car hire and guided island tours. Breakfast and dinner are served from a Continental set menu, in the main restaurant which is cooled by tropical breezes. No shorts or T-shirts are allowed in the restaurant and cocktail lounge after 19h00. A beach bar offers cool drinks and light snacks throughout the day. Once a week, there is a Creole theme evening, with traditional food, dancing and singing. Foreign currency and traveller's cheques may be exchanged at the reception counter. Credit cards may be used for payment. Prior reservations are essential:

Hotel L'Archipel, Anse Gouvernement, Praslin, Seychelles, tel. 23-2242, fax 23-2072.

Almost at the same entrance is the *Côte d'Or Lodge Hotel* (high tariff). Although its rates are high, the service, quality and staff of this hotel are a far cry from those of L'Archipel. It is, however, popular with families who want to be left alone. There is access to the southern tip of Anse Volbert beach from here. Activities are limited and cleanliness does not seem to rate highly. Still, a few people rave about the place, while others will probably change accommodation within a day or two of arriving:

Côte d'Or Lodge Hotel, Anse Volbert, Praslin, Seychelles, tel. 23-2200.

Beyond the hotels, dense forests give way to paw-paw and banana plantations, and then the road swings right towards the edge of **Anse Volbert**. On the left is an extraordinary plantation house. It is still inhabited, but the residents will let most visitors take a look inside. It is as though you have stepped back in time when you cross the threshold, into the colonial era and the lives of the traditional Seychellois. Ask before taking photographs and spend a while talking to the amiable people. Their home-brewed palm wine is delicious but potent: unless you have nothing else to do that day, do not have more than two glasses. On the other hand, it can be very pleasant lying on their back lawn chatting until the stars come out.

Octopus Diving, on the beach near the La Goulue Café, offers both day and night dives. It provides all equipment, a boat and experienced guide. You do not have to be qualified, as Octopus Diving offers a "Resort Course", which qualifies you to scuba dive here (but nowhere else).

La Goulue Café is often full of tourists. Prices are high, but the food is tasty and servings are satisfying. A few hundred metres north of the café the tarred road forks. By keeping right, travellers will arrive at the settlement of Côte d'Or.

Côte d'Or

Café d'Arts has a small restaurant, set in a garden on the edge of the sea, an art gallery and accommodation. The owner, renowned photographer Paul Turcotte, has a collection of his best works on display. There is also a collection of artworks by his wife and other Praslinois artists. Curios are also sold, and the staff have in-depth knowledge of the Seychelles – useful to solo travellers. In the restaurant, at which reservations must be made, diners may choose from an extensive menu of Creole dishes. For the accommodation (low-medium tariff), speak to the owners or book about 10 days ahead:

Café d'Arts, PO Côte d'Or, Praslin, Seychelles, tel. 23-2131, fax 23-2155.

Other accommodation worth considering on the Côte d'Or includes:

Praslin Beach Hotel and Casino (high tariff). There are 68 rooms in this mediocre hotel, set in an expansive garden. The hotel can arrange trips to the neighbouring islands, notably to Chauve Souris and St Pierre. A swimming pool and restaurant provide respite from the vendor-filled beach, while a casino pulsates every evening from Monday to Saturday. There is also a water sports centre and weekly theme evenings: PO Côte d'Or, Praslin, Seychelles, tel. 23-2222, fax 23-2244.

Village du Pêcheur (medium-high tariff) has 10 rooms at Anse Volbert beach. Its small restaurant serves mostly Continental cuisine and offers weekly Creole entertainment: PO Côte d'Or, Praslin, Seychelles, tel. 23-2030.

Where the road becomes gravel, tourists keen to go fishing will want to contact La Tazar Boat Charter. It offers trips as much as 30% cheaper than those booked through hotels. All equipment is provided, as is lunch, but bring your own drinks. Côte d'Or Bicycle Hire is located close to the rear entrance of Praslin Beach Hotel. Rates are charged per half-day. Make certain that you check your bike before setting off and that a padlock and chain are included. Bife Disco is recommended on a Friday and Saturday night. Rather forego the hotel discos and casino in favour of this local haunt. The people are friendly and unused to seeing foreigners in one of their nightclubs. A small entrance fee is charged, which includes one free drink. Count on dancing until sunrise.

You now have the option of either returning to the fork in the tarred road or proceeding onto the property of another of the Seychelles' top-class hotels, the Paradise Sun.

Paradise Sun Hotel *(medium-high tariff)*

Spilling onto the glorious Côte d'Or, the Paradise Sun is situated on what many tourists claim is the best beach in the world. The hotel's 80 rooms unobtrusively blend with its tropical gardens. Accommodation is in traditional Creole-style buildings that allow fragrant breezes to waft through each room. All have bathrooms en suite, fans and a patio. Coffee and tea can be made in each room: the necessary ingredients and equipment are supplied. This hotel has none of the aloofness and austerity usually associated with large hotel chains. At the Paradise Sun each visitor is made to feel special. The staff are attentive and friendly.

The hotel's entertainment department arranges and displays a list of the day's recommended activities each morning on a notice board. Volleyball and tennis are available and the hotel has extensive water sport facilities. A daily boat excursion takes snorkellers and walkers to the offshore islands, where knowledgable guides lead them through thick jungle vegetation and the alluring marine world. On the memorable evening cruise along the east coast, passengers are supplied with snacks, cocktails, light music and drinks. A well-stocked boutique sells curios and a few supplies.

Meals are excellent. Theme evenings have delicious set menus and a real holiday atmosphere. A resident band plays Seychellois music and any requests. On the beach, lunch and snacks can be eaten at Le Beach Restaurant. The essence of the Paradise Sun is a beautiful beach, excellent service, comfortable accommodation and the friendliest staff of all the Seychelles' hotels. Reservations are necessary, at least 60 days ahead:

Paradise Sun Hotel, PO Côte d'Or, Anse Volbert, Praslin, Seychelles, tel. 23-2255, fax 23-2019.

La Réserve *(high tariff)*

This hotel, west of the unmanned lighthouse on **Pointe Zanguilles**, offers superior accommodation in plantation-style bungalows. The interior of each house is a sheer delight and transports guests to the era of planters and pirates. Rooms have bathrooms en suite, huge double beds shrouded in gossamer mosquito nets, ceiling fans and a veranda complete with table and deck chairs. Reservations are advisable about 60 days ahead:

La Réserve, PO Anse Possession, Praslin, Seychelles, tel. 23-2211, fax 23-2166.

Nearby **Anse Petite Cour** has a shallow lagoon which shelves into what must rate as one of the top 10 snorkelling spots in the world. Non-residents are allowed to use this tiny beach off La Réserve. Wade in the shallow water along the hill to the south. Beyond the granite rocks the water quickly gets deep; here a submarine paradise starts. An abundance of sea life, which few tourists ever see, fills the crystal-clear water all along the rocky coast to below the lighthouse. The water is admittedly deep here, but there are no strong currents and it is warm. You could easily spend three to five hours drifting above this oceanic wonderland.

North of La Réserve is **Anse Possession**, with its expanse of coral beach and reefed lagoon, where the first French Stone of Possession was laid in 1744. Beyond it the gravel road winds through and over wooded hills before becoming a two-strip cement track which peters out at **Anse Lazio** beach, at the south-eastern end of **Baie Chevalier**. This beach is extremely popular with hotel guests and package tourists. Forget about solitude here. It is a great place for watching sunsets, though. Just before the beach, at the busy car park, is the *Bonbon Plume Restaurant* where the Creole food is excellent. It always seems busy and you may have a long wait before being served. It may be better to take along your own food and drinks for the day.

A good shore break creates fine bodysurfing waves, and a little beyond these waves is a large area of flat, calm sea. As there are few rocks in the water here, snorkelling or scuba diving is not fruitful. This is a swimming beach, an idyllic place where you can ride a horse along the fine white sand, suntan at the water's edge or meditate beneath softly singing palms.

20 ISLANDS AROUND PRASLIN

COUSIN ISLAND

Declared a bird sanctuary in 1968, this 30 ha island, less than 3 km south-west of Anse Kerlan, is owned and managed by the International Council for Bird Preservation. The Seychelles Nature Conservancy declared all wildlife on Cousin, in addition to birds, protected in 1975. Home to the unique Seychelles bush warbler (*Brebornis seychellensis*), Cousin is a must for all birdwatchers. Its rich avifauna includes red turtle doves, fodies, fairy terns, frigatebirds and Audubon's shearwaters. An estimated 300 000 birds nest on Cousin each year.

No independent travel is allowed to Cousin. Tour operators offer day trips to the nature reserve on Tuesday, Thursday and Friday. Only 20 people are permitted per tour. Book early to avoid the waiting list that inevitably builds up between April and May. A beach barbeque is usually included in the tour, and there will be enough time for a swim in the shallows. Remember that you are not allowed to wander about without a guide. The guides, anyway, are a fount of knowledge about the island's flora, fauna and fragile offshore ecosystems.

Birds are not the only drawcard to Cousin. Eleven species of reptile also live on the island, including giant tortoises, the Seychelles skink and the green tree gecko.

There are only six permanent human inhabitants on Cousin, all involved in the study and preservation of the island's wildlife.

ARIDE ISLAND

About 16 km north of Baie Chevalier lies Aride Island. The first Europeans stepped ashore here in 1756. Also a nature sanctuary, Aride has been owned by the Royal Society for Nature Conservation since 1973. An encircling coral reef makes it difficult for boats to land on the island.

No independent travel is allowed. You must go with a guide on an organised tour. These are offered four times a week by the major tour operators on the Seychelles. After a guided tour and lunch, visitors are permitted to walk along the south coast and swim.

Aride, one of the most attractive of the granitic islands, has lush tropical vegetation and a maximum height of just 134 m. There is a settlement on the southern coast at La Cour, on the Côte Désiré, where the boats land.

Birds are the attraction of Aride. Literally millions of birds arrive to nest on the island each year. These include the plume-tailed tropicbirds or *paille en queue* (the national symbol of Réunion), frigatebirds, lesser noddies, sooty and fairy terns, and recently introduced Seychelles bush warblers.

One of the highlights of any trip to Aride is enjoying the beautifully scented jasmine and the fragrance of the endemic Wright's gardenia growing on the low forested slopes of the island.

CURIEUSE ISLAND

Curieuse Island Marine National Park is about 2 km north-east of Anse Boudin. Most people go to Curieuse Island with a tour group from one of the Praslin hotels or with a tour operator. Such tours end with a barbeque on the beach before the return to Praslin. Independent visitors are also welcome. It is fairly easy to arrange a boat from Praslin. The best places to try for a dawn journey to Curieuse are from Praslin's north-east coast, for example Anse Boudin. Faster, more expensive vessels are available along Anse Volbert and can be arranged by the Paradise Sun Hotel.

The best way to explore Curieuse is to set off alone or with a local guide through the forests, valleys and hills. The island is only about 3 km by 2 km, so it is virtually impossible to get lost – ubiquitous children will assist you if you do lose your way.

Of the 300 Aldabra giant land tortoises translocated here, only about 100 remain – the others have been poached. They lay their eggs between May and June in the soft sand, and are constantly monitored by the rangers who live on the little island.

A concrete causeway had been built across **Laraie Bay** to form a protected turtle pond, but the pond is no longer used for breeding turtles. The ruins of a leper colony, dating back to 1833, can be visited near the beach of **Anse St José**. This is the better of the two beaches on Curieuse. You reach it by following the path that starts at the causeway, contours a shallow saddle and exits at more buildings near the beach. There is also a good swimming beach at **Grande Anse**, on the eastern part of the island. To get there, follow the coastal path northeast past the staff housing and then take the track going to the beach.

Snorkelling off Curieuse Island is wonderful, although relatively few people ever venture into the water around Roche Canon or off Rouge Point. Speak to the island manager or one of the rangers about the most suitable time to go.

If you arrive on Curieuse alone, the residents rush to greet you. The five families who live on the island devote themselves to caring for the wildlife, guiding tourists and cultivating crops of mangos, bananas and tangerines. They are keen to invite you into their homes, thrust food and drink in front of you, arrange a suitable guide and send children along as companions. This is certainly the best way to visit Curieuse. If you are hoping to stay overnight, take along some food to contribute to the islanders' simple meals.

ST PIERRE AND CHAUVES SOURIS ISLANDS

These clusters of granitic boulders lie north-east of **Anse Volbert**. There is not much to see or do on these islets, but the snorkelling around them is superb.

You can easily walk out to **Chauves Souris** from the beach at the Paradise Sun. There is a *lodge* (high tariff) on Chauves Souris. Eating a meal in its restaurant, lapped by sky-blue, clear waters, gives you a feeling of being suspended in space. The experience of sleeping in one of the five rooms on this rocky outcrop in the Indian Ocean is highly recommended for those who can afford it. Reservations are essential: Chauve Souris, PO Box 117, Victoria, Mahé; or PO Côte d'Or, Praslin, Seychelles, tel. 23-2003, fax 23-2133.

Located about 800 m further north-east is **St Pierre**, an even smaller mound of granitic rocks. The fishermen along the Côte d'Or are willing to bring passengers here, after about 7h30, and fetch them at 16h00. Take along your own food and drink for the entire day. The hotels along Anse Volbert also arrange day trips, and include a packed lunch. Speak to the reception staff at the Paradise Sun Hotel.

21 LA DIGUE

La Digue, the Seychelles' most photographed island, lies 43 km east of Mahé. The fourth largest island in the group at 5 km by 3 km, La Digue is frequently called the jewel of the Indian Ocean. And indeed, its beauty and strange rock formations sparkle in the warm tropical sea.

Until a few years ago, La Digue was largely unaffected by tourism and population growth. Today, however, the situation is rapidly changing. Hotels, guesthouses, restaurants and guides proliferate. All along the western side of the island, construction is under way. Where only ox carts and bicycles once passed, now buses and 4x4s rush about. However, the highland forests and stretches of beach on the east coast are still unspoilt.

Perhaps the most striking feature of La Digue, apart from the captivating beaches, is the pink granite boulders that litter the island, as though thrown down from the heavens in anger. They edge secluded coves and poke their shimmering tops from the jungle interior. Every visitor should spend at least one sunset or sunrise watching the changing shades and hues of these pastel pink beauties.

There is no airstrip on La Digue, so all visitors are forced to arrive by boat, either from Mahé or from Praslin. The shortest sea route is from Baie Ste Anne, on Praslin. The 7 km crossing takes about 30 minutes. The crossing from Mahé takes at least three hours.

Visitors arrive at the concrete pier in **La Passe** harbour. The gateway to the island is marked by a small lighthouse and Christian cross. At the end of the pier, tourists are offered a ride to their destination in wooden ox-drawn carts. Taxis wait for guests staying at the upmarket La Digue Island Lodge. Budget travellers can walk or hire a bicycle from one of the rental agencies here.

Accommodation touts also wait for arriving foreigners, concentrating their attentions on backpackers and those who have obviously turned up without reserved lodgings. If desperate, then use one of these chaps, otherwise simply find your own room by asking at the little stores along any of the gravel roads.

There is no actual town on La Digue. The shops, accommodation, restaurants and islanders' houses are scattered all across the granitic

LA DIGUE

0   1   2 km

Anse Patates

Anse Severe

Anse Gaulettes

La Digue
Veuve Reserve
(Flycatcher Reserve)

Anse Grosse Roche

LA PASSE

Anse Banane

Nid d' Aigles

Anse
Fourmis

Anse
Caiman

La Digue
Island Peak
333 m

Anse la Reunion

L'UNION
ESTATE

Anse Cocos

Pointe
Source d' Argent

Pointe
Turcy

Petite Anse

Pointe Belize

Anse
Pierrot

Grande Anse

Pointe Jacques

island. The post office is located near the end of the jetty, in the harbour of La Passe. Close to the National Library, and opposite the La Digue hospital, along the main west coast gravel road, is the Seychelles Savings Bank. Traveller's cheques and foreign currency can be exchanged here, but you cannot draw a large amount of cash from a credit card. Barclays Bank has a branch opposite the La Digue Island Lodge, next to Gregoire's Boutique.

By far the best way to discover La Digue is to take a day-pack with some water and food and just set off in any direction. There are countless paths and tracks crisscrossing the island's hills and forests. Many are frequently used, others go to remote settlements and isolated vanilla farms, where the hospitality of the locals will be one of your most enduring memories of La Digue.

SOUTH-WEST LA DIGUE

Where the path from the pier of **La Passe** harbour forms a T-junction, travellers will see a mass of signboards, dominated by those advertising Choppy's Bungalows and PADI Diving. La Passe Store is immediately to the right. Several shelves full of curios are available here, as are groceries, drinks, books and clothing. At *Tarosa Cafeteria*, light lunches, drinks and snacks are served throughout the day. The *Tournesol Restaurant and Guesthouse* (low-medium tariff) is seldom busy. It offers reasonably priced meals and provides clean rooms. No reservations are necessary, as yet. If the guesthouse is full, the management will send someone to find you another room in the area for the same price.

Beyond the magnificent Community Centre, where concerts are sometimes held on Friday nights or Saturday afternoons, lie the bank, hospital and *Chez Marston Restaurant*. This is the best place on La Digue for authentic Creole cooking. There is no menu as such, and you must tell Marston the morning or evening before what you would like to eat. He then goes out, buys the ingredients and prepares the meal. Prices are low, Marston is a character and the food is unsurpassed on the island.

In the converted Odeon Cinema is the Odeon Bar, which also serves as the reception area and dance hall for Choppy's Bungalows.

Choppy's Bungalows (medium tariff)

Having been in business for the last 26 years, Choppy's has built up something of a reputation among visitors to La Digue. There are, however, conflicting reports. Some tourists love the place, returning annually.

Others hate their treatment by the management and decry the standard of cooking. While this author did find the staff a little off-handed and the rooms in need of renovation, the quality of the food and the personal attention of the new manageress were beyond reproach.

Choppy's Bungalows was the first tourist accommodation on La Digue. The premises are rented by Harry Choppy from his relatives – his daughter is now in charge. Accommodation is offered in 10 rooms, all with bathrooms and verandas. One of the attractions of Choppy's is that locals also use the facilities, which allows visitors to get to know them.

The open-air restaurant provides a comprehensive set menu, bound to satisfy even the hungriest visitor. Non-residents may eat here as well. Book well in advance. Once a week there is traditional Creole dancing on the beach, a barbeque and wonderful opportunity for meeting young islanders.

Bicycle hire is available from reception. Rates, both daily and weekly, are lower than at rental agencies. Guides and tours can also be arranged, as can scuba diving and fishing excursions. For glass-bottomed boat outings or trips to **Frégate Island**, speak to the management, at least 24 hours ahead of intended departure. Book accommodation at least 60 days ahead: Choppy's Bungalows, Anse Réunion, La Digue, Seychelles, tel. 23-4224, fax 23-4088.

The beach off Choppy's Bungalows, **Anse La Réunion**, is protected by a reef and fringed with palm trees and pink granite boulders. This is the best place on La Digue to watch the sunset. Snorkelling along the reef will yield dramatic sights of brightly coloured coral, shoals of fish and intricately patterned shells.

Opposite the wooden clock tower is the *Sunshine Guesthouse* and Bicycle Rental, tel. 23-4033. Lodgings in this small, dirty place are only for real shoe-string travellers, used to spartan and basic living conditions. The accommodation is nevertheless somewhat expensive, given its standard.

Mason's Travel Agency has an office near the fascinating Zimaz Kreol Art Gallery (in the Social Security Fund building). Beyond this is the most costly and overcrowded accommodation on La Digue: the *La Digue Island Lodge* (high tariff). This hotel is popular with package tours. It has 43 rooms and two restaurants which serve Continental and limited Creole fare. The hotel can arrange excursions and tours of La Digue and the neighbouring islands. It has a splendid stretch of swimming beach on Anse La Réunion, and a water sports centre caters for guests wishing to windsurf, snorkel or paddle. Guests and non-residents may use its PADI scuba diving facilities and attend the courses offered. You may also change money here and pay bills with credit cards. Be warned, prices are very high, and if travelling on a tight budget you will soon find yourself broke. Book accommodation through Mason's Travel or directly with the lodge:

La Digue Island Lodge, Anse La Réunion, La Digue, Seychelles, tel. 23-4232, fax 23-4100.

Continuing south along the coast road, you pass the Phoenix Store, Creole house and La Digue school. A quiet church, Maison de Dieu, is situated on the left of the sand road. Anse La Réunion is a long, wide beach that extends from just south of the landing pier in La Passe, all the way down to the entrance of L'Union coconut estate. You are free to swim anywhere along here, although some people feel safer within the confines of the island hotels or with a guide on the protected beaches south of the coconut estate. Those visitors who swim off the beach opposite the Paradise Flycatcher Lodge will be alone for most of the day. In this stretch of wilderness you may be fortunate enough to spot the rare, and endangered, black paradise flycatcher with its impressive plumage and glossy black sheen. Local fishermen land with their catches on this section of coast early each morning. You will also be able to arrange boat rides around La Digue from here. Talk to any of the youths who laze about under the palm trees. Negotiate the price beforehand and try to get them to include a packed lunch for the day.

At the fork in the road going south, turn right to reach **L'Union coconut estate**. This is one of the few working copra sites remaining on the Seychelles, and is open Monday-Friday 7h00-16h30. The estate and factory charge a small entrance fee, but people on bicycles are seldom stopped, ride through into the coconut groves. You can get details and an informative brochure from the women who staff the entrance kiosk. There are no restrictions on visitors wandering about the estate, but neither are there any official guides. The tour operators bring their clients in air-conditioned buses or jeeps, and provide a guide for the excursion. As you near the factory part of the estate, there is an old cemetery on the right. Many of the graves date back to the early days of La Digue's history.

The factory seems to have changed little since the 19th century. A bullock still walks mindlessly in circles crushing the de-husked coconuts and draining off the precious oil, which is exported to countries like India and Sri Lanka. Opposite the grinding mill are the drying houses, kilns, storerooms and mounds of coconut shells. Although there is no estate guide, one of the women working with the copra will usually offer her services for a while. Unless you are familiar with copra production, it is advisable to accept the offer of a guide.

In front of the administrative offices is the original plantation house. As it is still inhabited, access is denied to casual visitors. On the lawn in front of the fountain, vanilla quills are dried on long trestle tables. The fragrance of vanilla mingles with the scent of copra and the sound of the waves nearby to create a special ambience. At the estate's curio boutique, shoppers can buy bottles of coconut oil, vanilla, spice essences and silk-screened T-shirts.

The path leading south through the estate takes walkers alongside the apiary and to the base of the enormous L'Union rock. To reach the summit, walk around the sad tortoise enclosure and behind the stables. From here it is a difficult climb up the granite to the top, where there is a water reservoir. The effort is worth it, though, for the expansive views up and down the west coast.

If you keep to the left path through the coconut grove you will reach the vanilla plantation. Each estate punctures its identifying mark into the green pods on the vines. L'Union's mark is a U. Near the vanilla creepers are trellises of passion fruit, and behind those the intensively cultivated vegetable gardens. By continuing across the river and through the steel gates, visitors finally arrive at a large, modern piggery. If you are interested, the farm manager will take you on a lengthy tour of the piggery and finish off by giving you a bunch of bananas and coconut!

On **D'Argent beach** there is a boatbuilding yard, where La Digue schooners are built in the traditional manner. Unlike the shipwrights near Château St Cloud, those at D'Argent are not at all friendly.

By taking the south-westerly path from the boatyard, visitors will arrive at **Anse La Source à Jean.** There are several little beaches all along this boulder-strewn coast. The best swimming beaches here are at **Anse Pierrot, Anse aux Cèdres** and **Anse Bonnet Carré.** The path continues south to end at **Pointe Jacques,** the most southerly point of La Digue.

NORTH LA DIGUE

From **La Passe**, proceed north along the coast. You will pass the police station and come to La Digue fish, vegetable and meat market. This is a hive of activity on Fridays and Saturdays. Self-catering travellers can do some of their food shopping here. The quality is good and the selection wide. At the Moonlight Craft and Curio Shop, a variety of local items are for sale, from seashells to coco de mer nuts and clothing.

Alongside the tree-lined beach, past the cemetery and beyond **Pointe Cap Barbi**, is the *Anse Sévère Bungalow* (medium tariff), open only to visitors staying for longer than three days. It has excellent views, is close to the reefed **Anse Sévère** beach and is situated in one of the least populated coastal areas of the island. Book about three months ahead: Anse Sévère Bungalow, La Passe, La Digue, Seychelles, tel. 24-7354.

Turquoise water and pink granite boulders line the sand road all the way round the northern tip of the island to *Patatran Bar and Restaurant*. Located in an idyllic setting, this restaurant and bar overlooks the sea and is very popular with tourists for lunch. After sunset its terraces are less busy and you will probably end up with a group of La Digue residents at the bar.

From here the coastal road dips to the east, passing huge hotel construction sites and skirting isolated beaches and bays. Some of these bays offer good snorkelling. Where the road drops from the Patatran Bar there is a strip of beach where the shallow reef is covered with gaily coloured fish and swaying marine plants. A Catholic shrine marks the end of development and the start of La Digue's receding wilderness. This road is ideal for cycling. Traditional housing dots the interior, while empty beaches and achingly blue lagoons entice all visitors who venture this far.

At **Anse Fourmis** the road ends and becomes a footpath. Continue south on this path to reach the remote beach of **Anse Caiman**. Passing through thick vegetation you will arrive at this dream-like beach. Few visitors bother going this far to find a beach, and you will probably find yourself alone with the palm trees, tropical breezes, big skies and open ocean.

SOUTH-EAST LA DIGUE

To reach this area of the island, take the road that goes left (east) at the entrance to **L'Union coconut estate** on the west coast. It passes the Helicopter Seychelles helipad and a plant nursery, and proceeds into a dense fern and bamboo forest. At the T-junction, turn right (south) to bypass the plantation mansion. From here, start looking for the enormous flying fox fruit bats. Unlike most bats, these ones fly about all day and spend much of the night asleep. These furry fox-faced bats have become a tourist attraction on La Digue, to the extent that a few unscrupulous individuals have caught some and keep them cruelly caged for visitors to gawk at.

If you leave the road and trek into the forests in this region, you will come upon small settlements deep in the woods. The people are unused to seeing foreigners this far off the beaten track and may initially be suspicious, but with lots of smiles and humility you can change their reserve, and they may offer you something to eat and drink. If it is late afternoon they may invite you to spend the night.

Little fields of sugar cane, palms and screwpines dot the landscape as far as the south-east coast beach of **Grande Anse**. Granite boulders, gleaming white beach and azure sea make this beach spectacular, but swimming can be dangerous. There is no reef here, and currents are strong. The waves are good for experienced bodysurfers, though. The long Indian Ocean swells rising over the shelving seabed create tubes and glassy walls for those experienced enough to swim out beyond the pounding shore break.

A rocky footpath goes north, past Grande Anse, across the promontory of **Pointe Bélize** to the protected bay of **Petite Anse**. Even further north, through the coconut groves of Pointe Turcy, is **Anse Cocos**, a haven of unspoilt natural beauty.

INLAND LA DIGUE

Take the road going east from the post office at **La Passe**. Along this road are reasonably priced lodges, hotels and guesthouses. Prior reservations are not necessary. *Le Romarin Guesthouse* is reached just before an area of swamp. Costs are low, the rooms are comfortable and Creole meals can be arranged, but hygiene standards are dubious. The Dilippe Gilbert Craft Maker shop near the *Guesthouse Calou* has masterly works made of local materials.

Further up on the hill is *Bernique Guesthouse and Restaurant* (medium-high tariff). The accommodation is clean and suitable for families. The restaurant is well known on La Digue and serves delicious Continental and Creole dishes. Prior reservations for accommodation are necessary: Bernique Guesthouse, La Digue, Seychelles, tel. 23-4229, fax 23-4288.

On the same section of road is the *Sitronnel Guesthouse* (medium tariff). Beyond this is the magnificent *Château St Cloud Guesthouse* (medium-high tariff), one of the best preserved plantation houses in the Seychelles. The Château St Cloud was for years favoured by backpackers and budget travellers, but since it has come under new management prices have skyrocketed. All rooms have bathrooms en suite and the outbuildings will soon be converted into additional accommodation.

Follow the path that goes west from the château and you will come to a traditional boatbuilding yard among the takamaka and badamier trees. The schooner builders are talkative, friendly and quick to explain what they are doing. Outside of Southeast Asia, the art of crafting boats from wood has virtually disappeared. Yet here on the remote island of La Digue, the methods remain unchanged.

South-east of the château the road rises and forks. To reach the summit of the mountain ridge, the Nid d'Aigles, which extends across central La Digue, follow the **Belle Vue** signs. The road climbs incredibly steeply towards the centre of the island. Proceed beyond the pig and poultry farm, through the forests and up to the Belle Vue water pumping station. From here the road gradient is almost 45 degrees, and it is virtually impossible to push a bike. At the top of the steepest section, the tarred road becomes a narrow track. Stay on this as it contours the hill and then makes a final climb into the virgin forest and up onto the summit ridge. Views in all directions are awesome, and La Digue's houses look like miniatures. Fruit bats hang upside down in the tall trees which cloak the hillsides here, and occasionally spread their giant wings to soar for a few moments above the green canopy.

Having succeeded in scaling the heights above Belle Vue, return to the junction in the main road and proceed south. At Mr S Papet Shop, where groceries and imported drinks can be bought, budget travellers can ask about cheap accommodation. Two rooms are let out to visitors, but as this is not an official guesthouse, residents are requested to maintain a low profile. Although meals are not included in the low tariff, the owner, Lucien, will cook for you if you supply the ingredients.

Around the corner, south-west of the shop, the road forks. If you go west you will come to lily ponds just before Madline Rose Boutique, which has little to interest curio hunters.

Beyond the shop you enter the rainforest and **La Digue Veuve Reserve**, open Monday to Saturday 9h30-16h30. If you want to visit the reserve on a Sunday or after 16h30, you can purchase an entrance ticket at C Louis Artist and Craft Boutique, on the same road. This is one of the places where a captured flying fox bat is kept in a wire cage, in atrocious conditions. In this forest reserve, which has an information centre, you may spot the extremely rare and endangered black paradise flycatcher. There is no need for a guide; the trails are clearly marked and well maintained.

This road continues to the west coast and joins the coast road opposite La Digue Island Lodge.

The gravel road leading south from the junction below Mr S Papet Store passes a woodcarving workshop and a large shrine to Mother Mary before reaching the *Villa Mon Rev Hotel* (medium-high tariff). Situated on the higher, cooler slopes of the island, this small hotel offers superb accommodation in a forest environment. Usually reservations are not necessary, but it may be safer to book about 30 days ahead: Villa Mon Rev Hotel, La Digue, Seychelles, tel. 23-4218.

Beyond the hotel are Luce Pierre Store and a public water tap, and then a T-junction. This junction is where the route described in the preceding section, on south-east La Digue, starts.

22 ISLANDS AROUND LA DIGUE

PETITE AND GRANDE SOEUR

These small granitic islands north of La Digue are cloaked in secrecy. They are reputedly owned by the children of the late Shah of Iran, but I could not establish their ownership with certainty. There is nowhere to stay on the islands, visitors are not encouraged and getting to them is difficult. The north coast of La Digue is the best place to enquire about a crossing, which will be expensive. Diving around Petite and Grande Soeur requires knowledge of drift-diving as there are strong tidal currents. The attraction of these islands is that adventurous visitors who arrive with their own tents and food can explore the thick virgin forests and deserted, boulder-stewn beaches. You will need a machete to make your way inland. There are no real paths, and the wilderness remains pristine.

FÉLICITÉ

Félicité Island lies 4 km north-east of La Digue and less than 2 km from the Soeurs islands. Getting there independently is difficult, but a fisherman may be prepared to take you across from north-east La Digue in his boat. There is accommodation in a three-roomed house for a maximum stay of three days. Enquire about this and about getting to the island from a tour operator, La Digue Island Lodge (tel. 23-4233) or Choppy's Bungalows. Campers will have no problem finding a suitable pitch on this sparsely inhabited island. Most of the island's inhabitants live on the north-west coast. The islanders may invite you to eat or stay with them. They will not expect any payment, but contribute something to the meals or make them a gift of something they will find useful. Penknives, pens and T-shirts are appreciated.

Félicité's biggest attractions are its tracts of primary forest and vast stretches of unexplored coral reef. Without a guide and machete you are unlikely to make much progress into the interior. Local children make the best guides. After sweating your way up to the forested summit of Mt Félicité (231 m), you can enjoy clear views of Petite and Grande Soeur, La Digue and, to the west, Praslin.

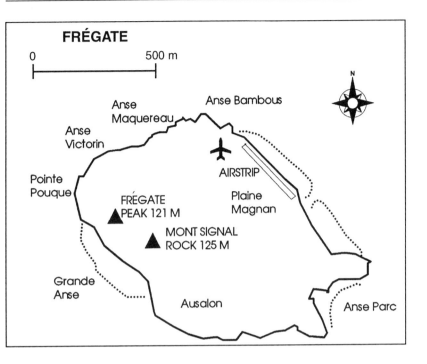

FRÉGATE

Frégate, 56 km east of Mahé, is the most remote of the inner islands. It is a mere 2 km by 800 m. Getting there by boat is almost impossible, unless under charter. There are weekly flights to Frégate. They last only about 15 minutes and land on the north-eastern side of the island. Frégate is privately owned.

Legends of pirate treasure have lured numerous people to Frégate over the years. Most famous of these was the writer Ian Fleming, who visited Frégate in the hope of deciphering the strange symbols on some coastal rocks, not unlike those at Bel Ombre, on Mahé. Some digging has been done, but so far nothing worthwhile has turned up. If you should be lucky enough to stumble upon a big find, the Seychelles government will be entitled to 50% of it.

A striking feature of Frégate is the two hills which dominate the island: Mont Signal (125 m) and Frégate Peak (121 m). The island's strange geology has a preponderance of quartz. Frégate is covered by a green blanket of lush vegetation. For ornithologists, one reason for going to Frégate is the chance of seeing the threatened, extremely rare and melodious magpie robin (locally called the *pie chanteuse*), which is unique to Frégate. Other birds include fairy terns, frigatebirds, fodies, sunbirds and Seychelles blue pigeons. Tortoises are much in evidence, as are geckoes, frogs and several other species of reptile, including a harmless snake. The island's still uncharted reefs offer fine snorkelling and scuba diving. Travellers wanting to mix with islanders will find those on Frégate friendly and eager to chat to interested foreigners.

Sugar cane, vanilla, coffee and bananas are grown on Frégate, mainly to cater for the one hotel on the island: the *Plantation House* (high tariff). It has 10 charming rooms in the main house, and two villas. The restaurant serves full-course meals and specialises in Creole cooking, using local ingredients and often fresh seafood. Meals are included in the rate. Reservations for accommodation are essential. These are made through the Central Reservations Office in Victoria: Plantation House, PO Box 330, Victoria, Mahé, Seychelles, tel. 22-3123, fax 22-4152.

A stunningly beautiful walk is along the path west of the airstrip along the Bambous river. Climb through the coconut groves onto the saddle between Mont Signal and Frégate Peak. The climb to the summit of Mont Signal is strenuous, but the views are worth it. Frégate Peak is easier to climb and also provides panoramic vistas.

The best swimming beach on Frégate is on the west coast, at **Grande Anse**. To get there, take the path going north-west from the Plantation House and then the one branching west through the groves. The path skirts a hill and leads all the way to the beach and its lagoon.

The southern coastline of Frégate has no real beaches but is spectacular. Walk south-west from the Plantation House to **Anse Coup de Poing**, and from there west along the coast to **Anse Felix**.

Another pleasant walk is north, past the airstrip, to **Anse Bambous** and around the northern tip of the island to **Anse Maquereau** and **Anse Victorin**. There are extensive stretches of sparkling white tropical beach all the way. There is no protective reef here, so the beach is exposed and swimming can be dangerous. The back-line waves are big and rideable. Beware of the rip current that surges around the point between Anse Bambous and Anse Maquereau. West of Anse Victorin snorkellers will see multitudes of fish feeding in the shallow water off the half-submerged rocks. Off **Pointe Pouque**, those who drift out into deep water may be surprised by another curious but harmless white-tipped reef shark. (The other one lives off Petite Anse Kerlan, on Praslin.)

23 BIRD ISLAND

Almost 98 km north of Mahé, on the edge of the 2 km deep Seychelles Bank, lies Bird Island. This coral island is a must for birdwatchers. Each year, from May to October, millions of sooty terns, boobies and noddies arrive to nest, and avian rarities and specials abound. The variety and numbers of birds are stunning. It is also on Bird Island that the world's oldest tortoise, Esmeralda, lives. Estimated at 200 years old, this tortoise is a male, despite its name. A white coral beach encircles Bird Island, making it ideal for sun-lovers, divers, fishermen and those who just want to relax. Staying on Bird Island must rate as one of the most idyllic things left to do on earth. There are no locks, no keys, no guards and no crime. Bird Island is probably the closest you can get to paradise in this life.

No independent travel is allowed to this privately owned island. All visitors must have booked an entire package through the Bird Island booking office in Victoria. You will not even be able to buy an airline ticket to the island otherwise. Be sure to book well ahead: accommodation at the one lodge on the island and seats on the daily Air Seychelles flights between Mahé and Bird Island are limited.

The flight cruises at 2 000 m for about 30 minutes from Mahé. Once the plane has stopped on the bumpy grass runway, the frightfully English managers of the *Bird Island Lodge* (medium-high tariff) come out to meet you. Luggage is shoved onto a tractor-trailer and guests are invited to the reception and lounge area. The Bird Island tour package includes flights to and from the island, all meals, accommodation, use of non-motorised water sport equipment (including snorkelling gear) and information literature. Visitors wanting to go boating or game fishing will need to pay an additional fee for the excursion, which will be arranged by the lodge.

Accommodation is in 24 plantation-style chalets along the west coast. Each chalet has its own bathroom, enormous double bed, mosquito net, fan and uninterrupted ocean views. A veranda offers shade from the fierce midday sun. In the open-sided restaurant, lavish buffets are served at breakfast, lunch and dinner. Dinner is usually a barbeque of fresh seafood and line fish, with crisp salads and ice-cold drinks. The

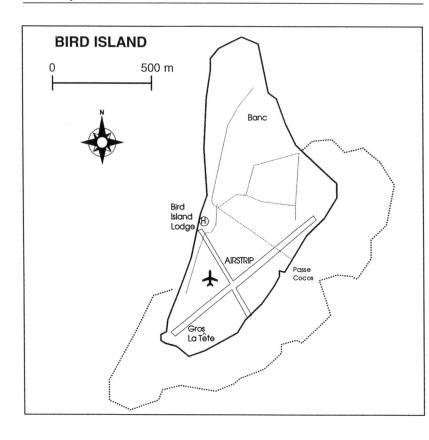

atmosphere is informal and the emphasis is on relaxation, tranquillity and bonhomie.

French and English are spoken by the management and most of the 35 staff members. Their attention to detail is refreshing after the frequent mediocrity of tourist-jaded Mahé. The manager's wife is an expert on the island's flora and fauna. She has put together a detailed brochure which informs visitors of Bird Island's geology, climate, vegetation and birdlife. Each visitor is given a "bird-spotter's guide" upon arrival. Guests are also given torches, because moonless nights can get very black.

A well-stocked boutique sells curios, suntan lotion and T-shirts, and runs a little library stocked with novels in several languages.

A minimum stay of two nights is required, but during the high season you may get away with a single night. Reservations are vital, preferably 90 days in advance. Confirm 15 days before leaving home:

Bird Island, PO Box 404 (on Independence Avenue, near the Pirate's Arms), Victoria, Mahé, Seychelles, tel. 22-4925, fax 22-5074.

There are several paths that link the coasts of the island. They lead through the forests, papyrus clusters and abandoned coconut groves of the interior onto soft sandy beaches. Because it is only 71 ha in extent, it takes just two hours to walk around the entire island along the beach. The west coast is exposed and swimming can be dangerous, but the east coast has a reef and a shallow seabed, and is perfect for lazy snorkelling or floating.

Sitting on the beach of Bird Island and gazing up at the stars is not to be missed, especially on a moonless night. Bird Island is so far from any artificial light sources that an astounding number of stars can be seen brightly glittering in the inky heavens.

Quite a few giant tortoises trundle around Bird Island; all are friendly and love having their leathery necks scratched. Esmeralda is, of course, the showpiece. You can normally find him sleeping against the side wall of one of the chalets. This docile tortoise will peer at you from what looks like tear-stained, rheumy eyes.

24 DENIS ISLAND

Denis Island was claimed for the king of France in 1773 by the explorer, adventurer and navigator Denis de Trobriand, and is named after him. This remote coral island is approximately 80 km north-east of Mahé. Just 1,8 km by 1,3 km, Denis Island will be a delightful experience to all who make the journey there. Owned by Pierre Burkhardt, Denis is only accessible to those visitors who book a package through the island's reservations office in Victoria. The minimum stay is three days.

Air Seychelles has a daily charter flight between Mahé and Denis Island, which lasts about 30 minutes. The price of the return flight is included in the Denis Island tour package.

Covered in tropical vegetation, thanks to the enormous guano deposits on it, and suspended on the edge of the Seychelles Bank, Denis Island offers a tempting lure to game fishermen and divers. Holding several international game fishing records, the warm, deep waters off Denis frequently host fishing competitions.

The south and east coast is surrounded by a lagoon which offers safe swimming all year round. The entire island is surrounded by a white beach.

There are only about 50 people living on Denis. All are connected to the Denis Island Lodge. Of historical interest is the lighthouse, built in 1910, and an Ecumenical chapel, the only one of its kind on the Seychelles. An abandoned prison and a copra production facility can also be seen on Denis Island.

Coconut groves and dense vegetation provide visitors with hours of pleasant meandering. Several paths cross the island. From the manager's house, cross the airstrip and take the track leading south, along the west coast. This walk takes visitors all the way down to the southwestern tip of Denis. An equally interesting walk is down the east coast from the lighthouse. Take along a towel and swimming costume; there are many opportunities for a dip along the way. Between La Mère Boeuf and Muraille Bon Dieu, in the south-west, lie the caves, a good example of the geomorphology of a coral island's growth.

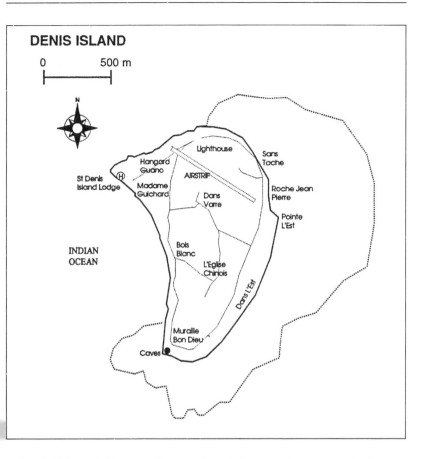

Denis Island Lodge (medium-high tariff) has 24 self-contained bungalows right on the beach, on the north-west of the island. The restaurant serves excellent Creole and French meals. Staff are cordial, drinks are cold and the general atmosphere is one of relaxation. Snorkelling equipment, windsurfers and tennis kit are supplied. Deep-sea fishing boats and tackle, scuba diving gear and a glass-bottomed boats are for hire. Reservations for accommodation should be made about 60 days ahead:

Denis Island, Denis Island Development Company, PO Box 404, Victoria, Mahé, Seychelles, tel. 24-4143, fax 24-4405.

During the low season, from March to November but excluding August, travellers may be able to book a package at short notice through the island's representative office in St Joseph Street, Victoria. To get to the office, go north past the Hindu temple and continue across the road leading to the Sir Selwyn Clarke market; the office is on the right. Note that it is only open Monday to Friday 8h30-10h00. If you have any problem making contact with the frequently absent agent, call Denis Island direct, tel. 32-1143, fax 32-1010.

25 OUTER ISLANDS

Far to the south-west of Mahé lie the "distant isles", as the outer islands are sometimes called. Closer to Madagascar and the Comoros than the inner Seychelles islands, these coral islands were once known as the oil islands because of their copra production. The islands can be divided into the Aldabra, Amirantes and Farquhar groups. Most are difficult, if not impossible, to reach. You need time and money to visit these remote island archipelagoes. Details of sailing to them can be obtained from the Island Development Company, PO Box 638, New Port, Victoria, Mahé, Seychelles, tel. 22-4640, fax 22-4467.

Information on flights to Desroches, in the Amirantes group, and Assomption, in the Aldabra group, is available from Air Seychelles, PO Box 386, Victoria, Mahé, Seychelles, tel. 22-5220, fax 22-5159.

The most pleasant, but an expensive, way of getting to any of the outer islands is by chartering a yacht for a few weeks. Contact Marine Charter Association, PO Box 469, Victoria, Mahé, Seychelles, tel. 32-2126, fax 22-4679.

ALDABRA GROUP

The Aldabra group is more that 1 000 km from Mahé. Many of the coral islets were pushed up from the bottom of the Indian Ocean aeons after they had been formed. They exhibit a strange mushroom-like shape caused by pounding waves and wind erosion. The group is named after the largest coral atoll in the world: **Aldabra atoll**, which actually consists of four islands encircling a lagoon rich in marine life. The islands are Picard, which has a busy scientific research station, Grande Terre, Polymnie and Malabar. The lagoon is the largest on earth.

Of all the outer islands, Aldabra is the group that determined visitors should see. In the words of Sir Julian Huxley, "Aldabra is one of nature's treasures and should belong to the whole world." Charles Darwin was the first European to bring Aldabra to the attention of the world, when he delivered a lecture to members of Great Britain's Royal Geographical Society.

Aldabra atoll is one of the most famous of all natural heritage sites. Scene of major international conservation efforts, Aldabra is the ancestral home of the giant tortoise. Twice in its modern history Aldabra was targeted for interference. In 1964 the USA showed a strong interest in leasing the islands from Great Britain in order to carry out bomb tests and establish a military base there. Fortunately, numerous environmental lobbyists thwarted the attempt. Then, in 1970, plans to build an airfield on Aldabra were leaked to the press. The efforts of wildlife enthusiasts ensured that the plans were scrapped. Tourism is now carefully controlled by the Seychelles Island Foundation.

Interesting fauna on Aldabra include the unique giant robber or coconut crabs. They really do steal things, so make sure that your cameras, bags, clothing and food are securely stored away. These large crabs use their powerful claws to crack open coconuts, which are their principal diet. A real peculiarity is the flightless whitebreasted rail. Sea turtles lay their eggs on the isolated beaches of Aldabra. Of all the islands, this is the place where visitors are most likely to see these prehistoric creatures struggling ashore at night to dig holes and plop their leathery eggs into the warm sand.

Aldabra's ecosystem is based on the ebb and flow of the tide in and out of the lagoon twice a day. With only four openings in the ring of islands, the pressure of the flowing water causes raging tidal streams that make a boat entry virtually impossible. As the water flows into the lagoon, sometimes raising the level by up to 2 m, it carries in several species of predatory fish including sharks and barracuda.

Unless you can arrange for accommodation with the scientists or fishermen on Aldabra, you must have your own tent and supplies. A great deal of paperwork is required for any independent visit to Aldabra. Try to obtain a letter of introduction from some scientific organisation or museum, detailing your specific interest in Aldabra. It is possible to take a day trip to Aldabra atoll from Assomption Island, which is more accessible (see below).

An island in the Aldabra group that has recently been opened to tourists is **Assomption Island**. There is an airstrip on Assomption. The main source of income for its few inhabitants is fishing. Fish is filleted and salted before being shipped to Mahé and exported.

Assomption is Seychelles' eco-tourism destination par excellence. There are tourist bungalows on the island's north coast, at **Anse Prenses**, and a guided boat trip takes visitors to Aldabra atoll, about four hours away, for the day. Assomption has sections of beautiful coral beach and an empty hinterland.

AMIRANTES GROUP

Comprised of roughly 24 islands, the Amirantes group is about 300 km south-west of Mahé. Named the Admiral Islands (Ilhas do Amirantes) by Vasco da Gama in the early 1500s, this archipelago includes African Banks, D'Arros, Poivre, St Joseph and the more southerly Alphonse islands.

The Amirantes are mostly privately owned, but their owners are keen to exploit their tourism potential. This makes them the most welcoming islands of south-western Seychelles. This group also has the most accessible of all the outer islands: Desroches.

Almost 200 km from Mahé, **Desroches** is the most visited and developed island of the Amirantes. Named after the governor of Mauritius in 1770, Desroches still has large areas of wilderness and exquisite beaches. There are three Air Seychelles flights per week between Mahé and Desroches.

The island's main attraction is scuba diving. While many divers rave about Bonne Aventure, off Grande Comore, some experts claim the 80 square km of vibrant coral reefs around Desroches offer the best diving sites in the entire Indian Ocean. From late May to early September, visibility here often exceeds 50 m. Equipment, refills and guides can all be arranged through the Desroches Island Lodge. Ask a guide to take you along the plummeting sea-walls of the reef. The caves, arroyos and canyons here will beguile even the most experienced of divers. Fish are prolific, as are swaying marine plants. The island's divemaster has in-depth knowledge of this underwater world, and no diver comes away feeling uninformed.

Ashore, 400 ha of coconut plantation and indigenous forest will entice most visitors to set off exploring this magnificent island. It is possible to arrange with the Desroches Island Lodge for boat excursions from Desroches to the neighbouring islands of **D'Arros**, **Poivre** and **African Banks**, further north. If you decide to go on one of these trips, remember to take along snorkelling gear and lots of sun-protection cream.

Accommodation on Desroches is at the *Desroches Island Lodge* (medium-high tariff), which has a sliding scale of rates depending on what time of the year you visit. The lodge, on the south-western part of the island near the airstrip, has 20 self-contained bungalows. A restaurant and bar offer delicious meals and drinks to residents. The lodge has a water sports centre, diving and fishing amenities. Prior reservations are necessary:

Desroches Island Lodge, Desroches Island, Seychelles, tel. 22-9003, fax 22-9002. Manager: tel. 22-9009.

FARQUHAR GROUP

Scattered within an enormous coral reef, the coral islands making up the Farquhar group are about 700 km south-west of Mahé. These islands are the most difficult to reach from Mahé or anywhere else. You will need to have your own vessel or one under charter to visit them. Very occasionally Air Seychelles flies between Mahé and the rudimentary airstrip on **Île du Nord**. Passengers are carried. Contact Air Seychelles, PO Box 386, Victoria, Mahé, tel. 22-5220, fax 22-5159, for their flight schedule to Île du Nord.

The islanders live exclusively on what they can produce: fish, coconut and a few vegetables. Most of the islands' cultivation is still devoted to coconut palms. But as copra and coconut oil prices continue to drop, the future looks bleak for the Farquhar islanders. Already some of the families have been forced to go to Mahé in search of work.

Flat, sandy and shrouded in vegetation and coconut groves, the Farquhar islands have retained the air of colonial plantations. Visiting them is an unforgettable experience. If you have the time, can endure discomfort and want to meet people still rooted in ancient traditions, then the Farquhar islands are a must.

For current information on getting to the Farquhar group and assistance with accommodation, contact the Island Development Company, PO Box 638, New Port, Victoria, Mahé, Seychelles, tel. 22-4640, fax 22-4467.

INDEX

REPUBLIC OF SEYCHELLES

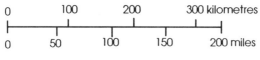

| 0 | 100 | 200 | 300 kilometres |
| 0 | 50 | 100 | 150 | 200 miles |

INDIAN OCEAN

Outer Island

See front for Comoros map

REFERENCE

▬▬▬	Main road
───	Secondary road
～～～	Road or track
───	City street
·····~···	Coral reefs
✚	Hospital
❶	Information bureau
⊠	Post office
✈	Airfield
▲	Places of interest
🚌	Bus terminal
Ⓟ	Police station
▲	Spot height
Ⓗ	Hotel
Ⓡ	Restaurant
⛴	Port

Aldabra Group

Picard Malabar
Grande · Aldabra
Terre · Atoll
Assomption   Cosmolédo
              Atoll

          ✈ Astove

Far
Gro

St

Bar

Far